MIND YOUR HEAD

THE ULTIMATE HOW-TO BRAIN TRAINING BOOK

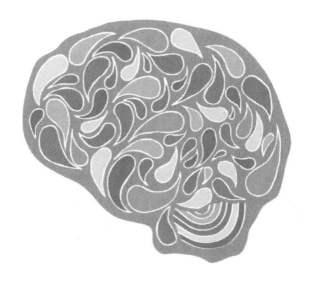

Rewiring Your Brain for
Success, Happiness, & Health

Sue Stebbins & Dr. Carla Clark

MIND YOUR HEAD

First Paperback Edition

Table of Contents

Summary Outline

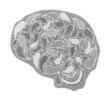

THE WAVE-MAP OF THE BRAIN

Neural networks, neuroplasticity and brainwaves.

SUPER BRAIN OPTIMIZATION PRACTICES

How to influence neuroplasticity and become the sculptor of your brain: meditation, Cognitive Behavioral Therapy, Neuro Linguistic Programming, brainwave entrainment and more.

THE ULTIMATE NEW LIFE SYSTEM

A complete system to fully integrate the benefits of Brain Optimization Practices (BOPs) seamlessly into your life.

CHAPTER I: FOCUSING ON THE SELF

How to de-stress, love yourself and upgrade your beliefs in order to transform your life.

RAPID DE-STRESSING

Understanding the brain mechanisms of stress is the first step toward de-stressing.

THE NEW AGE OF SELF-COMPASSION

By loving and caring for yourself and others you can boost your brain and body and enhance your caring for others.

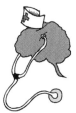

BRAND-NEW BELIEFS & HABITS

Understanding beliefs and desires in the brain and how they influence our behavior and the formation of habits. How to create encouraging beliefs and boost your brain to bolster your behavior towards, healthy habit formation for positive and happy outcomes.

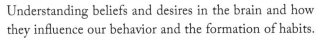

CHAPTER II: FOCUSING ON HEALTH

How to boost your happiness, physical health, brain performance, and overcome pain by re-balancing your mind-body relationship.

MAXIMIZING THE MIND-BODY CONNECTION

How to use your mind to boost your brain's level of happiness in order to boost your immunity and overall physical health.

FIT BODY, FIT MIND

How exercise boosts mental performance to improve learning, memory, attention and behavior and prevent cognitive decline across your lifespan. BOPs for creating the desire to exercise.

PAIN AND PLEASURE

How you can alter your experience of pain without drugs by making use of both the pain-pleasure relationship and associated emotion (pleasure) and attention (focus) related networks within the brain.

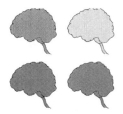

CHAPTER III: FOCUSING ON OTHERS

Learn how to create and experience more positive social interaction that will open the door to better health, relationships and other social opportunities.

TWO BRAINS ARE BETTER THAN ONE

How to retrain your brain, creating positive social skills thereby reversing past and present negative social influences on your brain and neuroplasticity. The result: A positive upward spiral of happiness, socialness and good health.

LOVE, FRIENDSHIP & FAMILY

How to create and maintain close, loving relationships that encourage positive emotions, promoting neuroplastic changes that protect us from negative feelings and depression. Love truly is the best medicine.

YOUR BEST COMMUNICATING BRAIN

Learn the art of communication as the secret for gaining access to other peoples inner worlds. This will strengthen your relationships, boost your brain and health, as well as open up many new doors of opportunity, that through miscommunication would otherwise have remained closed to you.

CHAPTER IV: FOCUSING ON SUCCESS

Success involves the ability to nurture creative thought, set and achieve goals and optimistically go about taking calculated risks. Learn how the science of your brain holds the key to activating these capabilities.

EXPANDING CREATIVITY

Explore the fine balance of contradictory abilities that nurture creative thought: working memory, defocused yet sustained attention, mental flexibility and cognitive control. You will utilize components of both DMN and TPN networks to stimulate more and more expansive and productive creative thought.

GOALS & DREAMS—THE NEW PATH

Learn the secrets of how best to set and achieve your life's ambitions, based on how your brain deals with goals. Explore brain based goal setting practices that make goal achievement habitual and carve a positive use out of the word failure.

DO & DARE

How well your reward and motivation related circuitry and your cognitive control network interact with one another dictate how successfully you will approach decision making and the taking of risks. Success comes from taking calculated risks and either achieving your goals or learning from setbacks. Learn how to engender an optimistic, no regrets attitude that can alter the course of your life!

POWER RESOURCES

GLOSSARY

REFERENCES

PREFACE

Why Mind Your Head?
Today's #1 Challenge: Stress—The Invisible Epidemic

You want to be healthy, happy, prosperous, and live a great life right? Of course! After all, that's what everyone wants! Yet take a look around you. How many of the people you know are truly happy? How many of them live in healthy bodies that they love AND have found their passion? How many people are earning the income they want, building healthy relationships, truly living an adventurous, fulfilling life and enjoying the freedom they've always dreamed of? Sadly, for many, that kind of life is a dream and is not currently a reality.

The culprit? More potential for us to stress out in life than ever before, without being shown a way to protect ourselves from being overwhelmed. As you probably know, stress related health issues account for an estimated 75-90 percent of all doctor visits. [Source: American Psychological Association, American Institute of Stress, NY (2013)]

Our 21st century lifestyles leave us overworked and over-stimulated. It is far too easy to succumb to media and work overload combined with job, relationship and money problems and everything in between. And as a result, our bodies, brains and minds are impaired and disrupted by stress, culminating in the growth of an estimated $2 trillion stress epidemic that is affecting 2 billion people worldwide. [Source: www.sharpbrains.com, Digital Brain Health Market Report (2012)]

Rewiring for a Better Life

If I told you it was possible to be free from your frustrations, stress, weight concerns and a recurring negative overloaded life, and that we and a handful of scientists and researchers compile the latest scientifically proven program that takes the guesswork and trial and error out of living a better life, would you believe me?

You may not know that help exists and we are learning new, improved and more targeted ways to help every day. The groundbreaking, drug-free, easy and instantly effective brain science based program you'll learn about in this book will instantly begin to transform your life, your habits and your energy levels. The science, brain and life-optimizing practices we will be sharing with you here have never been more vital for regular day to day living than now, with the added commonplace stresses of the 21st century.

What you will be learning in Mind Your Head is our biggest weapon against these struggles and stresses. The approach outlined in the following pages has been brought together to give you the edge you need to live beyond 21st century pressures, compulsions, and confusions, so that you can begin to design your own future and regain control to create a life of health, wealth and happiness.

Minding Your Head Isn't Rocket Science

Fortunately, this book addresses what you'll need to do in order to meet the new demands and possibilities of 21st century life, to love doing it as you create happiness, health and wealth and all while being fully immersed in a fast-paced, information-rich life. Imagine starting today by reading this book and exploring our other resources. With the techniques you learn, you could instantly begin to feel your stress and struggles melt away.

The beauty is that it's something we can ALL learn to do; you don't need to be in a certain wage-bracket, be a certain age or sex or be part of a special group or clique. With the groundbreaking research and practices put forth in this book, you can discover how to re-shape your brain, your future and finally, achieve your dreams. And best of all, Mind Your Head makes it simple, clear and fun to do.

The Answer: Self Directed Neuroplasticity

Your brain actually responds to how we live our lives. It rewires itself and alters its and your functioning depending on how we experience the ups and downs and ins and outs of daily living. This thought, habit, health and behavior shaping ability is called neuroplasticity. We unwittingly shape our brains to behave and respond to life in certain ways by the way we currently think, feel and do. Learning ways to alter how you think, feel and do now, allows us to rewire the functional networks in our brains and in turn, improve how we think, feel and do in life.

The fact that you were drawn to and are now reading this book is indeed significant and forward sensing. It shows there is a part of you that recognizes that while most people believe their lives, habits, and dreams are fixed, limited and like their brains, can't be easily changed, it doesn't have to be that way. By understanding neuroplasticity and how best to use it to our benefit, we know now that we have the infinite potential to grow and expand our capacities and capabilities throughout our lifetime.

Techniques that will change your life!

Mind Your Head presents the new 21st century science of brain training's promise: You can literally rewire new habits and new behaviors and learn to thrive if you have the tools to do so. In Mind Your Head, and through www.ultimatenewlife.com, we'll give you the healthy brain training technology that allows you to more quickly model and train your neural circuits for optimal functioning in all aspects of life, be it confidence, focus, beliefs, habits, behaviors, love, friendships, family or goals, dreams and everything in between.

Why Sue Wrote This Book:

Like many of my clients, I was conditioned to look good on the outside, and seek out demanding, high stress and highly competitive career paths. Along with so many others, I had been trained that becoming relevant or worthwhile had to be hard. In order to live a "Real Life," I thought that stress and being in survival mode with my adrenaline always pumping was the only way.

My efforts, though they led me to success, never gave me peace, happiness, or true fulfillment. In fact, inside I felt like a mess, completely lost and adrift. I felt guilty a lot of the time, even though by outside standards I was very successful, and was even 'living the dream.'

Truthfully, I was too driven. I was leading a brain-toxic lifestyle that led to chronic self doubt and anxiety. And I was over-compensating by 'trying really hard' and using overwork, overeating, over-exercising, over everything in a compulsive attempt to fill the hole using something outside of me. Sound familiar?

I had two major wake-up calls. The first was the death of my mother when I was 21. The second was complete burnout at 37. At 21, I started to find the answer. I was introduced to a new reality—beyond death—and it led me on an over 30 year research path, which fully matured when I turned 40.

My own therapist came to see me at that time and told me what a profound change she saw in me. "I have never seen such a profound shift, so fast, in anyone in my 20 year career!" she excitedly told me. "Look at how great your life, and balance is! How did you do that? I want to see you!"

It was then that I decided that my team and I needed to make this technology and research available for others. Today, with *Mind Your Head*, I bring to you the nearly 30,000 hours of research and work my team and I have conducted over the past 20 years. It has changed so many lives, mine included, in such powerfully fast, profound and miraculous ways. I've often been known to ask my colleagues, "Why don't more people know about this?" Now, they will.

So my friend, thank you for believing in the promise of this book. Thank you for believing in yourself enough to know that you can un-practice most of what you have learned, and practice 're-training' or re-wiring to the true you. Thank you for being open to finding your genius and being brave enough to create a new you.

Take comfort in knowing you won't be doing it alone. You will do it with the intelligence and resources we will share with you in *Mind Your Head*. Knowledge that will allow you to discover the science and magic of making your dreams a REALITY.

I must add that Mind Your Head wouldn't exist without the great researchers and committed partners around the world whose sole passion is to bring the secrets we reveal in Mind Your Head to a world that seems on the brink of overload. I am also glad to say how fortunate you will be to contribute to the new you with new solutions and the ability to joyfully navigate the new 21st century life.

Why Carla Wrote This Book:

It was winter again and I could feel it coming. Those same old feelings that, if left unchecked, morph me into an antisocial creature of the night, with routines plagued by irregular sleeping patterns, unable to think clearly and unable to care. The only words to describe how I felt during such times is dark emptiness.

The first time it happened I was unprepared. Kicking ass at 17 at university, having aced the first years exams, holding two jobs to pay the bills and with an almost nightly nightlife centered around underage clubbing, drink, drugs and general trouble making (a continuation of my rebellious early teen years), I was all systems go. Whizzing around at full speed to make sure that nothing slipped. So fast in fact that taking my eyes of the road for just a second could spell disaster.

And that's exactly what happened. Winter came and my body wanted to slow down, but my demanding life didn't have room for it. Something had to give, and seeing as I couldn't change the seasons, or indeed stop time in its tracks, it was my mind that gave and buckled under the pressure. The happy, daft, young, gifted and energetically spirited young girl I was vanished in a matter of months to be little more than a shadow of her former self.

In fact, some of the strongest, most influential and most inspiring people in my life have suffered a far, far worse relationship with depression than I have. My heart breaks to say, that some of those amazing people have been lost to a life of misfortune, poverty, drink and drug abuse.

Unhealthy daily habits, pressure coming from all angles and the monthly fight to scrape enough money together to eat and pay the bills is sadly commonplace for the majority of us. What's more is that those of us with the lowest incomes are hit the hardest, with studies showing that even if therapy is available, you are less likely to get the wondrous benefits that are easier to access for those of us a bit better off at the time.

I know now in my heart of hearts that if I had been able to share with them then, what I know now, I could have helped those amazing people whose lives have been claimed and to those still living in pain. This is why I wrote this book.

Now, there is far too much valuable knowledge out there about how to optimize our brains and protect ourselves from life's downwards spirals for the benefits to reach just select cliques and groups of people. Training my brain literally saved my life that first troubling winter and gave me the tools to not just be protected from but enjoy the yearly change in my mental state as winter rolled around.

Some of these live saving brain optimization practices have been used for literally 1000s of years and it's about time that we give them a modern day makeover and make them accessible to as many people as possible.

The more we understand , develop, grow and add to our understanding of the brain, body and mind and the repertoire of totally free brain boosting techniques, the closer we will be to ensuring that no matter where you come from, what you do, what you look like or how much money you have, YOU have the power to be happy and fulfill your life's hopes and dreams, all the while being armed with a brain that is so strong, so proud and so resilient that nothing short of Armageddon will bring you down.

How to Get the Most from This Book:

We hope you find this book filled with discovery, insights, and "wow" moments that lead you to the astonishing realization that you've got the blueprint for achieving your dreams and goals right inside your mind. Whether you have picked up this book to learn a few tricks to help you perform better in life or you feel your brain could do with a thorough re-wiring, boosting your brain has never before been so doable.

Don't just read this book! The exciting, groundbreaking research and fascinating science we share with you in Mind Your Head can be practiced in just 5 to 20 minutes a day! Clearly the more time you dedicate the faster the results, but simply regular practice and application of these techniques will set you on the steady and sure path to the results you are after—unless the results you are after are telekinetic and mind reading abilities, you will need to read another book for that! In easy to follow steps and with the latest proven practices, you'll be able to learn a set of techniques that simply have to be practiced and applied.

You don't need to work with just one area of your life at a time either. With Mind Your Head and the brain training practices we cover, you will begin to gently reshape and open your life and habits so that they are aligned more and more with your goals, desires and passions in your life. These feel good techniques should instantly start to repair old, damaging emotions, memories and habits and retrain your brain towards intuitive use of positive *Brain Optimized Practices* (BOPs).

For Additional Support and Tools, Visit Our Website

Although this book contains everything you need to know to get started with experiencing—not reading, but experiencing—and applying the latest mind strengthening technology of the 21st century: neuroplasticity fueled BOPs (*Brain Optimization Practices*), you'll find invaluable, additional resources at www.ultimatenewlifesystem.com.

Acknowledgments

This book is dedicated to the thousands of scientists, engineers, medical doctors, therapists, brain based futurists and visionaries who tirelessly work to share and bring forth the latest new research in brain plasticity, positive neuroscience and positive psychology.

Interpretations and conclusions revealed in this book represent the endowment and legacy from their scientific findings and efforts. We are honored to bring you this peer reviewed, groundbreaking information to be used to strengthen and grow your brain and throughout your life.

Mind Your Head is the result of over two decades and 30,000 hours of clinical practice and research and is a synthesis of the work of many generous and forward thinking individuals and institutions. It is grounded in the research, insights and passion for optimal brain health, human flourishing, learning and productivity that is the heart of the new mind, brain education science.

Dr. Mehmet Oz, we thank you for leading the way and highlighting how important brain optimizing (BOP) practices are for the 21st century:

"Sue, I liked your CD'S' very much this kind of empowering imagery and music can change the course of dis-ease."

Many other's research, beacons of wisdom, and new insights are in Mind Your Head that we would like to honor and thank: Dr. Norman Doidge, Dr. Michael Merzenich, Ph.D., Rick Hanson, Dalai Lama, Dr. Michael M. Merzenich, Dr. Daniel Siegel, Dr. Richard J. Davidson, Dr. Jeffrey Schwartz, Dr. David Rock, Deepak Chopra, Dr. Martin E.P. Seligman, Srini Pillay, M.D., Dr. Andrew B. Newberg, Dr. Daniel Amen, Mark Robert Waldman, Dr. David A. Sousa, Sharon Begley, Raymond C. Kurzweil, Barbara Fredrickson Ph.D., Howard Gardner, Dr. Les Fehmi, Jim Robbins, Teresa Aubele Ph.D., Cathy N. Davidson, Alvaro Fernandez, Dr. Carol Kershaw and J. William Wade Ph.D.

Special Significant Thanks

Sue

To David, Carla, Tom, Mary, Rachel, Leonaura, Shelly, Peg, Fran, Doug, Jeff, Guy, Kahlia, Becky, Luke, Dana, Clarisse, Thiru, Zubair, and my beloved clients of the past 21 years: thank you for believing in our work together, and making the journey so meaningful. To My Parents for Inspiring a New and Better Way.

Carla

To Lucas, Sue, Ruth, Lauren, Phil & Mousie, Sarah & Cara, Julie & Gianni, Gran & Puppa, Ali Kamenova (Youtube Yogi Master), Toni, Purna & Om: for your endless selfless support, love and encouragement that undoubtedly makes me a better person.

To my Greek family and friends who have welcomed me into their lives and hearts and been a never ending source of love, laughs, kindness…and food!

And last but by no means least my Mum, whose beauty, hard work, kindness and selflessness have fueled my belief that you can achieve whatever you dream in life!

Special Joint Thanks:

To our beloved UNLS (Ultimate New Life System) team that continue to inspire and support us every day: David, Shelly, Becky, Luke, Dana, Clarisse, Thiru, Zubair, Leonaura and Andrei.

About the Authors:

Sue Stebbins

CEO of Successwaves International LLC—Creator Of Ultimate New Life System

 Sue Stebbins loves and lives to use new brain science to improve people's lives and businesses by transforming their brains and minds. Considered an expert in the field, Sue achieves remarkable results for her worldwide clients through the use of the new science of brain plasticity.

In 1993, Sue founded Successwaves International LLC. For 21 years, the boutique consulting and training company has specialized in using applied brain science to help clients achieve peak performance and well-being. She and her team are among the world's top pioneers in the brain research and training space. With a primary mission of rewiring individuals and businesses by retraining their brains, the Successwaves team is known for the incredible results it gets for clients.

Sue's passion for new brain science and brain plasticity simply can't be matched. She has logged 30,000 hours coaching and training Fortune 100 executives, entrepreneurs, parents, children, celebrities, and many others with a deep desire to transform. A passionate teacher, Sue presents her clients with the new science-based strategies they can use to rewire their brains. As a result, improving their lives and businesses feels easier, and they are able to work and produce more effectively and see groundbreaking results.

In addition to her work at Successwaves, Sue is the creator of UltimateNewLifeSystem, which offers the world's only proven and simple audio brain training system, coaching and community for those seeking to make changes and improvements in key life areas, such as stress, weight, confidence, optimism, and peak performance. It is a revolutionarily effective brain plasticity training program, which instills positive changes for life.

Sue also created the Elite Neuro-Entrepreneur MBA Program, a groundbreaking results program designed to optimize well-being and increase profits for forward-thinking entrepreneurs, who want to achieve 6,7, or even 8-figure success without suffering toxic stress and an unhealthy lifestyle. She has personally worked in the most stressful environments, and understands what many of today's leaders face. She has dedicated herself to helping people with overloaded 21st century lifestyles optimize their performance and growth through best-in-class business strategies, business design, and brain science.

After her mother died when Sue was only 21, she felt she had been blessed with a second chance. She vowed to learn the "secrets" of health, happiness, success and well-being—what she calls the new 21st century skills and brain optimization practices. Since then she has dedicated her life to helping others use and learn the New Brain For Success™ methods found in UltimateNewLifeSystem™, her entrepreneurial Elite Neuro-Entrepreneur MBA Program and Life Makeover programs.

Sue and her team are passionate about sharing their evidence-based insights, results, and engaging learning programs through webinars, keynotes, seminars, media Interviews, group coaching, limited VIP Masterminds, and one-on-one training.

You can learn more about Sue here:

SuccessWaves.com

UltimateNewLifeSystem.com

Dr. Carla Clark

UNLS Neuroscience Executive Director and Future Innovation Engineer

 Dr. Carla Clark's scientific background gives her a sophisticated grasp on even the most theoretical aspects of brain science, but her real passion comes from rearticulating such knowledge for the empowerment of others. For Carla, the pursuit of knowledge has been the magic and mystery that filled her life from an early age—where she grew up in the majestic countryside of Scotland, developing a strong connection with nature and with books!

Her thirst for knowledge led her to discover the world of meditation and other useful techniques that helped her enhance her learning further. Troubles at home, where in fact her blessing, inspiring her to leave home at just 16 years old, to live life to the fullest and immerse herself in knowledge. Despite a rebellious teen life, her brain training and impeccable grades gave her the chance to go straight to University at sweet sixteen. Her ticket out was her brain!

By 20 years old she graduated as Edinburgh University's Honors Bio-chemistry valedictorian where she went on to complete her doctorate in Bio-physical Chemistry. Despite the wonders of science and even working in cancer research, she was quickly disillusioned by a research world dominated by the push for drug based therapies. Having herself used brain training to beat depression she began to re-think her role in science and how she could help bring these new powerful neuroscience based life improving discoveries to those in need.

Eager to take her understanding of the mind to a higher level she put down her test tubes and picked up the books again, immersing herself in the latest neuroscientific discoveries about drug-free therapies for re-wiring and reshaping people's brains, lives and well-being. While freelancing online, rel-ishing work where she could witness the benefits of helping others, Carla met Sue and an unforgettable partnership was forged.

Sue being living proof of inspiring and leading positive brain based change and track record in the applied brain sciences, combined with Carla's passion for innovative neuroscience ignited the thinking fires as they put their heads together to create a simple, effective, informative yet fun and us-able way to spread the good word and provide the tools for anyone to learn how to take health and happiness into their own hands.

Carla continues to live a sun-filled life in Greece with her partner, dog, cats and turtle! She simultaneously serves as the Executive Director and Proj-ect Lead for Ultimate New Life System.com™ (the soon to be released brain training and social platform of Successwaves).

Carla is also developing the next generation of expert online freelancing services, connecting other brainiacs and wizkids to innovative projects and businesses so that they too can find the perfect partnerships, reinvent the working world and generate innovative solutions and finally start giving our world the change it deserves.

INTRODUCTION

A little Learning is a dang'rous Thing;
Drink deep, or taste not the Pierian Spring:
There shallow Draughts intoxicate the Brain,
And drinking largely sobers us again

~ Alexander Pope

Integration Is Key

ATTAINING LIFE'S ULTIMATE VALUE

"The ultimate value of life depends upon awareness and the power of contemplation rather than upon mere survival."

~Aristotle

More Than a Book
Bought the T-shirt?

"Been There, Done That, Didn't Last." Have you ever dabbled with meditation, Cognitive Behavioral Therapy (CBT), Neuro Linguistic Programming (NLP), brainwave entrainment or any other bona fide brain optimization practice? Perhaps you were one of many that had a go, it was nice and all that but it didn't take long until life took over and you almost forgot about those sacred moments of bliss completely? Or you may go through 'healthy' phases, and then…poof! When your practice goes out of whack a little, your mind is back to the same old tricks.

Although sacred in its own right, finding ten minutes of morning bliss using meditation doesn't cut the mustard if within another 10 minutes your blood begins to boil as your ritualistic morning wind-up begins. Your blood may begin to simmer when the early morning key hunt begins; is ready to bubble over as you stumble and fly over the strategically placed house cat/kids toy/shoe/low-lying furniture; and may be ready to explode even before those Monday morning drivers have a chance to block your hurried path to the workplace.

Knowledge > Techniques > Integration

Mind Your Head is the fun, no nonsense practical guide to the Ultimate New Life System—brain technology for the life you deserve. We like to say: *"Train Your Brain & Free Your Life"*. We've seen thousands of our private clients benefit from truly remarkable results; be it their health, happiness, mood, weight, stress, career or wealth and money issues. These are people who got results after having tried everything.

With the recent and radical shift in global mindset regarding our health, freedom, rights and life, we feel that now is the time, for the rest of the world to benefit. As practitioners that have taught our clients proven and life changing practices for over thirty years we unquestionably know that you can make self and life improvements that can be hardwired into your brain and change the course of your life.

In Mind Your Head you will be introduced to powerful Brain Optimization Practices (BOPs) based on the latest neuroscience research. Standing alone, Mind Your Head is an invaluable brain optimization bible with unrivalled reports of the latest scientific developments and a unique way of integrating BOPs into every aspect of life.

BOPs are tailored for the improvement of four life aspects: yourself, your health, your relationships and your dreams and goals. BOPs are introduced in a manner that builds up your skills without throwing you in the deep end, with each technique learned priming you for the techniques to follow. All of which are specifically designed for achieving balance and heading, straight as an arrow, towards your targets.

Minding your head becomes habitual and effortless allowing you to make everlasting and continually positive changes to your brain, mind, body and life.

Part I

OUR 21ST CENTURY LIVES

"Learning is what most adults will do for a living in the 21st century."

~ S J Perelman

21st CENTURY LIVING
Back in the Day

Modern life is far from monochromatic. It is multifaceted, fast-paced and ever evolving as we charge full speed ahead into the heart of the information age. Yet, once upon a time in the not so distant past, life was a lot simpler, and a heck of a lot slower. Then, we were often defined simply by the place we were born in and our position in the family—breaking the mold and expressing true individuality typically took a back seat. Is it any wonder? Would you have time to tweet your thoughts on about Justin Bieber or Jersey Shore when back then, doing a task seemingly as simple as the weekly washing would require a full day of hitting the washboard hard, elbow deep in soapy water, scrubbing, rubbing, ringing and washing?

Similarly the modes of communication and transportation we had in the past operated at a snail's pace in comparison to the instant messaging and overnight, inter-continental flights that forge the vast webs of communication that we have today. Forgetting to extend wishes to your friend from the back end of Timbuktu on their birthday was perhaps less of a social blunder when the message may have taken 12 months, 6 wagons, 3 boats and a donkey to reach their destination. Or can you honestly imagine male pattern baldness, or stubborn cellulite patches being of great importance when simply using the public lavatory could have left you with a bad case of the bubonic plague? Fat chance!

Modern Stressors

Today, we have higher expectations for ourselves and more demands in life than ever before. Now, in the 21st century with labor saving inventions, advances in technology and ease of access to both knowledge and communication we have the potential to live a balanced lifestyle, healthy and fulfilling in every aspect. In recent decades, the Internet has literally placed knowledge at our fingertips, providing a virtual meeting space, where together we can contribute instantaneously to knowledge that may enhance all of our lives. Importantly however, gaining more knowledge leads to greater power—the power to shape our future—and with this greater power comes greater responsibilities.

With modern life's demands and responsibilities pulling our minds in a million different directions, it's not a shock that we sometimes struggle to keep up with the continually evolving, super-complexities of the modern world. It's only natural that juggling your work, lovelife, family and friends, without disregarding your own physical, mental and emotional well-being and still being able to maintain a sense of enjoyment and wonder in life is nothing short of a miracle.

Busy Bug Burnout

We tend to get stressed-out when we feel we don't have all of the resources we feel we need to meet life's demands. So how have we responded to this increase in stress and demands? Well, as my grandmother and count-less other wise ones used to say, "the rolling stone catches no moss" or "the busy bee makes the best honey." In other words, most of us have internalized the message: MOVE QUICKER! WORK HARDER YOU LAZY FOOL!

We catch the busy bug, where we get a genuine physiological adrenaline rush from whizzing through each day like a whirlwind, while at the same time keeping our bodies and minds in a seemingly "safely controlled" and prolonged state of…STRESS! Woooosh! That was the sound of your life flying by your head…yay! And while pushing the limits as to how much we can jam into one day can be exhilarating, catching the busy bug has its side-effects (and they ain't pretty!).

Raise your hand if you have ever been speedwalking down the street, in a minute-splitting hurry to have a sauntering couple or slow-poke family stop you in your tracks. How dare they; chatting away without a care in the world, their time may be unimportant, but yours for sure as hell is! Is there something wrong with their legs? Must they take up the entire bloody walk-way? Can't they walk faster than a frigging legless tortoise? ARG!! But come now. Where is the sense of ease and happiness in navigating through your daily life when your first compulsion is to punch these inconsiderate idiots squarely in the back of their progress blocking heads?

Simply "moving quicker," "working harder," and "keeping busy" just isn't going to cut it anymore. In the end it adds to modern stressors. Whether it harms yourself or those around you, that helpful little busy bug can meta-morphose into an uncontrollable, unwanted monster, which more often than not leads to an extreme sense of being overworked and feeling exhausted and overwhelmed.

New Tools for a New Future

To clear the hurdles of our rapidly evolving lifestyles with ease we need a *new* way to learn, a *new* way to operate and *new* tools for surviving and succeeding in the 21st century. How would you feel if you could be more successful with less work? More beautiful without lotions and potions? More healthy with less pain for your gain? More loved, respected and appreciated with less conflict, awkwardness, arguments and strife. And achieving your simplest and your wildest dreams without fear of failure? Impossible you claim?! Well, read on…

Neuroscience Leads the Way

Breakthroughs in neuroscience are unraveling the mysteries of how we can upgrade our brains for 21st century living, squish that busy bug once and for all and get on with truly and actually enjoying life. Mind Your Head disentangles the wealth of information and misinformation on brain training to provide you with the most relevant and evidence-based **brain optimization practices** (BOPs) which, with simple repetition, will easily begin to have your brain and life reflecting optimal well-being and have things running like clockwork, lickety-split. It's not rocket science… it's neuroscience!! What's more is that we break down the hardcore science into super fun, super easy digestible chunks, so that bit by bit you become your own brain expert.

Most importantly, we guide you in fully integrating these tools into all aspects of your forever turning wheel of life. While Mind Your Head is a stand-alone practical guide it forms the foundations of the "Ultimate New Life System," *the only clinically proven system,* from leading experts in brain training, for enhancing brain function and optimizing your life! That's right, the ONLY clinically proven system for enhancing brain function and optimizing your life!!

WELCOME TO THE BRAINIVERSE
Life Revolves Around Brains

In the eyes of us simple, earthly creatures, the universe wouldn't exist without our brains. Our brains ARE our universe. Equivalent in weight to a big bunch of bananas, this relatively small organ is the command and control center, working 24-7 to compose the masterpiece that we experience as our lives. How our brain functions determines every aspect of our lives, from coordinating the processes of the body and physical actions, to how we feel, think and behave. Ultimately, it orchestrates the music of our minds; whether we are up-beat or sad; whether we fly into a rage or stay cool, calm and collected; if we prefer Metallica or Bach; whether we dream of soaring through the sky or turning up for a big meeting to suddenly realizing we are in the nude.

Even our sexual preferences and how well we play the games of love are routed in the brain. How our brains operate is central to who we are and how we interact with and perceive the world, including how we get along with friends, co-workers and even the family dog. Without our brains, our legs may still kick when the local GP whacks our kneecap with a hammer, but sophisticated purposeful control of action, thought and behavior requires the powerful capabilities of the brain.

Your Brain is the Engine, Your Mind the Driver

Today, in the midst of the information age, we are bombarded with the stuff. Information, it's coming at us at lightning speed, from every angle and showing no signs of stopping. Our brains are now expected to work harder, better, faster and stronger than ever before. But just like a car's engine your brain can succumb to stress when overloaded. Imagine for a second that you are a Subaru race car: your brain is the engine, with your mind behind the wheel and you are about to compete in the race of your life. Upon arrival to the track an official suddenly informs you that you are to race at ten times the speed, with a ten ton elephant in the backseat! Before you have time to question how the elephant got there in the first place, the horn blows, the green flag is flown and you're off...you screech past the start line, foot to the throttle.

Brain addled and a little stressed to say the least, you zoom along, desperately trying to pick up speed. Approaching maximum velocity, the elephant in the back seat begins to take its toll; the car starts to succumb to the added stress. With the extra weight, you can't go anywhere near as fast as you could before, and you certainly can't go ten times as fast! The smell of burning rubber begins to fill your nostrils as the tires start to overheat, and every bump in the road makes the car shudder fiercely. Just around the first S-curve, and with a resounding snap the suspension fails and you begin to rattle around like crazy, flying uncontrollably towards the gaping mother of all potholes. You frantically twist the wheel to avoid it, but the steering doesn't respond like it used to, it's got a life of its own! Having completely lost control, the car donuts wildly off the track before...BANG! You are brought to an abrupt and inglorious stop, nose down in a nearby ditch.

Like our very own brains, vehicles react differently and can malfunction when the maximum weight which they are designed to carry are exceeded, especially when running at full-speed. Just as an overloaded car can become less stable, difficult to steer and take longer to stop, an overloaded mind can cause both our brains and bodies to breakdown and malfunction, making it difficult to control our thoughts, actions and emotions. As a result of such overloads we can take far longer to switch off our minds and cool down its engine—the brain. And when we do happen to meet one of life's unavoidable bumps along the road, it gets much harder to keep the engine running and the car on track.

Upgrading Your Brain

So what do we do to win the race? Why are high performance drivers called high performance? We pimp our rides to suit our needs, of course! So why not pimp our brains? It's the same thing with so many everyday things we rely upon. When your mobile phone's features are lacking and the phone works inadequately for your purposes, you get an upgrade. Why not upgrade your brain? "My brain is not a mobile phone or a car" I hear you cry. "I can't just take it into the nearest chop shop". Well yes, you are right, brain transplants are still in the realms of science fiction, well kind of.[BB1]

Shall we throw down our gadgets, pick up the nearest club, grab our women by the hair and run for the nearest cave? I think not. Thanks to the collective knowledge obtained from our research partners around the globe— neuroscientists, psychiatrists, psychologists, educators, therapists, physicians, sports trainers, counselors and clinicians—we have a far less messy alternative. That is, to simply train and optimize our brains for heightened states of mental functioning.

Before we get on to the "how," let's focus on the "why." Simply put, in these heightened states us "ordinary people" are capable of breathtaking athletic feats, sublime works of art, profound scientific and philosophical insights and rock-steady emotional and mental control, both when relaxing, and when the pressure is on. We can modify our brain just like that race car and zoop it up a bit, allowing you to masterfully navigate the ups and downs of modern life with ease.

BRAINY BITS

1.   There are some success stories with regards to monkey head transplants, creating real life Frankenmonkies! Just this year a provocative science paper outlined how to perform a human head transplant, which thanks to today's technology is well in the whelms of possibility.

2.   **There is a surprisingly common urban legend that humans only use 10% of their brains, the other 90% remaining an untapped resource. TOTAL BALONEY! In fact, most of our brain is active all of the time, some parts more than others depending on the task at hand, even when we sleep!**

3.   If you were to have a lazy day approximately 20% of your daily calorie needs are fuel ONLY for your brain (~400-600 calories). While your muscles would only need ~13%. Unlike your muscles, your brain is never truly at rest.

SUMMARY

• 21st century life has many more potential lifestyle stressors to juggle.

• Stress and mental overload is a key player in both physiological and mental health problems.

• Brain training and optimization can not only overcome stress and mental overload related problems but take control and performance to the next level.

Up Next...

Now that we are focused on minding our heads—and more importantly, what's inside them—we will draw from the latest neuroscientific research coming from the world's leading universities and research laboratories to provide you with clearer blueprints for understanding the brain and how it works than ever before. More importantly you will get to know the tools needed to optimize your brain for peak performance and how they can drastically alter your brain. Then we shall reveal the best recipe for brain and life optimization success, the Ultimate New Life System!

Part II

YOUR AMAZING BRAIN ATLAS

"The neuroscience area – which is absolutely in its infancy – is much more important than genetics."

~ Leon Kass

THE FUNCTIONAL BRAIN ATLAS
The Era of the Brain

Now it's time to get geeky and tell you all about neuroscience. We certainly aren't going to bore you with dull and dreary jargon and unnecessary details that distract us from having a solid understanding, nor are we going to give you half-assed explanations. In the following pages we will sort the wheat from the hay, bringing you THE MOST up to date, research-based account of the current understanding of our brain and its functional role in our lives. With literally all descriptions supported by the latest peer-reviewed (that means expert science geeks have approved it) scientific journal articles, we leave no wiggle room for misinformation.

Yet despite this recent boom in our knowledge and understanding of the brain, we are still at the tip of the iceberg, with new groundbreaking articles popping up near enough daily, so don't forget to keep up with the latest and greatest developments on our blog following the launch of www.Ultimate-NewLifeSystem.com

Thankfully, science is now on the right track with new tools, techniques and technologies to overcome one of man's final frontiers, the human brain. We have cut the fat and unnecessary science mumbo jumbo and diced-up the info into bite-sized chunks to give you a clear and balanced overview of our advances in unveiling the blueprints of our minds.

The "Average" Brain

Importantly, none of us are average. And our brains in fact are far from average, even for the 'beigest' of characters. Primarily composed of around 100 billion cells, called neurons, your brain controls your body, processes information from your senses, generates experiences and churns out your thoughts at 1000s of miles per second. So how do these teensy weensy cells (called neurons) do so much and so quickly? They use electricity to communicate with each other, literally faster than lightning.

The "Average" Neuron

Neuron cells look kind of like trees (Fig. 1), with extensions that look like the tree's branches, called dendrites. Instead of collecting light energy like a tree, these dendrites fan out to detect incoming information from neighboring neurons. The signal detected by the dendrites is then passed through the main body of the cell. Then, this detected information is converted into electrical energy and rapidly travels through the cell where it travels through the second type of extension in a neuron, a singular, stalk-like projection called an axon.

The act of passing the electrical signal from the tip of the axon to a nearby axon's dendrite is actually a chemical process and occurs where the axon and dendrite meet called the synapse. At the synapse, the electrical message is converted into a chemical message that unlike electricity can jump the 100s of millionths of a meter gap and fire-up the next neuron. But that's not the only cell in your noggin, about half of your brain is made up of glial cells. These guys were pretty much wall flowers and little more than neuron helper cells until recently, as science is just beginning to discover what they can really do.

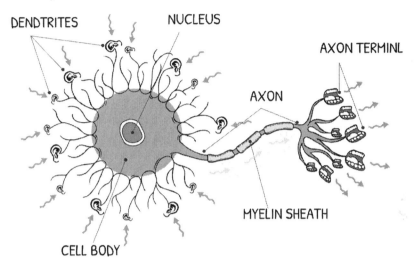

Figure 1. Your Average Neuron. Using verbal communication as an analogy for communication between neurons: We hear a message with our ears (dendrites), and our brain's process this message into electrical energy (cell body), which is propelled through your spinal cord (axon), that for some varieties of neuron cell types, is coated by glial cells with a special substance called myelin that speeds up transmission of the electrical message to the mouth (axon terminus). At the mouth the electrical energy is converted into vibrational energy in verbal communication, which is actually an electrical to chemical energy conversion with communication between neurons.

Mapping out the Brain

But long before the Neuron was discovered in the 1820s, never mind the glial cell, scientists literally poked around and picked brains to figure out the main functions of each physical part of the brain. The gruesome past of mapping the brain was sparked by a French surgeon Paul Broca. He was busy dissecting the brains of stroke patients, when he realized that all patients with difficulty speaking had the same damaged bit of their brain responsible for the problem. Today, we have a continually refined, updated and highly detailed brain atlas that maps out functions of all the bits of our brains.

Now, we could get bogged down in all the fancy pants words for the different parts of the brain and its inbuilt complexity, but really it boils down to this: there are three main, broad regions of the brain: the brain stem, the cerebellum and the forebrain (Fig. 2). An overview of each follows.

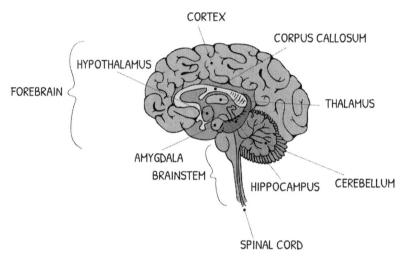

Figure 2. The Brain Atlas. Shown here is a view of the brain as if we had sliced the brain in half, right between the hemispheres and cracked it open like an apple. The brain stem and cerebellum are at the bottom of the brain, closest to the body, depicted with darker shading. The largest section is the forebrain, formed predominantly by the cortex (the large lightly colored outer layer) which encapsulates many other forebrain structures inside.

Brain Stem

In evolutionary terms, the brain stem is the most ancient part of our brains—the part we had before we could contemplate sophisticated masterpieces like the infamous Jack Ass movies or the intellectually invigorating Twilight saga. It controls a broad variety of essential, primal functions such as breathing and heart rate, as well as pain sensitivity and the sleep cycle. It is also the seat of our most fundamental emotions producing the primary chemicals that control our moods, such as playfulness, fear or lust. Attached to the spinal cord, it passes all of the information that comes from it to the rest of the brain and is arguably the most vital part of the human body. It's crazy but true that a human can live a full, healthy and fulfilling life with less than half of the brain, but don't touch the brain stem or you're a goner.

Cerebellum

The cerebellum is easy to recognize. At the back of the brain, attached to the brain stem, it kind of looks like a pair of...well you can decide that one for yourself. For years it was thought that the cerebellum's only function was to provide precision and control for the movement of your body; making the difference between blending in on the dance floor, or writhing around uncontrollably, much like Uncle Jim at your cousin's wedding last year (yes, we all have an Uncle Jim).

The old view of the cerebellum is now changing and its roles in memory, learning, language, behavior and emotion—including the feelings of pleasure and affection—are being discovered. Cerebellum activity has even been associated with the female orgasm! These new discoveries have fueled a surge in research into the cerebellum, so keep an eye on this mysterious guy.

Forebrain

Next we have the forebrain, which has four main structures particularly worthy of note, which are the thalamus, the hypothalamus and the hippocampus found inside the forebrain and the cerebral cortex that forms the outer layers.

Thalamus

At the brain's core, sitting on top of the brain stem, are two important structures, the thalamus and hypothalamus. The thalamus looks a bit like a mini-brain, itself composed of two halves. The primary role of thalamus is to be a switchboard for the hotel that is your brain. The switchboard operators (your neurons) process the messages they receive and open up connections to pass the message through the switchboard to the correct room—or parts of the brain. These messages include all the information from your senses, which have small groups of neurons within the thalamus that act as specialized control centers.

Hypothalamus

If the thalamus is the gatekeeper to the cerebral hemispheres, the hypothalamus acts as the middle man between the brain and your hormones. It receives information about the body and tells your glands what hormones to produce to keep your body stable without you having to think about it. The hypothalamus also controls functions such as body temperature, hunger, thirst, mood and sex drive.

Hippocampus

LEARNING AND NAVIGATION

Wrapping around the thalamus, looking like a pair of futuristic headphones is the hippocampus. Perhaps you have heard that this bit of the brain is super developed in cabbies as it encodes, stores and retrieves information for learning and memory. By training it at work every day cabbies have super navigational powers, with a finely detailed internal map of their driving routes, allowing them to expertly steer you towards your destination...or to take you on the scenic route (for a marginally higher price of course.)

MEMORIES AND EMOTION

The hippocampus is the largest component of a set of structures in the forebrain called the limbic system, which have long studied roles in memory and emotion. As the largest part of the limbic system, the hippocampus is the main structure involved in consolidating information from short-term memory into long-term memory.

The pair of amygdalae that are also members of the limbic system and whose functions include controlling the fear response (you will hear more about on the chapter on stress), are physically attached to the hippocampus and have a close relationship with the hippocampus in the processing of emotional memories. Strong emotional memories are those that when recalled give you a glimmer or even a surge of the feelings you felt in the past during the emotional event. These memories are normally associated with major life events, such as your bashful first date, your prideful graduation day, the joyous birth of your first child and the somber death of a loved one.

Emotional memories, good or bad, often produce very powerful and vivid memories that are easily recollected. This is in fact due to the concerted action of your amygdalae and hippocampus, where your amygdalae influences the consolidation of hippocampal memories, making those emotionally heightened moments easier to remember. In a survival sense this is practical. If you were overjoyed when one person saved your life or distraught when another tried to take it, you would want to clearly remember who was who right, right?

STRESS IS ITS KRYPTONITE

The hippocampus is one of the brain structures most sensitive to stress, as the encoding of relatively stressful events is important for our survival. Chronic stress and continual over-stressing however, eats away at the hippocampus, making you forget recent memories and struggle to recall old ones. Have you ever wondered why over-stressing in an exam can make even the simplest of answers vanish from your head? Well stress is like kryptonite to the hippocampus, which you will learn all about in the next chapter where we will teach you how to eliminate stress.

Cerebral Cortex

The outermost layers of the brain cover the entire forebrain and are collectively called the cerebral cortex or neocortex, dominated by grey matter (predominantly consisting of unmyelinated parts of neurons). The cortex is supported by a much larger layer of white matter beneath it (predominantly consisting of myelinated parts of neurons like long axons). A deep fissure in the cerebral cortex marks where, like an apple, the brain can be split exactly in two, right down the middle, from front to back, marking the line of symmetry that defines the two near-identical halves of the brain, the left and right hemispheres.

CEREBRAL ASYMMETRY

The left and right halves of the brain have almost all structures shared between the two halves. However there are important anatomical differences and many brain functions have marked lateralization, i.e. they use the structures on one side of the brain more than the other for a given function. This is called cerebral asymmetry, one cerebral hemisphere, or parts of it, being more active than the other equivalent part.

BRAIN ASYMMETRY AND WHY IT IS IMPORTANT

Contrary to many wild claims about balancing your hemispheres and 'hemispheric synchronization', having uneven activity between the left and right side of your brain is essential for normal functioning and allows our brain's to multi-task even further. Taking computers as an analogy, the more and more advanced they have become the more we have split their brains, the processors, to allow for more multi-tasking, i.e. dual-core or quad-core processors. When one core is running your web browser the other can be scanning for viruses. Having asymmetry is what has shaped our abilities to perform complex tasks and having more pronounced asymmetries than other animals is likely one of the main reasons we are at the top of the food chain.

A FISHY TALE OF TWO HALVES

An experiment in fish, highlights why asymmetry is an evolutionary advantage. The experimenters had two varieties of the same type of fish, let's call these two fish asymmetrical Alex and symmetrical Sam. Both of these fish can handle single tasks equally well, such as catching shrimp for dinner. However if we add a predatory fish into the mix, Sam's brain has a bit of a meltdown as he can't focus on both the catching of food and the avoidance of the predator too well. Alex on the other hand, with his asymmetrical brain doesn't need to split his time between focusing on the prey and dinner separately, he can focus on both tasks at once and they can catch their dinner just as easily as if the predator wasn't even there. If these fish were our ancient ancestors it's clear that we are more likely to have evolved from asymmetrical Alex.

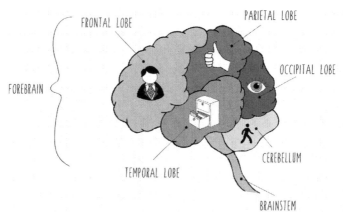

Figure 3. The Four Lobes of the Brain. *Here is a whole brain with the four lobes outlined and containing a symbol representative of its general function: frontal lobe (business executive for executive functions), parietal lobe (hand for the senses, particularly touch), temporal lobe (filing cabinet for information storage), occipital lobe (eye for processing vision).*

A HUMAN TALE OF TWO HALVES

Movement, hearing, talking, smelling, practically everything we can do requires asymmetry for the multitasking in the brain that we take for granted. For example when listening to a friend tell you about their day your left brain will process the words being used, but the right side of the brain will process those details that can signify the true meaning of a sentence, such as tone or inflection. Without this asymmetry it would be impossible for us to function at the advanced level that we do.

HEALTHY VS. UNHEALTHY ASYMMETRY

In a healthy, intelligent brain, the two halves are communicating fluently, and working closely together. There are clear hemispheric asymmetries, however when comparing to an unhealthy brain it is clear that the healthy brain has a reduction in dominance of one hemisphere over another for many tasks. More pronounced asymmetry than the norm can be a causal factor in many diseases and disorders. From depression or anxiety to Alzheimer's or Parkinson's, over pronounced (and in some cases under pronounced) asymmetry can cause a whole host of problems, be it thought and emotion related or something more physical.

Divisions of the Cortex

Found only in mammals, the cortex controls the higher functions that define us; like how we interpret the world around us, or plan and organize a party, or how we get down and shake our thangs, as well as how we communicate. It all looks like it is made of much the same, slimy, pinkish, noodle-like wiggly stuff. But in fact it is divided up into sections that have specific roles. While only 2-3 mm thick, this wrinkly layer makes up three quarters the volume of your brain and is made of more than 20 billion Neurons. These Neurons are in six layers that stack like Lego bricks, with each stack forming a functional module. If the neocortex was a Lego board, the modules that share the same function would click together in groups, with the end result being a patchwork of functional groups.

This patchwork of functional groups has varying degrees of complexity. The closer we investigate a region of the cortex the more we can divide it up into even smaller functionally distinct sections. The broadest divisions of the cortex are naturally divided by some of the bumps (gyri) and grooves (sulci) of each cerebral hemisphere into the four lobes of the brain: frontal, parietal, temporal and occipital (Fig. 3).

The Frontal Lobe

The frontal lobe is considered to house what makes us human as it is concerned with executing our behaviors. It is associated with reasoning, planning, strategizing, self-monitoring, attention, emotion, motivation, reward, retrieval of memories from the past, memories of the task at hand (working memory) and houses the primary motor cortex for control of movement. Broadly speaking the frontal lobe deals with the executive functions of the brain, much like a business executive. It allows for successful integration of loads of information about your thinking, feeling and doing to then evaluate and actuate the best course of action. As such the frontal lobe needs lots of information to help make complex decisions and has a high level of connectivity with the rest of the brain.

The Occipital Lobe

Found at the back of the brain the occipital lobe processes visual input that is sent to the brain from our eyes. Determining color and depth and detecting motion are all part of the parcel. The information that dictates our sense of vision is further processed by the parietal and temporal lobes.

The Parietal Lobe

The parietal lobe is involved in integrating information from our senses. It receives sensory information from the tongue and skin, and processes sensory information from the ears and eyes that come from the temporal and occipital lobes respectively. By integrating this information it helps us generate goal-directed voluntary movement. Sensory information such as pressure, touch, and pain are of particular importance to the parietal lobe.

The Temporal Lobe

This lobe is the location of the primary auditory cortex, which is important for integrating visual information from the occipital lobe with auditory processing allowing us to interpret what a sound is and where it is coming from and to understand the language we hear. It's no surprise that memory and learning is closely associated with language and is reflected in verbal memory storage in the temporal lobe. The hippocampus is found in the internal part of this lobe which reminds us of the temporal lobes involvement in the intentional recollection of facts (such as when your dentist appointment is) as opposed to unconscious memories (how to ride a bike). Generally, we can think of the temporal lobe as a 'filing cabinet' for verbal language and other memories and facts.

Modules within Modules within Modules

Each of the four lobes of the brain are further and further subdivided down to tiny areas that are specific for certain functions. By connecting up spatially separate groups within and between different lobes, both at cortical and subcortical levels, that have different functions, the cortex has the astounding ability to give us an accurate representation of the world. It makes complex inferences about both our social and physical environments, and how to use these ideas to plan and implement our behavior. Without your neocortex you'd likely have the emotional, social and intellectual depth of a goldfish.

Corpus Callosum—White Matters

Myelin is the substance that sets white and grey matter apart. Being white, those cells and parts of cells that are covered in myelin are considered white matter, those without are considered grey matter. Grey matter mainly consists of the cell bodies, dendrites and unmyelinated axons while white matter mainly consists of myelinated axons. As myelin helps speed up the transfer of the electrical signal across myelinated axons, white matter is the tissue through which messages are shot at super speed to the different grey matter areas of the cerebral hemispheres.

The left and right hemispheres are not fully separate; in fact they remain connected through the corpus callosum (Fig. 2). The corpus callosum is the largest white matter structure in the human brain and is crucial in maintaining the independent processing of the hemispheres and in communicating information between the two sides. The corpus callosum develops at 6-8 years old and deteriorates in old age and as such we have less asymmetry when we are very young and very old. It is connected to the white matter networks that exist within each hemisphere, the underground cables that connect different parts of the outermost grey matter layer, the cortex, together.

BRAINY BITS

1.   Giraffes have neurons with incredibly long axons that transmit information from their toe to neck that are over 5 meters!!

2.   Although glial cells do not transmit electrical energy there are actually more glial cells in the brain than neurons!!! We are still discovering new functions for the many kinds of glial cells, which so far include cleaning up cellular 'debris' (brain litter!), structural, nutrient and insulation support (myelin) for neurons and dead neuron digestion.

SUMMARY

- Neurons are the building blocks of the brain, communicating information electrochemically from one neuron to another where a dendrite of one neuron meets the axon of another, the synapse.
- **These neurons form many structures within the brain which have been being mapped in greater and greater detail for almost 200 years.**
- There are three main regions of the brain, the brain stem, cerebellum and the forebrain
- **The brain stem controls a variety of primal bodily functions and emotions and is a conduit for information passed between the body and the rest of the brain.**
- The cerebellum is best known for control of motor control (organizing and executing of our physical movement) with new roles in memory, learning, language, behavior and emotion.
- **The forebrain has five main structures worthy of note here: the thalamus, the hypothalamus, the hippocampus, the cortex and the corpus callosum.**
- The thalamus is the switchboard operator between the outside world and us that receives information and outputs it to the correct destination within the brain.
- **The hypothalamus is the middleman between the brain and release of hormones.**
- The hippocampus encodes, stores and retrieves information for learning and memory.
- **The corpus callosum is the largest white matter structure in the human brain and is crucial in maintaining the independent pro-**

cessing of the hemispheres and in communicating information between the two sides.

•   The cerebral cortex is formed of predominantly grey matter with stacks of neurons or modules that are clustered together in functional groups. The broadest functional divisions make up the four lobes of the brain: the frontal, occipital, temporal and parietal lobes.

Up Next...

Perhaps now you are wondering just how it is possible to coordinate this insanely complex partitioning of function within the brain. Not only coordinating the Lego stacks of the cortex, but modules of neurons in the primal brain stem; the slightly mysterious organizing center that is the cerebellum; the mighty memory geek the hippocampus and the super organizers, the thalamus and hypothalamus. Well that is exactly what the subject of the next section is all about, the rapidly evolving worlds of neuroplasticity and brainwaves! Priming your brain with the latest neuroplasticity and brainwave know how is the fundamental stepping stone needed to orchestrate the creation of your ultimate new life!

Part III

THE WAVE-MAP OF THE BRAIN

"There's a revolution going on. The present era in neuroscience is comparable to the time when Louis Pasteur first found out that germs cause disease."

~ Candice Pert

Neural Networks and Neuroplasticity
Unacknowledged Beginnings

Now let us go back to the 1800s. Doctors were so busy slicing, dicing, poking, prodding and electrifying brains in attempts to map out brain function that no one took notice of a remarkable discovery—the brain can miraculously reorganize this so-called hardwired map of itself, ON ITS VERY OWN. Said another way, the brain possesses the capability to re-organize itself! A few scientists were ahead of their time in the mid to late 19th century, realizing that the damaged brains of infant animals (including humans) can reorganize themselves to recover lost function. It wasn't until 1948 that a polish scientist, Jerzy Konorski, coined the term neuroplasticity, and even then no one made much of a fuss.

Popular Present

Science clung to the idea that the functional modules of the brain stem and cerebral cortex in particular were permanently fixed after childhood and that only the hippocampus was plastic (it has the ability to develop, grow and change) as it was associated with memories, which clearly change with time. Only now in the 21st century is a real paradigm shift underway. Science is finally appreciating that ALL areas of the brain can be plastic.

Simply put all of the functional parts of our brains, like putty, can be molded for better or worse throughout the entirety of our life spans—they have neuroplastisticity. The recently re-established potential of neuroplasticity has transformed it into a bit of a buzzword, and it should be for the foreseeable future. There is a relentless stream of neuroplasticity based behavior, thought and life changing discoveries being revealed year after year and showing no signs of stopping.

Neural Networks

To understand the importance of neuroplasticity we must first begin by consolidating how we think about neural networks. As we mentioned to you earlier, neurons are highly specialized cells with long wire-like extensions coming from their main body, through which they talk to one another electrochemically. Through axons and dendrites, the mouth and ears of the neuron, they connect up the different functional regions of the brain, forming large and complex networks. Just how large and how complex can it get? Well what we didn't tell you is that the average neuron can be connected to tens of 1000s of other neurons which gives rise to enormously complex networks.

You thought the universe was complex? Well your mind blows its complexity out of the water. The number of potential connections that neurons can make in a single brain, is larger than the number of particles that exist in our entire observable universe! Your mind is an intricate mesh of interconnected and overlapping networks. It is the communication within and between these networks that form the basis of how the brain does what it does and makes us who we are. Thanks to neuroplasticity these networks are not set in stone, we have the power to change, grow and optimize our networks, better our brains and improve our lives—anytime, anywhere, over and over and over again!

Neuroplasticity
Neuroplasticity Basics

Broadly speaking neuroplasticity is the brain's natural ability to form new connections between neurons and change its structure and functioning in response to both internal and external experiences—essentially what and how you think, see and do. The brain's ability to mold, change and adapt to suit our needs—neuroplasticity—is brought about by a collection of processes that work together to cause changes in the structure, function and strength of communication within and between brain regions. Essentially neuroplasticity is an umbrella term that covers all changes in the brain occurring at the cellular level that alter the connectivity of networks in the brain in response to everything that we experience.

Enhancing Connectivity

At the molecular level new neurons can be generated in a process called neurogenesis. The neurons themselves can be structurally upgraded to enhance connectivity. They can be zooped-up or down to have more or less dendrites or axons sprouting in multiple directions and they can also have their synapses fine tuned (synaptic plasticity) to increase or decrease the amount of neurotransmitter (the chemical message) they can release at the end of the axon and how well the dendrites respond to these chemical messages.

Use It Or Lose It

But what fuels neuroplasticity? What makes the new networks form and old networks dissolve? Well that's where the saying "Neurons that fire together wire together. Neurons that fire apart wire apart," comes in. Basically, it boils down to "you are what you do, not what you think you will do" The more you do, think or feel something the more a particular set of neurons communicate with one another and the stronger the neural network involved becomes.

Similarly, the less you do, think or feel something the more a network is broken down. What is it that orchestrates these neurons within a network to work together as one for a common goal? What is this fuel for network functionality that can also act as a fuel for neuroplasticity? Well that is what the next section is all about, the magnificent world of brainwaves.

What Are Brainwaves?
A Confusing Past

I'm sure you have all heard of brainwaves before, but as with neuroplasticity, there is a ton of incomplete truths, confuddled explanations and general confusion about what exactly brainwaves are, how they are made and what they do. This isn't surprising as it reflects split views and incomplete understandings in the scientific past of brainwaves. Until the past couple of years, brainwaves haven't been getting the full credit they deserve. Often, they have been thought of as a by-product of the brain that reflects our brain functions, not a tool that the brain uses with specific purpose or importance to control the brain's functions. Oh boy, were we wrong!

Brainwave Basics

When many neurons are chatting with one another they operate in synchrony, firing their electrochemical signals in bursts at the same frequency. The heartbeats of the brain, these synchronous beats of electricity are called brainwaves. Just like the electrical activity of your heart is measured using an electrocardiograph (ECG), telling the cardiologist about your heart's status, we can measure the electrical activity of the brain using electroencephalography (EEG) which tells the neuroscientist about your brain's status.

An ECG reading is a graph of repetitive increases and decreases in the electrical activity in the cells of the heart, up-down-up-down, with time. These rhythmic waves of electrical activity cause the muscle cells of the heart to become coordinated and contract together to pump blood around the body, making the audible beating of our hearts. An EEG reading on the other hand shows the electrical activity in the cells of the brain, up-down-up-down, with time. These rhythmic waves of electrical activity cause the neurons within and between networks to become coordinated in their communication and work together to generate thoughts and control your body.

Brainwaves Are Classed By Frequency

The speed of electrical brainwave beats are measured in hertz (Hz), a unit of frequency also used to describe radio waves. Generally speaking, Hz measures the number of times per second a periodic phenomenon occurs, called the frequency. In this case, the frequency is the number of times per second the neurons are firing in synchrony. When it comes to your brain, different radio bands or radio wave frequency ranges within your brain, allow your neural networks to tune into different radio stations, depending on the task at hand.

In order of frequency from low to high, slow to fast brainwaves, we have infra-slow waves at less than ~0.1Hz, then delta waves up to ~4 Hz, then theta to ~8 Hz, alpha up to ~13 Hz, beta up to ~30 Hz, gamma to ~80 Hz and then we have even faster ultra gamma oscillations, with the latest recordings reaching up to 600 Hz.

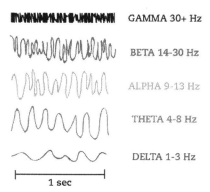

Figure 4. Brainwaves in the Brain. Graphical examples of broad classes of EEG recordings with a 1 second scale bar.

Brainwave Mapping

During an EEG, patients wear a pretty daft looking hat to say the least. Dozens of wires poke out of their heads, connecting them to sensors that measure the electrical activity coming from their brains at precise positions on the scalp. Using sophisticated math and computers, the brainwave data from each precise point is analyzed and converted into a series of heat maps of brainwave functioning called brain maps or quantitative electroencephalographs (QEEGs, Fig. 5). This map shows where a particular brainwave (or range of brainwaves) is stronger or weaker in the cortex than for the average brain of someone of the same age, that has the same handedness and is doing the same task. Basically it highlights which brainwaves are doing something different or unexpected than in your average, healthy Joe and roughly where in the cortex this is occurring.

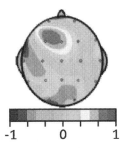

Figure 5. Quantitative EEG Brain Mapping. Here is a representative QEEG map for 8Hz (Alpha). The heat map shows where on the cortex the strength of the 8 Hz signal is pretty standard (lighter shades), stronger or weaker (darker shades) when compared to the average Joe's healthy brain from a normative database. The front of the brain and frontal lobe is situated at the top of the diagram, the back of the bead and occipital lobe at the bottom facing the scale bar. Darker shades show 1 standard deviation from the norm.

What Do Brainwaves Do?
There Is No Such Thing as a Solo Brainwave

Just like your heartbeat, your brainwaves go faster or slower depending on the task at hand, charging the brain with its operating power, the modes or speeds in which the functional sections using that brainwave are working at. And we are never experiencing just one frequency. Your brain consistently cycles through each of these brainwave states, pulsing with all of these brain-wave states simultaneously. The dominant state dictates our state of mind and level of consciousness, as well as what mode the different modules and networks within the brainwaves' influence are working. With brainwave science still in its infant years, we are even discovering and defining previously immeasurable brainwaves and only just beginning to hint at the roles they play in the brain.

Changing Stations

The dominating frequency in a brain network tends to change depending on your mood, where you are and what you are doing. You are unlikely to listen to thrash metal when your ancient Aunt Aggie comes to visit or classic FM when you are trying to get a raving party started. Brainwaves behave exactly like radio waves. Different brainwave frequency ranges or brainwave states (Fig. 4) allow us to set the mood and tune into different states of mind which are both caused and changed by our thoughts, our conversations, our interaction with our environment and our bodies. Broadly speaking, delta dominates during deep sleep; theta in sleep and semi-awake states; alpha when you are relaxed and awake; beta when you are engaged and attentive and increases in gamma power are associated with fast and complex brain functions.

Networking

It turns out that not only do they have a purpose but they are in fact paramount and integral to how we coordinate the super complexity of the brain for all our thinking, feeling and doing. The evidence suggest that brain-waves are actually controlling the little functional modules of the brain, al-lowing modules that are far apart to become one, forming a complex network that functions in synchrony, performing as one for a specific task. Or perhaps more profoundly, brainwaves synchronize all the different functional net-works in the brain, including the different parts of your brain that deal with our senses. Of course, it is our combined senses that generate our perception of the world. Incorporating this with our thinking and feeling is what helps to generate our conscious awareness. As such, brainwaves are inextricably linked to every fiber of our being, and through nourishing particular brainwave states we can enhance our being from the way we think, feel and act to the way we perceive the world itself and how we enjoy our own life experience.

Brainwave Frequencies Explained

Current Research

Our understanding of brainwaves is growing in leaps and bounds. From the molecules that are involved in creating them and the genes that control them, to identifying abnormal patterns that are indicative of diseases and mental health problems, to identifying the brainwave patterns that can transform ordinary people into super-functioning, high-achieving Zen masters. Decades of research on EEG activity have led to defining the frequency ranges for the brainwaves found in the brain (alpha, beta etc.), based on the fact that some of these frequency ranges are characteristic of particular brain regions, functions and states.

The Evolution of Brainwaves

Ultimately each brainwave state provides a different system for organizing the brain, with higher and higher frequencies being obtained to allow for an additional level of organization as you follow the evolutionary ladder of animals. For example delta oscillations are the most ancient system, swamping the brains of our scaly ancestors, the lower vertebrates (reptilian, amphibians, and fish). Theta oscillations on the other hand tend to dominate in lower mammals. Alpha oscillations are associated with a more advanced system, which is the wave that dominates our waking lives. Brains that are used to a regular overflow of gamma waves, particularly the ultra-fast kind, include fast thinkers, masterminds and yogi masters.

The Need for Speed

There is a strong link between the brainwave frequency and the speed your brain processes information. The faster the frequency the more supercharged those brain regions are. Recent studies suggest that the gradual slowing of our brain functions as we get a bit soft with age is caused by the gradual slowing of the fastest waves on the scale, the gamma waves. This fits well with the very broad classification of brainwave functions where delta dominates during deep sleep; theta in sleep and semi-awake states; alpha when you are relaxed and awake; beta when you are engaged and attentive and increases in gamma power are associated with heightened network functioning needed for fast and complex brain functions.

Local and Global Networking

Have you ever stood outside a party or club, or have been rudely awoken by your neighbors when you hear the dull, rhythmic thud of a bass line blasting out of speakers and through the walls? Ever wondered why you can hear the bass and not the singer or the melody? Well it's down to the physics of waves. Take two rather irritating serial snorers for example, one male one female, both equally as loud as one another, disturbing your sleep from the neighboring room. The female has a high pitched squeak of a snore, which in wave form is super fast, much like beta or gamma waves. The male on the other hand has a deep resonating snore, which in wave form is much slower and more like theta or delta waves. Low frequency waves have a long wave length.

That means that every up and down on a graph takes longer and is more stretched out than for high frequency waves, were the wave length is shorter. As such, low frequency sound waves, like those of our male snorer, travel farther than high frequency (short wave length) sound waves, with the short wave lengths being more easily absorbed by the molecules in the air and surroundings. So while closing your bedroom door and putting in ear plugs might just drown out the squeaky high-pitched snore of the female, the male's mountainous snore can penetrate these barriers and disturb your sleep.

How does this traveling distance-frequency relationship relate to brainwaves? A current theory is that fast high frequency brainwaves of beta and gamma work on coordinating areas on a more local scale, within and between close knit networks. While, on the other hand, the slower low frequency brainwaves of delta, theta and alpha tend to operate on a more global scale, integrating networks separated by greater distances to generate your real-time perception of the world.

In combination, this intertwined maze of multi-level, overlapping networks generates the sense of self that makes us conscious creatures. So not only do brainwaves unite distant regions in a network to operate together for the same function, they integrate all your individual functional networks to represent real-time reality and allow you to make complex decisions, and set goals for your future. This intricate integration of overlapping brainwave systems for organizing your brain is the magical glue that makes you you.

Infra-slow (<0.1 Hz)
Binding Brain Glue

Infra-slow brainwaves were first discovered over 50 years ago. Yet, they have been considered little more than noise until recent technological developments. As a result, very little is actually known about them. Found nestled and closely linked with the faster brainwaves (described below) the present belief is that infra-slow waves are the rubber bands that hold together these large overlapping, interconnecting networks that are dominated by different brainwaves depending on the situation. Infra-slow waves have been found all over the brain, but they seem to be particularly important for thalamus activity, which is unsurprising considering the thalamus is the connection center of the brain.

Delta (1-3 Hz)
Sleep, Memory, Learning and Motivation

Delta waves are considered the most ancient of brainwaves. In humans, delta waves dominate the realms of slow wave, deep and restful sleep. They are also the most prevalent waves in the brains of babies in the womb, but are quickly overridden by higher frequencies as we develop. During slow wave sleep it is thought that delta waves are involved in the transfer of your days memories from the hippocampus into long-term storage in the cortex. In waking life, delta waves are involved in the acquisition of new information in learning, further increasing in strength the more difficult it is to learn something. Delta waves also control networks linked with motivation and increase when you are hungry or a bit randy. They are pretty primal actually.

Delta's Dark Side

But the delta wave has a dark side. Normally the higher frequency brainwaves overshadow delta, keep it in check and let you make logical assessments (like whether making your neighbor's yappy Chihuahua "disappear" to appease those delta controlled hunger pangs is really such a good idea). However, unusual increases in delta waves are found in many diseases and disorders. Too much delta (as well as theta) is thought to play a role with the brain's attention and concentration generating networks and is unsurprisingly characteristic of ADHD. Delta has a reputation for sometimes taking over and wreaking havoc within us. For example, delta activity spikes during panic attacks. On the flip side, it is also integral to slow wave sleep, when we consolidate new memories in our brains and in learning and motivation. A double-edged sword, you need to watch your step with delta.

Theta (3-8 Hz) and Friends

Sleep and Memory

The next slow brainwave range in the frequency scale is theta, the long waves that take you into the first stages of sleep and are characteristic of REM sleep. REM sleep is where emotional consolidation of memories occurs in relation to delta dominated slow wave sleep. During REM sleep theta begins to take over the delta waves in the hippocampus. The current theory is that while delta waves help encode memories, the theta waves are involved in refining memories, consolidating connections and enriching them with stored memories and emotions. This could be why we have very vivid memories of extraordinarily detailed REM sleep dreams, but the rarer slow wave sleep dreams are much fuzzier (you 're too busy at that time storing the memories). Essentially, during this process delta first uploads the pictures and then theta adds the tags.

Waking Life and Memory
Theta and Gamma Like to Work Together

Theta has strong ties with gamma waves. They like to get cozy and couple up, syncing up their beats with one another. The faster gamma waves are nestled in a background of theta waves and they tend to come hand in hand. This theta-gamma code may have many roles, one of which is in how our memory works. Theta-gamma interplay is thought to link your short-term memory of recent events with your past memories and long-term memory, and allows you to have multiple items in your working memory such as your daily "to do" list.

Gamma forms the representation of the events occurring around you, while the theta links this to your past memories. For example, being aware of bouncing a bundle of joy giggling on your lap shortly after feeding (gamma), you all of a sudden recall that last time this happened you were rewarded with a healthy coating of baby puke (theta)! Maybe ceasing the baby jiggling would be a smart move? Evidence also suggests that you are more likely to make the right judgment call the more your theta and gamma waves are humming as one.

Theta Digs for Details while Alpha Waves Desync

But what happens when you don't quite recognize what something is straightaway, or you're finding it tough to hear what someone is saying? This is when theta is busy playing tag with the faster, more dominant waking life brainwave alpha during waking consciousness (when you're not asleep). When you need to focus your attention to make sense of something and probe deeper into your memory for help, alpha, your general knowledge or knowing wave, becomes less synchronized and its signal goes down.

For example, if you struggle to hear what your pal is screaming at you over the music in a busy bar, theta will come to your aid to help you make sense of it all. The rate at which syllables are spoken is roughly 3-7 Hz, which low and behold is the theta rhythms' frequency. This slower rhythm allows you to sink up with your friend's chat, putting greater focus on interpreting and understanding the words. Scientists are still trying to make sense of the intricate relationship between different types of brainwaves and our memory. Highly detailed work is currently underway.

Navigation and Emotion

Theta waves are pretty fond of the hippocampus—the enlarged memory headphones of the brain that are beefed-up to give cabbies super navigational powers. It's no surprise then that theta waves are also involved in navigation. Can't find your car in that ten story parking lot in the center of town again? Missed the turn on the bypass? When you are awake theta (and to a lesser degree delta) is busy helping your hippocampus get you around when you need to dip into your internal map.

Not only do theta waves help you navigate the world, they also help you navigate your emotions. Theta, and to a lesser extent delta and alpha (the comparatively slower waves), have been recently studied to understand their roles in regulating our emotional interpretation of the world and our interpretation of other people's emotions.

To that end, we have two main systems in our brains that deal with our emotions that reside within the forebrain, one that represents emotions and the other which deals with regulating these emotions. In a science paper released online in June 2013, it has been shown that theta waves regulate the crosstalk between these two regions allowing us to modify our emotions based on our environment and well-being. What's more is that greater emotional control is gained when the synchrony between neurons pulsing in theta is finely tuned.

The Dark Side of Theta

As with delta, theta also has a dark side. Abnormal increases (and also decreases) in theta and irregular interplay between theta and higher oscillations (going out of whack), are common in many diseases and disorders including dementia, Alzheimer's, Parkinson's, ADHD, Autism, OCD, alcoholism and addiction, and the list goes on. A common pattern is emerging: if a brain imbalance is rearing its ugly head, theta and delta brainwave pattern disturbances may be part of the problem.

Alpha (8-13 Hz)
More than Just a Wandering Mind

Along with the fast wave beta, the slow wave alpha was the first brainwave to be discovered in around 1908. The alpha signal is strong when you are awake and deeply relaxed with your eyes closed, when your attention is focused inwards and when you are daydreaming. When you open your eyes and come back to reality beta may begin to outshine the alpha waves.

Sadly, alpha waves were snubbed from the get go and for nearly 100 years it was considered brain noise, or, the random, unimportant, smoky wanderings of the idle brain. In truth, however, alpha waves give you access to the roots of your conscious awareness, operating at the boundaries between the slow delta and theta waves of the sleeping subconscious and the faster beta that dominate caffeine-fueled hectic 21st century brains.

Online there are hoards of websites talking about the amazing benefits of controlling alpha waves for relaxation (which you will hear all bout in the next section). These claims are true, alpha waves are the easiest of brainwaves to consciously control and they can also bring bliss, but as with all brainwaves it's when, where and how they are used that makes the difference between brainwave benefits and brainwave botch-ups.

Now, the concept of alpha waves being the brain's idle wave has been turned on its head and we are finding that alpha waves have functional roles all over the brain including visualization, memory, learning and concentration. Increased alpha activity in brain areas not directly involved in processing information is thought to reflect inhibition of task relevant brain areas.

More simply put, a current theory is that alpha waves, may be inhibitory waves that stop a brain area from carrying out its regular functioning. It seems that alpha might be able to excite a brain area and to inhibit it from doing its regular job, but in all honesty the current picture isn't that clear and a simple inhibitory role may be an oversimplified concept. Despite the clear benefits to health and well-being that alpha waves bring, and the fact that alpha waves are strong and dominate EEG signals, its widespread roles and lack of early interest mean that our current scientific understanding of alpha waves is pretty juvenile. Nonetheless, the little that we can currently gleam is profound.

Memory and Dipping Into the Subconscious

The alpha wave works to untie the brain and provide you with a real-time perception of the world, the knowing of one's existence in the here and now. It is thought to control the access to information that represents your knowledge of the environment, the stuff you just intuitively know without feeling like you have to think. 'I let go of the glass, it will fall.' That's why when there is a clear meaning in your knowledge base about what is happening around you, alpha dominates. For example when you struggle to hear your friend at the bar over the general hubbub, and a clear meaning to their words is lost, alpha activity recedes and then theta waves help you out. They allow you to recollect info from the past to help you interpret and store this new information and update your general knowledge base for future use by alpha.

Alpha waves are associated with intuitive memory and this is likely why alpha waves don't take over your brain until adulthood. When you are a child, theta is busy establishing a solid knowledge base for alpha to work with in the near future. Science is also hinting that individual differences in alpha activity may reflect different ways of perceiving the world, with links to personality traits. This would explain why for some people alpha band activity is not so dominant; their minds might not rely so heavily on a sound knowledge base and may rely more heavily on emotions or working memories to unify their view of the world. You will hear loads more about alpha and its benefits when we get started on some brain optimization practices.

Beta (14-30 Hz)
The Action Stations Wave

You would think that being one of the first to be discovered, along with alpha, would mean we know all about beta. Long story short, we don't. It's probably the least well characterized of the bunch, but recently identified roles in mental illness have fueled further research. Beta is associated with alert consciousness unlike the relaxed conscious awareness of alpha. It is your alert and ready to respond 'action stations' wave. It's busy when your body and mind are set on a task and as such it tends to dominate the motor system, keeping you poised for action.

Theta and Control of Beta and Emotions

The exact role beta plays in the motor system remains unclear, but it is clear they are extensively interlinked with many cognitive processes and involved in cross-talk with other waves, notably in regulating your emotions. Well, how you respond to negative and stressful situations depends on the interaction between theta in the frontal lobe and beta in the motor cortex.

When you feel emotionally unstable and we see something that gives us icky negative emotions, theta goes out of control and it is completely unable to work with the beta. The beta waves spike out of control resulting in a lack of emotional control. If on the other hand you're feeling pretty Zen your theta waves keep the balance in your emotional system and carefully regulate your beta. By maintaining the status quo, theta-beta interplay allows you to think clearly in emotionally upsetting situations.

The Beta Burden

All in all beta waves are important for getting the job done. With your brainwaves going faster, you can think quicker and feel more energized, making us more motivated and socially outgoing. The most recent theory is that beta activity provides us with an internal measuring device to decide if action is needed and if so, then to instigate it. Too much beta however, easily translates to stress, anxiety and restlessness and beta waves are botched-up in substance abusers.

We have all enjoyed the beta buzz from zooming through our day, mowing down your to-do list like nobody's business. But beware, while beta has been fueling humanity's race from A through Z and back again, modern society is seeing the side-effects of too much beta with stress related health problems running a muck in 21st century society.

While you need some beta in your frontal lobe to charge your brain's executive planner with the alertness needed to get stuff done, if you don't also have a dash of some chilled out alpha waves in your right hemisphere nothing is there to stop fear, stress and anxiety from rearing its ugly head. You will hear plenty more about balancing your beta in the next chapter, where we beat back the beta and iron out life's stresses.

Gamma (30-80 Hz)
A Promiscuous Wave

Being some of the fastest waves in the brain it's unsurprising that gamma waves are directly related to fast brain processing, states of peak performance (both physical and mental), high focus, concentration, mystic and transcendental experiences. As such, gamma has captured the limelight in recent years. With its fingers dipped in so many higher brain functions, it's hard to keep up with new developments.

Changes in strength, frequency and synchrony in gamma have been linked to every brain function imaginable. It is found literally everywhere in the brain, when we are knocked unconscious and when we are asleep. It originates from the master organizer, the thalamus, and sweeps through the cortex. Involved in so many brain functions and found literally everywhere it has taken some time, and might take some time yet, to exactly pinpoint gamma's true function.

Short-range Integration

Many scientists think the evidence points towards gamma waves as being the key to how we can integrate short-range information. Let's imagine you are out marveling at that Lamborghini of yours that you have parked out back. When you look at your car, many different regions of the visual cortex process different aspects of the visual image. Specific regions deal with aspects such as corners, lines, colors, motions, categorization and shape recognition to name a few. Gamma waves integrate and unite the spatially distinct regions allowing you to perceive the car as one object.

Binding Theory

This is why gamma has been considered the binding rhythm of the brain. One that unites all the parts of our brain so we experience life as a unified whole, integrating the individual objects and background of our environment, our emotions and our thoughts into a single, unified experience. This is not surprising considering both novice and expert meditators as well as non-meditators describe a feeling of oneness, bliss and joy when enhancing their gamma waves. However, the physics of waves suggest that this theory may be a misinterpretation of the results as fast waves like gamma would be more suited to integration over shorter distances, not across the whole brain.

Peak Performance

Another theory is emerging that is equally plausible and makes up for some of the flaws in the binding rhythm theory. The theory is that gamma is needed solely to tune your brain's functions for optimal performance only as and when needed or directed. Whenever brain function demands are high and the more complex the tasks at hand are, the more a gamma wave boost will have your brain singing and programmed for winning. This theory is pretty attractive to scientists as it would explain why gamma is so promiscuous and found involved in literally all higher brain functions, whether it's attention, memory, communication , emotion, decision making, reward circuits, memory, learning, consciousness, peak performance and other heightened experiences.

Neuroplasticity Booster

The peak performance theory would also support the belief that gamma synchronization is the best wave for enhancing neuroplasticity, with strong roles in making synapses multiply and strengthen. If the brain needs to operate at a higher level, in comes the gamma waves to work at super speed, the perfect time to pimp up those brain regions so that next time the task gets easier and easier. No matter which theory is correct, nothing can detract from the fact that gamma is a pretty special wave with astounding benefits to both health and well-being.

Epsilon: Fast to Ultrafast (80 Hz and Beyond)
Be Wary of HFOs

The muddiest waters of information are about recordings of electrical activity in the brain that have been described as fast (80-400Hz) or even ultrafast (400-800Hz) and are collectively known as the epsilon band or high frequency oscillations (HFOs). If you come across any websites that talk about these waves, they may also refer to them as ultra-gamma, epsilon or lambda waves—be wary. Not one non-scientific resource that we have laid eyes on refers to anything factual with regards to these waves. This makes sense as along with the infra-slow waves, we don't have a very concrete scientific understanding of HFOs.

Spikes Spoil Results

Fast waves come in two main forms, genuine intracellular HFOs and spikes. Spikes refer to the electrical energy from the communicating neurons that leaks outside of the cells and rhythmically spikes out of control to generate high frequency 'brainwaves'. We have only just recently realized that these spiky guys have confused matters by masking the genuine high frequency waves, making the complex task of understanding the genuine fast wave's jobs even more difficult. What's worse is that it makes the majority of earlier HFO discoveries potentially spurious.

We have only just started to truly distinguish genuine high frequency brainwaves (>80Hz) from the spikes, so there is extremely limited reliable information. One thing we can say for certain is that they, just like gamma waves and their spiky counterparts, like to sync up their beat with theta waves. Theta waves that are commonly associated with memory, sleep and emotion are consistently found in the literature to influence and/or be influenced by gamma waves, alpha waves, beta waves and seemingly by HFOs too—theta is a very social brainwave. Fittingly, in a spike-free experiment in rats, HFOs (60-150 Hz) were found to pass spatial information from the cortex to the hippocampus during both active exploration of an environment and in the dream world. It won't be long before we start hearing about spike-free assessments of what is going on in the human brain.

BRAINY BITS

1.   Brainwaves allow neurons to communicate together, however, where is the information that they are communicating, such as a memory, stored? A theory currently being explored is that little tubes that provide cells with structure (much like scaffolding for a house) called microtubules, might be involved in information storage using principles of quantum physics to operate.

2.   **The master organizer, the thalamus, may be the pacemaker for alpha and theta brainwaves...and perhaps other brainwaves too!**

3.   Many different kinds of experiments are helping us create technology to read people's brainwaves for making prosthetic limbs move or to generate speech in those that are disabled. But did you know that you can now even play simple computer games on your smartphone with the latest futuristic mind reading tech. Researchers have even designed a small helicopter, whose flight can be controlled solely with your mind!

SUMMARY

- Measurable brainwaves are different speeds of an electrical wave signal coming from the beat of neurons working together.
- **Connectivity between neurons creates a vast series of interconnected networks.**
- Communication within and between these networks allow the brain to integrate functions depending on the task at hand through coupling and syncing up of different brainwave frequencies.
- **Brainwave frequencies are categorized based on the fact that they are characteristic of particular brain regions, functions and states.**
- Brainwave changes are influenced by our thoughts, our conversations, our interaction with our environment and our bodies.
- **Infra slow—little is known, could be the glue that links networks together.**
- Delta—deep sleep, memory encoding during sleep, motivation, has a dark side.
- **Theta—REM sleep, memory fine tuning during sleep, memory-short and long-term, navigation, emotional regulation.**
- Alpha—Relaxed wakefulness, bridge the conscious to the subconscious, general knowledge ('knowing'), easy listening and calm reasoning, inhibitory roles.
- **Beta—Alert wakefulness, action stations, motor system.**
- Gamma—Fast brain processing for peak performance, short-range network integration and neuroplasticity booster.
- **HFOs—Super-fast brain processing, function in humans largely unknown, conveys spatial information in rats.**

Up next...

Now that you are all experts on brainwaves, in the next section we give you the latest news of what's happening with brainwaves and neuroplasticity in the world of BOPs (Brain Optimization Practices). We explain how BOPs can be used to master your brainwaves, allowing you to master your mind. And with this great knowledge, comes the power to be happy in life despite the complexity of today's world; to gain confidence and raise self esteem; to be healthy and maintain a healthy weight and feel good about your body; to strengthen your relationships and find love in life as you reach, with certainty for your true goals and dreams.

In the next section you will discover just how much is possible with Brain Optimization Practices, and learn how to apply them and integrate them with every aspect of your daily life.

Part IV

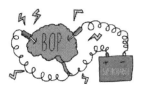

SUPER BRAIN OPTIMIZATION PRACTICES

"Every man can, if he so desires, become the sculptor of his own brain"

~ Santiago Ramón y Cajal

THE SUPER BRAIN
One Wave to Rule Them All

We all now know that via brainwaves, your brain operates, adapts and upgrades with the aid of neuroplasticity. So what is the ultimate brainwave for upgrading the brain and achieving success in life? It's a bit of a trick question really as no single brain wave is best for all of life's challenges; and, all brainwaves are essential for a healthy and well-balanced brain. In principal the brain of a well-balanced, peaceful and happy person versus a stressed, unbalanced and unhappy are not that different. They are both optimized through neuroplasticity—the former for success, and the latter for distress (Fig. 6). Willingly or unwittingly each brain has been shaped and molded by the brainwave training that is life.

Super Brain vs. Blooper Brain

It's the little daily habits you have acquired throughout life, both your interaction with the world and your internal thoughts, that influence the neuroplastic shaping of your mind. Many of us have well established habits that are clearly not good for us (drugs, alcohol, diet, smoking, apathy, stagnation, laziness—just to name a few). As the old computing saying goes, 'garbage in garbage out.' Nonetheless, caught in the intricate web of modern life we blindly charge ahead with the same old habits and routines, resulting in the actual strengthening of the neural connections and associated brainwaves and behavior patterns that promote stress and dysfunction! Until now, that is no one's faux paux.

How could you have known that a regular outburst in cross-town traffic or routinely rushing to get ready in the morning were bad BOPs? But, with this book, no one can further use the excuse "Who knew?" To that end, we have a new saying for you, 'excellence in excellence out.' There are many techniques, tools and tips, namely BOPs, that promote healthy brainwave states and neuroplastic changes to enable you to retrain your brain; sever old unhealthy habits, routines, and practices; create new connections (synapses); and have new found control over your state of mind for any situation, in any aspect of your life—anytime, anywhere.

BOPs Influence Neuroplasticity

The super brain takes advantage of the cyclic relationship between the brain and the mind with BOPs: using your own mind to train your brain to change your mind for the better. BOPs influence the mechanisms of neuroplasticity, enabling you to slowly disintegrate and chip away at unhealthy connections through misuse and override them with new optimal connections (synapses) for not only a happy and healthy life, but for greatness! Using the gifts of brain science knowledge and your mind, you have the power to achieve this by yourself through self-directed neuroplasticity.

However, we aren't going to blow your mind, spin you about and then expect you to find the path to excellence all on your own. In the following chapters we will show you how to apply BOPs to every aspect of your life, from expanding your creativity to boosting your immune system, to conquering unhealthy habits, to eliminating, self-doubt, dependency, additions and everything else in between. For now we will introduce you to the main techniques and reveal the Ultimate New Life System's secret recipe for success.

Brain Optimization Practices
What are BOPs?

BOPs can be anything from intense training exercises to minute adjustments to your daily lifestyle. Importantly, BOPs can, and will, make lasting changes to the way your brainwaves shape how your brain operates and your mind thinks. While many BOPs can bring near instantaneous release from unhealthy brainwave patterns, to enduringly modify your grey matter and neural networks to superhero status you have to practice, practice, practice what you preach.

What makes a BOP successful?

Scientists around the globe have investigated the brains of celebrated artists, monumental geniuses, mathematicians, top physicists, monks, yogis, professional athletes and numerous field leaders, discovering that these exceptional individuals can make rapid brain state changes and enter amazing states of cognition. The primary characteristic in common among these exceptional individuals (and the soon to be exceptional you) is: **practice, practice, practice.** Practicing is the essence of BOPs, they're not called brain optimization one hit wonders!

Practicing is Easy

We realize that practice is a bit of a dirty word, and can sometimes conjure up feelings of past frustrations (being forced to 'practice' violin in school when you would much rather be rocking out with a killer set of drums). That is why BOPs are fun and are meant to *never* be laborious as there is no exam

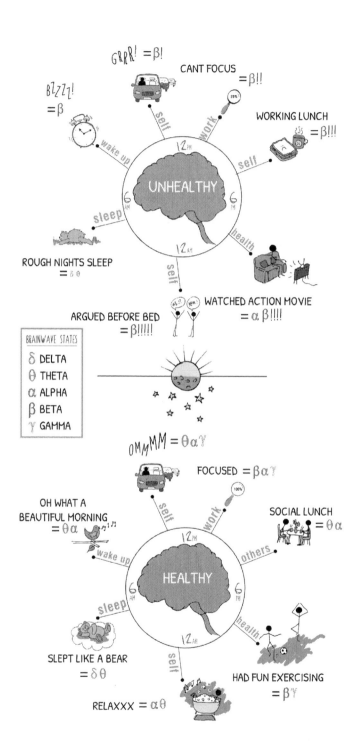

date to prep for or strict set of rules or laws that mean failure if not abided by. And most of all, they are surprisingly very simple. They require no fancy equipment or special skills to practice, no degree or qualifications and no money. Just a simple set of instructions that are to be **practiced, practiced, practiced** and almost played with.

You can become fascinated with your BOP practice, and making it fun, not 'serious'. We want to create a movement of people who BOP—brain optimize—because it feels good, life gets better, you feel lighter, happier, healthier, wealthier and more confident. YES! BOPs, will do that for you, that's what all the "best masters, and practitioners, know—life becomes more fun and easy as you sustain your practice. If we aim for the sky with our practices we can train the brain like any muscle. You can operate in these heightened states of mental functioning as default and on demand, not just in isolated moments. By achieving the brilliant brain of a mastered mind, you will always be in the perfect state of being for the situation at hand.

BOPs Are Universal

Putting aside those people that are using BOPs unwittingly, BOPs are being used both in and out of the clinic to treat a whole host of diseases and disorders of the mind, from stress, anxiety and depression to Alzheimer's, epilepsy and schizophrenia. At the opposite end of the scale, BOPs have been used to consolidate and perfect heightened states of cognition in a range of professions.

Professional athletes, like golf guru Tiger Woods, tennis star Jimmy Connors and heavyweight boxing champ Kevin McBride, brought BOPs

Figure 6. Super Brain vs. Blooper brain. (Opposite page) Depicted is a comparison of a healthy and unhealthy brain's daily experiences. As you know the brain is never experiencing just one wave, but we have highlighted waves that are worthy of paying attention to. For example when you're focusing on a friend during a social lunch (see the healthy brain at around 5pm), gamma, although reduced in the DMN, will be higher in the TPN, giving it a boost. However, we don't mention gamma, as the special waves of note are those relied on heavily during speech detection (delta and alpha). Laid out in front of you like this, the difference in brainwave patterns from a day filled with healthy or unhealthy BOPs are shockingly clear. Delta waves=δ; Theta waves=θ; Alpha waves=α; Gamma waves=γ.

into play to propel them to the top of their game. They used BOPs to their advantage, making entering 'the zone' and playing to perfection second nature. In the corporate world Successwaves has been using BOPs on executives, leaders and CEOs and their businesses for over 20 years with a proven track record of phenomenal million dollar profit boosting and of getting businesses up and running like well oiled machines.

Celebs world over such as Samuel L. Jackson, Lily Allen, Drew Barrymore and Ben Affleck have applied BOPs to quit addictions and to hone and perfect their performance skills. Even famous figures of the past used BOPs as the key to their success, such as the granddaddies of brilliance and innovation, Einstein and Edison.

Perhaps WWII may have ended differently if Winston Churchill hadn't used his daily BOPs to stay alert and focused regardless of the fact that he standardly went without sleep, while being under relentless and monumental pressure. So as you can see the use of BOPs have even shaped our history! Together, we can use BOPs to mold a brighter future for ourselves as well. Here is a rundown of some of the main BOPing tools and techniques, how they relate to neural networks, neuroplasticity and brainwaves and how this can translate to a super functioning you!

Mindfulness and Meditation BOPs

For De-Stressing and Upgrading Your Default Settings!

It's a tough game for us 'new worlders' If your granny, sitting cross-legged on the kitchen floor, chanting "ooooommmmmmm" is a familiar memory, you are one of the very lucky few. Originating from ancient Eastern traditions, meditation has been regarded by many as an esoteric, mystical pursuit. Now, mindfulness and meditation are finally going mainstream.

They are being used in schools and hospitals all over the world, with the brain benefits positively influencing countless aspects of life, from disease and pain management, to sleep and emotional control. Despite science's earlier misgivings there are pretty blatant reasons why mindfulness and meditation have been practiced and perfected for thousands of years!

What Are Mindfulness and Meditation?
Meditation

Meditation is usually thought of as a sitting practice that trains your brain and mind and alters your state of consciousness to a deeper state of calm awareness. Like different kinds of physical sports are sports of the body, different styles of meditation practice are simply sports of the mind. While we will focus on mindfulness meditation here in the introduction, you will learn about many different forms of meditation throughout Mind Your Head. All styles of sports and meditation have a common end goal: mastery. Sports deal with mastering the body and in turn developing the mind, while meditation is the mastering of your mind and in turn developing the body. Thankfully, meditation is not a competitive sport, there is no test, no failure, *only practice.*

Mindfulness

Mindfulness is a quality, ability or trait that is required to some degree for all forms of meditation. Mindfulness is the opposite of forgetfulness. Forgetfulness is the 'ability' to lose our focus, where we don't pay close attention to where we are and what we are doing. Mindfulness is the ability to stay aware and play close attention to the present moment, where you tune into everything both outside and within you with calm acceptance. The aim of mindful meditation is to become more aware of your environment, senses, thoughts and feelings in a non-judgmental way, so that instead of being overwhelmed by them, we learn to manage them better.

Mindfulness in Meditation

Mindfulness and meditation are two sides of the same coin. Meditation is the mind based action or active practice, while mindfulness is the ability to be passively aware that is, to some degree, found in virtually all varieties of meditation. A specific flavor of meditation, mindfulness meditation, is where we focus solely on being mindful of everything in and around us, not to zone out and be forgetful of some aspect of ourselves or the environment. While, mindfulness without a sitting meditation posture is generally considered to occur when you take your mindfulness based meditation practice into your everyday walking, talking life.

Yet all of the various types of meditation are mindful in essence. All types are aimed at being attentive, focused and mindful of something. This is true, whether you are cultivating awareness with all of your senses in mindful meditation; are engaged in spiritual meditation where you center your thoughts on god; or movement meditation where your mind centers upon repetitive movement. Whichever style of mediation is practiced, the end result is the same, positive and specific changes to how your brain functions and in turn how you feel, think and behave.

What Does Mindfulness Meditation Do To Brainwaves?
Meditation in General Makes Waves

Meditation is one of the most powerful tools to affect positive changes in the brain. EEG and other brain imaging experiments (such as acronym heavy fMRI[BB2] and MEG[BB3]) measurements prove that during meditation, the brainwaves with the most striking changes are the slow alpha and theta waves and the fast to ultra-fast gamma waves. Slowing of the alpha rhythm and increases in the power of alpha activity is the most prominent and consistent change with practically all forms of meditation that have been studied.

Mindful Alpha Enhancement and Theta Bursts

This alpha enhancement is associated with deepening relaxation and establishing a calmly aware state of mind, and providing emotional stability. Master meditators also have bursts of the slower wave theta, followed by the alpha rhythm, thought to signify a highly deepened relaxed state. While such theta bursts are normally associated with being asleep, with master meditators, these theta bursts during meditation are clearly distinct as they are associated with the master being bright-eyed and bushy-tailed, and keep up their appearance even after meditation practice is over.

Mindful Gamma in the Hear and Now

At the other end of the scale is the powering up of gamma (and ultra-fast waves in more experienced meditators). Increased gamma waves are deemed highly relevant for retraining one's brain. Increased gamma, particularly in the occipital cortex, better enables one to be in the here and now, enhancing our awareness of the present moment and is the ideal wave for positively impacting neuroplasticity in the creation of new processing circuits for the restructuring of the brain and learning.

Meditation Causes De-synching Too

But it's not all about enhanced brainwave activity, desynchronization of brainwaves in certain regions also occurs. Said another way, this simply means that instead of neurons firing in synchrony at a certain frequency, they fall out of step with one another and stop using that brainwave frequency to function together for the same goal. Now we will go a little deeper to see just what meditation induced brainwave changes can do for you, it's truly amazing!

Mindfulness Mediation and the Default Mode Network

DMN and TPN

Self-referential processing i.e. generating thoughts relating to oneself, has been attributed to a set of brain regions which were designated as the Default Mode Network (DMN). The DMN is basically a network within the brain that is in control when you are not busy or on task; but most commonly used when you are engaged in internal thoughts. When you are focused on a goal or task the DMN is deactivated and another network, the task-positive network (TPN) is activated. As these are the two most common states of mind your average Joe is in, it's imperative that we have extraordinarily organized, healthy and balanced DM as well as TP networks.

The DMN is spread out all over the brain. It spans regions of the cortex that are used for memory, attributing mental states to others and oneself (theory of mind or ToM) and information integration. It also includes hippocampus and amygdalae with roles in memory and emotion. This network is deactivated however, when attention shifts towards external stimuli. This is why the DMN is in charge when we are engaged in internal tasks such as daydreaming, envisioning the future, retrieving memories, gauging others' perspectives and indeed in self-referential processing.

Desyncing the Default Mode Network

When you meditate your brainwaves in certain regions (see following example) of the DMN desynchronize. Scientists think that this desynchronization, when repeated through practice, causes the severing of ties between previously well-connected regions. One example is the severing of ties between emotion related modules of the cortex and the amygdalae which puts a dimmer switch on your emotional response, particularly enhancing the mastering of fear, giving you greater control over fearful emotions.

These emotional modules of the cortex are also involved in retrieval of autobiographical emotional memories (a breakup for example) which might be an indicator as to why meditation can be a magic pill for trauma sufferers and those stuck in the past. It may also explain why I have yet to meet a meditation guru with a tendency to jump into egotistical and pompous stories of me, me, me, me. We all know someone who could benefit from a dose of meditation in that regard, someone you love dearly but have quietly thought of throttling if they mention themselves just one more time.

By gaining emotional control and dampening the influence of fear and past emotional memories even first time meditators can make some brainspace. The result is often the ability to be present and less focused on the self, and more receptive and open, with a sense of emotional calmness and bliss. Desynchronizing these parts of the DMN is also a shining example of "practice makes perfect." Comparing novice meditators with experts reveals that the longer you practice the stronger the desyncing is, creating master blasters of emotional control.

Increasing Alpha and Emotional Control

Conversely, other regions of the DMN have increased brainwave activity in meditators. Chilled out alpha waves cause certain regions of the DMN on both the left and right hemispheres to unite. In meditators, this balanced union is involved in creating emotional control. In contrast, majorly depressed and anxious individuals have alpha activity in the left hemisphere that far exceeds that in the right hemisphere; while individuals with depression without anxiety have alpha activity that is stronger in the right hemisphere than that found in the left.

And so through simple meditation you can balance out those hemispheres (particularly regions of the DMN in the frontal lobe) and punch your ticket to the land of emotional mastery, with meditation also re-wiring other networks outside of the DMN, including your emotional circuitry, that you will hear more about in the chapters to come. Just imagine being able to stay calm and collected and ready to take the best course of action no matter how crazy the situation may be.

Gamma Changes in the DMN
Influences Self-Referential Thoughts

Gamma wave decreases in parts of the frontal lobe (prefrontal to be exact) during meditation are thought to be involved in deactivating connections with other parts of the brain, resulting in the inhibition of thoughts that refer to oneself. The resultant neuroplastic dewiring keeps this area deactivated even after meditation. In meditation masters this is thought to be part of the rewards that the journey of mediation practice brings—the realization that there is essentially no real 'self'.

Awareness of the Present

During meditation, other parts of the DMN also sync up their beats, but they become super charged by gamma waves. Increased gamma activity in regions at the back of your head, in the occipital cortex, are thought to reflect our conscious awareness of the present moment. . Evidence also indicates that such gamma boosts enhance your powers of attention, concentration and focus.. Like a mind altering drug, the gamma band takes us away from our self-narrative focus in experiencing life and expands and heightens your experience, routing you firmly into the here and now. It makes sense that this sub-network is malfunctioning in people with high levels of stress hormones, who often are lost in stressful thoughts which keep them from feeling in touch with the world.

Protection from Depression

Scientific experiments have shown that artificially stimulating and activating gamma waves in these depression affected regions of the DMN results in a reduction of the symptoms of depression. The beauty of meditation however, is that you are your own neuroscientist and can achieve this without the need of expensive, fancy gadgets, software or medication.[BB1] And remember—always remember—the Ultimate New Life System community (us!) is here to support you every step of the way.

What Can Mindfulness and Meditation Do For You?

We have a whole load more to tell you about how you can benefit from the mind marvels of practicing mindfulness and meditation in Mind Your Head's 'how to' chapters. Here is a list of some of the scientifically supported advantages of mindfulness meditation:

- Reduces stress and depression in your body and mind (see Chapter 2: focusing on the self).
- **Enhances self-awareness.**
- Emotional control and stability: dampening of negative feelings (e.g. loneliness, anger, fear, pain) and bolstering of positive feelings (e.g. love, compassion, understanding, joy).
- **Enhances many higher brain functions (e.g. attention, perception, reasoning, problem solving, working memory and intuition).**
- Clarity of inner and outer perception and decreased reactivity to distraction.
- **Can give your brain more processing power by visibly growing more grey and white matter, pumping up the cerebral hemisphere with superhero style neuroplasticity effects!**
- Enhances body awareness.
- **Boosts immune system and weight loss (see Chapter 3: focusing on health).**
- Reduces addictive behavior.
- **Boost and refines social skills (see Chapter 4: Focusing on Others).**
- The brain network modifications and neuroplastic enhancements outlined above enhance and make room for further development in social communication and in achieving and expanding peak performance capabilities (see Chapter 5: Focusing on Success).

Cognitive Behavioral Therapy BOPs

For Gaining Control Over Your Thoughts and Behaviors

What is CBT?
The Basics

Cognitive behavioral therapy is an amalgamation of several different theories and a whole host of techniques. As the name suggests, CBT centers on how we think and feel (cognitive), which in turn influences the way we act (behavioral). CBT based BOPs help us gain control over this relationship (therapy). They have been quietly taking over mental health care for treating anxiety, depression and many other disorders. It isn't like old age psychiatry, all about tissues, tears and talking the ear off a therapist about your worries and troubled past. Rather, it's about quickly learning and mastering the skills you need to solve your own problems and take care of your precious mind in the here and now.

Thoughts, Feelings and Behaviors

CBT recognizes that it is our thoughts that cause our feelings and behavior, not other people or situations that make us behave in a certain way. So while one man can be at peace at a boisterously energetic kid's party and join in the fun, another may be reminded of his fear of having kids and feel overwhelmed and under attack by the horde of little monsters. Feeling overwhelmed may lead to an internal and/or external outburst causing one to slink off and miss out on the fun completely. Importantly, they were both at the same party and in the same situation, but it was their thoughts and state of mind that made the difference to how they acted. The benefit of this observation is that we can change the way we think and feel, even if the situation itself remains unchanged.

CBT helps us accomplish this result, by noticing that a thought, belief or idea is the seed from which our emotional state stems and that by controlling our thoughts we can influence our emotions, and ultimately how we behave. CBT is being used in clinical treatment of psychiatric disorders and outside of clinical cases worldwide for life optimization; to generate healthy mindedness and strengthen our ability to handle the emotional challenges life throws at us. The end result? Development of beneficial, positive and healthy life habits.

Neuroscience Based CBT Research
How Does CBT Affect Your Brain?

As you are now a brain expert, you already know that altering brainwaves and neural networks is the driving force of CBT. Agreed? If so, you are miles ahead of science in this respect. To our knowledge, there is only one recent, cutting-edge study that has scientifically investigated the existence of a neural basis of the contrastingly well documented positive changes that can be achieved through CBT. Well you already guessed the conclusion. The neural basis for the positive outcomes of CBT is of course, brainwave driven neuroplastic change!

What You Already Know

This particular neuroscience based CBT study focused on the coupling between two brainwave frequencies, beta and delta. We learned in the last section that different brainwave frequencies cozy up and sync their songs to integrate their functions, like with theta and friends. So when a regular, healthy you or I is presented with a potentially threatening situation, beta and delta sync up. We also learned that slow waves are more suited for integrating processes over larger distances in the brain and play a stronger role in the subcortical (underneath the cortex) and more evolutionary ancient brain structures.

Helpful Background Information

Scientists and scholars speculate from the current repertoire of data on the subject, that the syncing up of beta and delta during anxiety promoting situations transfers threat related signals between the subcortical regions (dominated by delta waves) and regions of the cortex (dominated by beta), particularly the motor cortex that control movement, having you ready for action. It has been found that individuals with high anxiety, clinical obsessive compulsive tendencies, panic attacks from social encounters, or avoidant and fearful behavior have a mega powerful coupling between delta and beta in their brains.

Results: CBT Rewires the Brain through Brainwave Changes

The brain based CBT study proved that even half way through a full 12 week set of weekly CBT sessions, the relationship between delta and beta waves was being broken down, reducing the symptoms of mental illness. And if theories are correct, this may result in putting a dimmer switch on states of anxiety. While such beneficial effects of CBT are realized world over, we are a long way from understanding the immense impact CBT has on our brains that are actually at the root of these therapeutic changes.

The Advantages of CBT:

- Reduces stress, depression and anxiety both physiologically and mentally (see Chapter 2: focusing on the self).
- **The long effects of CBT (long-term changes in behavior) can be observed and CBT completed within just 12 weeks.**
- Although traditionally a talking therapy, the highly structured nature of CBT and its techniques mean that CBT can be used on oneself and be taught and practiced in groups, self-help books and even computer programs and mobile apps.
- **Once learned, CBT principles and techniques can be applied to all aspects of life from enhancing your footy skills on the playing field (see Chapter 3: Focusing On Health) and enhancing interpersonal skills (see Chapter 4: Focusing On Others), to business development and sales boosting techniques (see Chapter 5: Focusing On Success).**

What Can CBT Can Do For You:

- Improved concentration on set goals.
- **Improved motivation and drive.**
- Improved self-control and self-discipline.
- **Improved self-esteem and self-belief.**

- Improved self-understanding and self-awareness.
- **Improved time management.**
- Improved work-life balance.
- **Improved stamina in physical training.**
- Improved mindset, and mental attitude.

Entrainment BOPs

FOR ENHANCING THE POWER OF YOUR BRAINWAVES

What is Entrainment?
Its All About The Beat

Its not ENTERtainment; its ENTRAINment (but it can be entertaining!!). Scientifically, brainwave *entrain*ment is any technique aimed at promoting neuronal electrical pulse frequency synchronization with the assistance of a periodic stimulus (like a drum beat or strobe light) that has a frequency equivalent to the intended brainwave state. For example, meditating to the beat of a drum; or experiencing a strobe light tied to the rise and fall of the beat of a song. Significantly, even without the assistance of these stimuli, you entrain your brainwaves naturally throughout your day from task to task.

With entrainment, where we use audio and/or visual beats, you can tie your BOP to a specific beat to enhance the power of a particular brainwave (alpha, beta etc). Sound odd? It's not. There are countless highly respected scientific studies that have proven the effectiveness of brainwave entrainment in altering your state of mind. Successful brainwave entrainment experiments have resulted in improved vigilance and memory and increases in students GPA, increased hypnotic susceptibility, reduced stress and anxiety, pain relief (including for migraines and even for premenstrual syndrome) and have been able to increase the power of all brainwave frequency ranges within the brain.

THE Ritual for Learning

Entrainment explains why drums have been used by both ancient and modern day cultures to induce meditative, trance-like altered states and are normally used as the keystone in sacred rituals. You may be one of those people who swear by listening to music when studying. Well science agrees with you. Learning information to a beat in a melody or rhythm causes your brainwaves to pulse in synchrony.

This makes the parts of your brain that are associated with learning and memory morph, upgrade, and grow. Learning to music creates a more balanced left and right frontal lobe with more symmetrical theta, alpha, and gamma frequency bands. Most importantly, learning to music plugs the studied info much stronger into your long-term memory. That's why it's easy to remember the lyrics to that childhood song you haven't heard in years word for word, but try and remember what your old high school history teacher was droning on about in any class...fat chance!

The Science of Entrainment
The Derailment of Entrainment

It's sad but true that the scientific understanding of brainwave entrainment is being walked all over by companies making wild claims: 'In Just One Hour, You Can Learn The Long-Lost (Almost Illegal) Mind-Power Secrets That Still Scare Professors, Priests and Politicians to Death!' Come on now, what do they take us for!? With brainwave entrainment, scientific EEG studies are essential to prove that the technology and methodology used to create the final audios used actually works....let us explain.

Getting Specific

You see, brainwave entrainment has had a mixed reputation among scientists. While one study shows clear significant, positive changes in brainwave patterning, other reports show about as much change as a stream of farts could make. Perplexing?! After much debate, scientists now believe that we need to take a step back and really establish: (a) which of the many methods actually work for producing and applying a brain entrainment audio and/or visual frequency; and (b) if mental focus is a necessity to generate positive results, or is just a bonus that enhances already positive results.

Essentially we need to pin down what is truly effective, with what techniques, under what circumstances and using which brainwave frequencies and why. By unearthing the key ingredients that unite the entrainment success stories we can perfect the technique and then get serious about studying and comparing effects under different situations.

Get the Proof from the Pudding

Can we believe it when brainwave entrainment audios come with the label "scientifically proven results?" Well the sad truth is you can't unless the results are accompanied by a scientific EEG study for their specific products. But guess what? That is precisely what we did with our audios. And we are the only ones out there that truly put their "money where their mouths are." Importantly, we didn't just throw a few sound files together and slap on some fancy packaging hoping to make a quick buck. Intense and meticulous research was used to select the best of the best that is out there and then finally put it to the test. Our truly astounding results are in the final section of this introduction for you to see for yourself.

Neuro-Linguistic Programming BOPs

FOR ENHANCING INTRA AND INTERPERSONAL COMMUNICATION AND THE MODELING OF EXCELLENCE!

What is NLP?
Made from a Meeting of Minds

Neuro-Linguistic Programming (NLP) arose in America in the 1970s as a result of collaboration between John Grinder and Richard Bandler. Bandler discovered that specific words and sentence structures enhanced the effects of positive suggestion given to psychotherapy patients. As his pal Grinder was a professor of linguistics they set to analyzing the work of hugely successful therapists and developed a method for achieving personal excellence through studying the way we think and communicate. But what does NLP actually mean? Read on.

It Does What it Says On the Tin

NLP has a threefold meaning. The term 'neuro' you know by now to mean neurological. In NLP terms 'neuro' relates to the brain and all the information it gleams from our senses in representing our inner and outer worlds. Linguistic is the part that relates to language, the foundations of our thoughts and communications. We all have that internal dialog, nattering away throughout the day and often, at times, well into the night. And the final term 'programming' is based on the concept that ideas and behaviors can be modified and managed to generate responses that make you shine. So all in all NLP means to use language and communication to reprogram the brain and enhance intra-personal AND inter-personal relations.

Understanding and Influencing Others

With an understanding of your own thinking and behavior patterns, NLP also provides BOPs that allow us to better understand and even influence changes in the thinking and behavior of others. If you aren't familiar with the mind boggling mentalist Derren Brown's TV shows, he is definitely worth the watch. He intricately weaves techniques used in NLP into his shows, mastering the art of communication and programming the mind with powerful suggestive words and actions. Once done, he can direct you as if you were a puppet on his string.

With the power of suggestion and an understanding of the human mind he even managed to make an innocent man truly believe he was guilty of murder and hand himself into the police! Perhaps even more outstanding, he even managed to turn himself into the invisible man using verbal and body language suggestions to make his volunteer think he could see straight through him! Once, he even made a whole audience of over 1000 people completely forget the live show they had just witnessed! The true power of suggestion is mind blowing.

NLP and Hypnosis
Getting Better Reception

Derren and many NLP therapists also add a pinch of hypnosis to seal the deal, warming the brain to a state in which it softens and becomes like putty in their hands. Hypnosis isn't some unnatural state of mind designed to enslave you. Rather, it allows you to easily enter a deeply relaxed, highly receptive state, calmly ready to accept verbal commands and suggestions. Hypnosis and meditation are much alike with gross changes to brainwave activity. They both result in a general increase in slow wave theta and alpha activity as well as gamma.

Hypnosis and Meditation

However, there is no clear-cut comparison between hypnosis and meditation to show how these brainwave changes may similarly or differently reflect changes in communication within neural networks. Hypnotic states and meditation have also been shown to have similar beneficial outcomes in clinical experiments such as in inhibiting the perception of chronic pain. As science expands our knowledge it may turn out that the effects of meditation and hypnosis upon our brainwaves are substantially similar with unique aspects that set the experiences apart. With meditation, it is you who is self-reflecting. With hypnosis, an expert is helping to guide you into a relaxed meditation-like state and mold and direct the rewiring process with the language of the mind using NLP techniques.

Uses of NLP
Personal Development

In essence, NLP is used to improve your internal dialog and self-representations of your inner and outer worlds. NLP allows the installation of positive useful behaviors that override old bad habits. Equally, NLP can be used to make a good habit even better. NLP techniques have a wide range of applications today, some of which are just beginning to be explored.

Fame and Fortune

Due to NLP's fame as a popular approach to communication and personal development, it is big business in professional fields such as sales, management and sports training. Fortune 100 companies such as American Express and BMW have employed NLP techniques for sales boosting and enhancing customer care. Successwaves uses the latest science based research on how these kinds of 'accelerated' learning and high performance evidence based strategies can more rapidly help people navigate 21st century business challenges—achieving extraordinary success.

Teaching & Learning

Recent articles have indicated that NLP techniques are inherently a part of successful teaching and learning with the potential for highly innovative education and teaching. In medicine, NLP is used to develop rapport with patients to maximize the benefits gained during medical consultation.

Therapy

NLP is also used to provide techniques for treating specific medical problems (such as irritable bowel syndrome, insomnia, substance abuse, obesity and chronic pain). If you can recall, NLP originated from the study of successful psychotherapists. As such, it is considered highly applicable for mastering the mind and modifying behavior. It provides powerful techniques for remedying disorders such as anxiety and depression as well as treating fears and phobias.

Research Is Coming for It

As we know, with practice (that dreaded word again!) any change in behavior can become long-lasting and deeply rooted in the brain. As the understanding, scientific development and fine-tuning of NLP models and techniques is in its relatively early stages, there are no current studies on what a course of NLP sessions (with or without hypnosis) can do to the brain, brainwaves and neuroplasticity. Born 10 years after CBT, hopefully we won't have to wait another 10 years to see the first EEG study on NLP. So we just have to sit tight and wait for science to fill in the blanks, while we benefit from the results

What Can NLP Do For You?

- Provide the keys to building successful relationships with yourself and with others.
- **Directly influence your own and even other's behavior and thinking.**

- Enhance your sensory awareness and mindfully gleam more from your senses.
- **Teach outcome based thinking allowing you to quickly and purposefully reach your true goals, without getting sidetracked.**
- Develop behavioral flexibility to be able to respond to yourself, others and your environment and always get the desired results.
- **Train you in the modeling of other people's successful performance to achieve excellence in life.**

BRAINY BITS

1.   Neurofeedback, also called neurotherapy, uses EEG to measure brainwaves while the results are displayed on a screen in real-time in order for a person to self-regulate their brainwaves . In other words they watch on a screen as they try and achieve the desired changes.

2.   **Functional magnetic resonance imaging (fMRI) is a form of brain scan that uses high frequency radio waves to measure blood flow in the brain, giving an accurate picture of how active a region of the brain is and where exactly is the activity in the brain.**

3.   Magnetoencephalography (MEG) is a technique for mapping brain activity by recording magnetic fields produced by naturally occurring electrical currents in the brain.

4.   **Discovering new biological changes in our body that occur from regular meditation practices is not uncommon. One example is where a study found that people that meditate have significantly higher telomerase activity than non-meditators. Telomerase is a buzzword at the forefront of anti-aging science as it is an enzyme that protects the ends of your DNA from degrading with time.**

5.   Meditation has even been shown to help treat HIV sufferers, by increasing white blood cell numbers (immune cells) as well as improving their happiness and general well-being.

SUMMARY

- Generally, meditation is usually thought of as a sitting practice that trains your brain and mind and alters your state of consciousness.

- Mindfulness meditation is a form of meditation designed to develop the skill of paying attention to our inner and outer experiences with acceptance, patience, and compassion.

- As a result of meditating, the slow waves, alpha and theta and the fast to ultra-fast gamma waves are the brainwaves with the most striking changes.

- Increases in alpha and for more experienced meditator's increases in theta contribute to a deepened state of calm and mental clarity. Increases in gamma are also reported for the modification and creation of new neural network connections and faster processing power which enable us to be fully present in the now.

- Through mindfulness meditation, and the resultant desyncing of brainwaves in specific parts of the DMN, we reduce or alleviate our focus upon mental self-reference and autobiographical memories and effectuate greater control of our emotions and fear response. Increases in alpha within the DMN iron out hemispheric asymmetry issues which influences emotional control. At the same time, gamma synchronization within the DMN is thought to expand and heighten your experience and further boost neuroplasticity.

- CBT is designed to help you understand the thoughts and feelings that influence your behavior and help to transform destructive thought patterns that have a negative influence on your behavior and change them into positive ones.

- To treat anxiety, CBT is used to cause more desyncing of beta and delta during anxiety promoting situations. This inhibits the transfer of threat related signals between the delta wave dominated subcortical regions and the regions of the cortex overflowing with beta, which in the absence of CBT, may otherwise have you unnecessarily ready for action.

- Brainwave entrainment is any technique that aims to promote neuronal synchronization with a periodic stimulus (like a drum beat or strobe light) that has a frequency equivalent to the intended brainwave state.

•   Studies have shown that entrainment audios (and visuals) have a whole host of benefits including vigilance, memory, attention, concentration and increased hypnotic susceptibility to reduced anxiety.

•   The methodology involved in entrainment is under study to ensure that every audio created has the desired effects, this is why it's important to see scientific proof that a certain entrainment technology has the desired affects.

•   NLP uses language and communication to help reprogram the brain and enhance intra-personal and inter-personal relations.

Up Next...

Wow! It seems that the four techniques outlined above can make a broad spectrum of positive changes regarding how your brain and ultimately you function. You may be thinking, "if only there was some way to benefit from all of these BOPs, zeroing in on where they are needed most and integrating them easily into my life." Well there is. You can use our Ultimate New Life System to engender permanent, positive and brain changing BOPs and positively impact day to day habits.

Part V

THE ULTIMATE NEW LIFE SYSTEM

"The ultimate value of life depends upon awareness and the power of contemplation rather than upon mere survival."

~ Aristotle

OUR ULTIMATE NEW LIFE SYSTEM
Been There, Done That, Didn't Last

It's great to have knowledge of BOPs and brainwaves pouring in, but it's of no use to us unless we get down to action. Have you ever dabbled with meditation, CBT, NLP or brainwave entrainment or any other bona fide BOP? Perhaps you were one of many that had a go, it was nice and all that but it didn't take long until life took over and you almost forgot about those sacred moments of bliss completely? Or you may go through 'healthy' phases, and then...poof!

When your practice goes out of whack a little, your mind is back to the same old tricks. Although sacred in its own right, finding ten minutes of morning bliss using meditation doesn't cut the mustard if within another 10 minutes your blood begins to boil as your ritualistic morning wind-up begins. Your blood may begin to simmer when the early morning key hunt begins; is ready to bubble over as you stumble and fly over the strategically placed house cat/kids toy/shoe/low-lying furniture; and may be ready to explode even before those Monday morning drivers have a chance to block your hurried path to the workplace.

Integration Is Key

The real trick is not only to get practicing, but to fully integrate the brain benefits of BOPs seamlessly into your life, each and every day, and especially during those trying moments when they are needed most. In this manner, minding your head becomes habitual and effortless allowing you to make everlasting and continually positive changes to your brain, mind, body and life. This is why the Ultimate New Life System is a magical recipe of four tools specifically designed to develop and integrate BOPs, to assimilate with and enhance all aspects of your life, and give you a full arsenal of tools at your disposal.

Integration Is Integral To Our System

To fully integrate BOPs into your life you need: a full and deep understanding; to discuss BOPs with others that practice; to monitor your own development; and to receive expert help and guidance needed to up your game. This is how meditation masters do it. Usually they join a monastery, are taught a deep understanding by their masters, they live eat and breathe meditation with their peers in the monastery and are monitored and nurtured into full bloom by their masters. And that's how the Ultimate New Life System does it, integration. It is your digital monastery of BOPs that makes BOPs integral to your life so that the improvements never end!

System Overview

Mind Your Head provides you with the framework to have BOPs at the essence of your super being and is an integral part of the Ultimate New Life System. It will give you knowledge, power and expert guidance and techniques to provide a solid foundation for your BOPs. But there's more. Our Digital Brain Training Audios are at your disposal to wave the wand of expertise, using an amalgamation of techniques to accelerate your success.

To make sure your BOPs don't fizzle out and you don't stray off the path to pure peace of mind, our system includes our NeuroLogical goals journal. This journal helps you with dream developing and goal setting techniques that you will master as your BOP develops. It will result in allowing you to integrate, document and evaluate your growth. And you can share the knowledge you acquire from your BOPing experiences with other fellow brain changers around the globe with a buzzing Online community—our Ultimate New Life System Community portal. Together us BOPers can play, share and grow together with the unified clarity and motivational energy needed to hippity-hop, skip and BOP our way towards the ultimate new 21st century life of our wildest hopes and dreams.

The Book

LATEST KNOWLEDGE & TECHNIQUES WITH LIFE INTEGRATION

Mind Your Head is the fun, no nonsense practical guide to the Ultimate New Life System—brain technology for the life you deserve. We like to say: "Train Your Brain & Free Your Life". We've seen thousands of our private clients benefit from truly remarkable results; be it their health, happiness, mood, weight, stress, career or wealth and money issues. These are people who finally got results after having previously tried everything. With the recent and radical shift in global mindset regarding our health, freedom, rights and life, we feel that now is the time, for the rest of the world to benefit. As practitioners that have taught our clients proven and life changing practices for over thirty years we unquestionably know that you can make self and life improvements that can be hardwired into your brain and change the course of your life.

Standing alone, Mind Your Head is an invaluable brain optimization bible with unrivaled reports of the latest scientific developments and a unique way of integrating BOPs into every aspect of life. BOPs are tailored for the improvement of four life aspects: yourself, your health, your relationships and your dreams and goals. BOPs are introduced in a manner that builds up your skills without throwing you in the deep end, with each technique learned priming you for the techniques to follow. All of which are specifically designed for achieving balance and heading straight as an arrow, towards your targets.

Digital Brain Training Audios

ADVANCE, FOCUS & EXPERTLY ENHANCE

Our experts are passionate about constantly adding the latest scientifically reviewed insights coming from leading universities and research centers to bring you the ultimate and best of the best BOPs. Our mission: to optimize human well-being in the 21st Century, concentrated and specifically tailored for brain optimization for specific aspects of your life. Our audios combine mindfulness based practices, CBT, and our proprietary in-house NeurotechTM audio, which utilizes the latest scientifically certified brainwave entrainment techniques, along with strategic neuro-remapping messages carefully designed by NLP specialists.

What's more is that for those of you seeking to take your practice to the next level we can tailor sessions specific to you and your needs! Our audios, filled to the brim with a mass integration of BOPs and their positive influence on brainwaves and brain states will leave both the expert's and your own jaws dropping. You can get the following audios at www.ultimatenewlifesystem.com:

- *Releasing Overwhelm, see Chapter 1, De-Stressing*

- *Quantum Weight Release, see Chapter 2, The Mind Body Connection*

- *Letting go of Pain, see Chapter 2, Pain and Pleasure*

- *Authentic Power, see Chapter 1, Self-Compassion*

Before sharing our audios with you, we pilot tested our audios and the feedback was phenomenal. So, in true Ultimate New Life System spirit, we decided to put our money where our mouth is and let science decide just how effective our audios are. So far, neuroscientists have performed both a pilot study and initial case study. Based on those test results, the scientific experts have coined our audios as "the first publically available, scientifically certified brain optimization audios proven to make truly instantaneous, positive changes to your brain." And with the powers of practice and neuroplasticity these positive changes can truly and permanently transform and invigorate all of our lives!

THE EFFECTS OF COMBINED AUDIO THERAPIES ON CHRONIC STRESS—AN EEG CASE STUDY

In connection with our study, three very different individuals with a history of chronic stress kindly offered to be a part of our study. In respect of their privacy, let's call them Mary, James and Jo. Each of our volunteers where hooked up to an EEG and their brainwaves were recorded both before and after listening to our 20 minute long Releasing Overwhelm audio. The EEG data was then computed using some intense mathematical formulas to compare our volunteer's brainwave activity with the average 'normal' brain for their age, gender and handedness (if they are a lefty or a righty).

Quantitative EEG (QEEG) heat maps, like in the diagrams below, were generated for every frequency measured (1-30 Hz), providing a heat map allowing you to see what parts of the cortex have increases (hotspots colored red) or decreases (cold spots colored blue) in a specific brainwave compared to the norm. By taking a snap of Mary's, James' and Jo's brainwaves, before and after listening to the audio, we were able to see some genuinely astonishing results.

CASE 1: JO

Background

14 year old Jo was the youngest of the group. He had previously been diagnosed with high functioning autism and as such, has a close relationship with chronic stress and is used to regular bouts of anger and frustration. He

PRE   POST

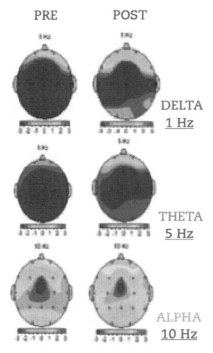

DELTA
1 Hz

THETA
5 Hz

ALPHA
10 Hz

Figure 7. Jo's QEEG Maps. *Pre (before listening to Releasing Overwhelm) and post (after listening to Releasing Overwhelm) for selected frequencies.*
Darker shades show 1 standard deviation from the norm.

also has troubles sleeping, focusing his attention and with organizational skills.

Results

The EEG clearly indicated that before listening to the audio Jo's slow wave delta, theta and alpha were severely low compared to your average 14 year old boy (Fig. 7), relaxing slow waves were next to none. Irregularities with slow waves are typical with autistic children as they are closely associated with memories, learning and attention and emotional control and reasoning. Generally, Jo's brainwave activity over all frequencies was reduced throughout most regions of the brain.

Yet, after just *one session* of our audio, Releasing Overwhelm, there were dramatic increases in delta, theta and alpha wave activity in the frontal lobe with alpha waves also spreading out all over the brain. With practice (daily listening), sustaining these increases in activity in the frontal lobe could lead to enhanced attention, memory, social awareness, character motivation, planning and emotional regulation, all of which would be highly beneficial for this troubled teen.

CASE 2: JAMES

Background

Our next volunteer, James, had been diagnosed with ADHD in his early 20's. He was 27 years old at the time of our study and was suffering from high stress levels making him feel edgy and hyperactive, which aggravated and perhaps even caused his then current health problems such as irritable bowel syndrome and stress induced overeating and excessive alcohol use.

Results

After listening to our Releasing Overwhelm audio James had a substantial and remarkable boost of alpha wave activity in the frontal lobe (recall, it is the CEO of the brain, responsible for being the master regulator of all your thinking, feeling and doing)! As you may remember, chilled out alpha waves in this region of the brain are maintained by master yogis and are a sign of relaxation. It's no wonder our usually hyperactive volunteer was feeling calm, relaxed and sleepy. What's more is that beta (both high and low frequency) were reduced in areas all over James' brain, transforming his ADHD-like action waves to brainwaves which are more reminiscent of a surfer dude hammocking away in the sun.

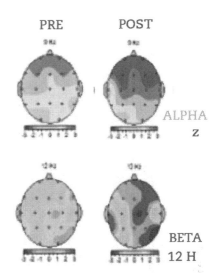

Figure 8. James' QEEG Maps. Pre (before listening to Releasing Overwhelm) and post (after listening to Releasing Overwhelm) for selected frequencies. Darker shades show 1 standard deviation from the norm.

CASE 3: MARY

Background

Mary is the oldest of our volunteer group at 63 years of age. She had severe troubles with sleeping and being consistently overwhelmed by stress. This left her feeling physically sick, so she turned to over-consumption of food and alcohol which worsened her problems of course.

Results

Mary had particularly lower than normal theta and delta waves, common of stressed out people having difficulties with sleep. Not only were these waves brought back into normal range, they were elevated to even higher levels than our 'normal' brain database not experiencing the effects of Releasing Overwhelm. Artificially causing the brain to experience delta and theta by small electric shocks (trans-cranial electrical stimulation) has been

PRE   POST

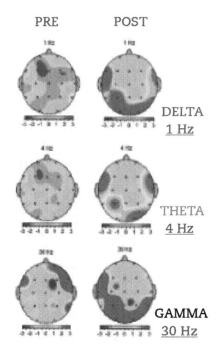

DELTA
1 Hz

THETA
4 Hz

GAMMA
30 Hz

Figure 9. Mary' QEEG maps. Pre (before listening to Releasing Overwhelm) and post (after listening to Releasing Overwhelm) for selected frequencies. Darker shades show 1 standard deviation from the norm.

shown to be effective in treating depressed and anxious patients with insomnia—go figure! Dramatic changes in gamma waves in the occipital region at the back of the head are indicative of enhanced processing of one's perception and the mindful shift in awareness that comes with it. This striking increase in gamma is of particular benefit for boosting neuroplasticity in this aging brain.

CONCLUSIONS

Like a magic pill specifically designed for each volunteer our miraculous audio resulted in changes that specifically benefit each individual. Just like a successful therapy session, our audio session cared for the ills of their individual brains in an age and condition specific way, with the same end goal: Releasing Overwhelm. Releasing Overwhelm caused our volunteers' brainwave patterns to change dramatically, and in every case for the better, which coincided with their mutual experience of calm relaxation.

Not only was the audio a phenomenal brainwave success story, it was a success story for those people most in need, with clinically diagnosed chronic stress and other disorders. With their brainwaves and state of mind instantaneously relieved from just one session, just imagine what daily listening—practice—can do (if the art of practice is simply to listen to an audio, imagine how easy that practice is!). As you can imagine we are now keen to probe the science further with many more experiments in the pipeline.

The UNLS Worldwide Community Portal
COMMUNITY & SUPPORT

In the Ultimate New Life System, Minding Your Head never ends, and you become the walking talking breathing books of knowledge to share with and be had by all. As balanced optimized individuals we are strong, but as an integrated worldwide community we are unstoppable. We can use our collective minds and help one another change our lives and world for the better.

Maybe you have tweaked and fine-tuned a BOP and are bursting to share your brilliant discovery or had a profound BOP experience that we can all learn from? Perhaps you want to join a group of like minded individuals who you enjoy practicing with. The grand opening of the Ultimate New Life System is coming soon so keep an eye on our website for the latest developments:

www.ultimatenewlifesystem.com

The Journal
RECORD, OBSERVE & DEVELOP

Practicing, but not seeming to get anywhere worthwhile, in our eyes is sacrilege. That is why we include our printable and editable NeuroLogical journal so you can easily track your progress and highlight those BOPs that are doing the magic for you. We don't believe in goal setting, we believe in achieving and exceeding our goals and dreams. So most importantly the journal teaches you the art of defining and achieving your core goals that fuel your drive, passion and happiness—the ultimate sign of success. Get set onto the path of success and access your journal and use your BOPs to go for gold.

A Taste of the Online NeuroLogical Journal, Offline

In Mind Your Head we have included some goal setting aids to help you progress through your brain training with purpose and direction. Try the satisfaction meter on the next page and get ready for the goals and notes pages at the end of each BOP section—have your pencils at the ready!

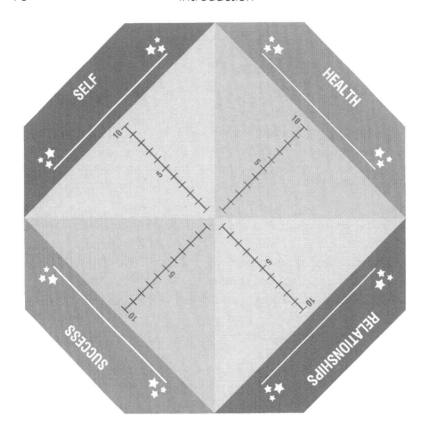

Satisfaction Guaranteed

Use this aid to give you a glimpse into what sections in life you want to be focusing you brain optimization energies towards. Granted the nature of the brain means that improving your performance and abilities in one sphere of life will spill over into other spheres of life. So your satisfaction in those areas will improve whether you want them to or not!

1. On the line between the stars, jot down what ultimate satisfaction in this life area means to you. Just a representative word or few words is fine for now. Once you have finished reading the book (the first time round) and by using the BOPs, you will have a much clearer understanding of what truly satisfies these life areas for you, it may have changed a little, although it will likely change a lot.

2. Simply take the centre of the above tool as being a satisfaction level of zero for each life area. Now mark down your level of satisfaction in each area. If you repeat these steps, weekly, or monthly you will clearly see the influence that the BOPs you are using has in shaping your life for the better.

Diamonds in the Rough

At the end of each step by step BOP section there are NeuroLogical goal setting diamonds. These allow you to note the steps you plan to take for training your brain with the BOPs described in that section. At the top of the diamond you can write the main goal you are aiming towards on the star spangled line. For example on the section on de-stressing you goal might be to eradicate regular daily stress. The first steps you plan to take can be written at the bottom of the diamond (e.g. practice BOP1 and BOP2 for 5 minutes daily) and then with the next rung in the ladder you write the next step you plan to take (e.g. practice BOP3) and the next (e.g. extend BOP1 and BOP2 to 10 minutes each) and the next etc. You may discover other BOPs that may be useful for achieving your goals. Keep coming back to and updating the diamond as you learn more as your progress and brain training develops. See the following page for an example of a filled out diamond. For more on goal setting see Chapter 4.

Take Note

The NeuroLogical goal setting diamonds are followed by notes sections for you to document any thoughts, experiences, questions or ideas you might have while practicing those BOPs. We would love to hear all about any experiences, ideas and questions you wish to share, either through the contact form on our website (www.mindyourheadbook.com) or by emailing us directly (info@mindyourheadbook.com).

Printable copy

We have included a FREE and printable goal setting aid from the NeuroLogical web journal that you can access at www.MindYourHeadBook.com/freegift.

DE-STRESSING

Stop regular stressing out!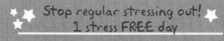
1 stress FREE day

Test and train myself with vents that WERE stressfull

Practice using negativity wave technique

Incorporate Mindfulness Training

Learn about other relaxing BOPs

BOP 1 and 2 10/day

BOP 13 5m/day

BOP 1+2
5m/day

CHAPTER I:
FOCUSING ON THE SELF

"Thinking: the talking of the soul with itself."

~Plato

Part I

RAPID DE-STRESSING

"Your mind will answer most questions if you learn to relax and wait for the answer."

~ William S. Burroughs

The Symptoms of Stress
Stress Can Be Found Just About Anywhere

Modern stress can rear its ugly head from a bazillion situations: from a pile of unanswered emails and your latest Facebook status to rattling through a to do list as long as your arm while still having time to look like you've just strolled off the catwalk. Today we can find a reason to be stressed at just about anything: the alarm-clock, the sock hunt, burnt toast, lost keys, late for work—and that's just the morning! Feeling stressed-out can wreak havoc in our modern lives, but from an evolutionary standpoint, the stress response, also known as the fight-or-flight response, is vital for our survival.

The Evolutionary Fight-or-Flight

A stress response, to a curious saber-toothed tiger or dwindling food supply would have ensured survival instead of being injured, eaten or starved to death. In this respect your fight-or-flight response is pretty handy. How does it work? Well, your brainwaves connect up the brain in a useful way to respond to the threat and your body is pumped with hormones like adrenalin and cortisol, giving you the near enough super human powers needed to survive. Granted, it's not every day that you encounter a saber-toothed tiger, however, even every day modern stressors, which linger day by day, or minute by minute, pile up on you and it is just like having a 200lb saber stalking you as you go about your daily business!

Continual Stress is a Health Pest
Pest of the Mind

This is where stress becomes a huge problem for most of us. When we can't seem to switch off the stress-response, our brains and bodies have become so continually overwhelmed by stress that it becomes your brain's default mode of operation, and even the slightest testy situation can feel like another tiring shock to the system. Stress and over-worrying are the first steps on the rickety road to the many flavors of anxiety and depression.

Pest of the Body

While stress in itself isn't medically classified as an illness, prolonged stress created by our minds, induces neuroplastic changes in the brain, that sustain unhealthy states of stress in the body. Such chronic stress has been linked with many physical ailments from anything as mild as a headache, back pain or thrush to the severe and life threatening such as heart attacks, cancer or even Alzheimer's disease. Ehealthcare leaders, WebMD, estimate that between 75-95% of all doctor visits are stress related. That's right up to 95% of both chronic and acute illness are related to stress. So, learning to manage and balance our stress levels, in the 21st century- is critical for maintaining a healthy body and a healthy mind.

Stress on the Brain
Frontal Lobe Degradation

When it comes to neuroplasticity and the structure of your brain, repetitive stress can even make changes to your brain's structure that are visible to the naked eye! Stress, anxiety, over-worrying and depression seem to all involve changes in similar regions of the cortex, particularly in the frontal lobe, which regulates your responses to people and the environment, your thoughts and your emotions. The bit of your brain that makes all those important life altering complex decisions, stops being able to make those complex decisions any more—when you think about it stress is kind of like man's own in built devolution mechanism. If you don't have the resources around you and within you to use the full life-balancing potential of a super evolved brain then, then the brain area's needing a boost to sustain it aren't needed and wither away—use it or lose it!

Losing Control of the Limbic System

Other regions of the brain are particularly stress-sensitive and backfire when we burnout. The amygdalae and hippocampus (as part of the limbic system) set your emotional circuitry out of whack: misinterpreting other peoples words and emotions, overreacting in stress-full situations and a general lack of emotional control. Stress not only eats away at your hippocampus, fuzzying-up your memory making processes, it actually makes your amygdalae grow! Neuroplasticity is actually boosted, inflating your amygdalae, making controlling fearful, angry and upset emotions and behaviors challenging. A shining example of neuroplasticity's unbiased nature; it makes brain alterations based solely on practice. It doesn't judge whether it's good or bad, that's *your* job.

Stress Alters Brainwaves

The understanding of brainwaves and stress related disorders is a bit fuzzy due to all the different classes of mental health problems and ways of studying them. Thankfully, in the past couple of years we are beginning to reach the crux of the matter. It seems that the chronic stress induced changes in the strength, frequency and synchronicity of brainwaves within and between these different brain regions define the difference between general worry and clinical anxiety or depression. Studies show that stress causes changes in all the major brainwaves, from delta to gamma. Here is a rundown of research results for each wave's involvement in stress and stress related disorders.

Delta (1-3Hz)
Hemispheric Asymmetry

People with depression and anxiety have more of an imbalance between the delta power in the right and left hemispheres than happy healthy people do. This is clear. Exactly how this imbalance relates to stress on the other hand isn't very clear at the moment as different individuals can have a variety of different delta related imbalances. A general picture is emerging, that too much slow wave delta and theta compared to the norm are commonly involved in over-activating our beta in a whole load of nasty life disturbing conditions, from OCD to anxiety and panic disorders and back again.

Theta (3-8Hz)
Hippocampal Overflow

Many studies have focused on the stress induced elevation of theta waves found in the hippocampus and how it disturbs emotional control and memory. An experiment conducted in 2013 shows that drugs currently prescribed for anxiety reduce this overflow of hippocampal theta. While of course we want to avoid depending on drugs, the most amazing part of this experiment was: that simply being in a new or unusual environment had the same affect in reducing hippocampal theta waves as the anti-anxiety drugs did. It makes a whole lot of sense; we have all felt that need for a change of scenery for a good resetting of our stress levels.

Soothing Your Beta

With theta, as with delta, there are strong ties with beta. As we mentioned earlier, the coupling between theta and beta regulates your emotional stability. Their relationship makes the difference between a potentially stressful event seeming like water flowing off a ducks back or adding fuel to the fire. Keeping frontal theta in check allows you to remain calm as it soothes your beta, maintaining the status quo and allowing you to think clearly when you need it most. Feeling like stress is building up and hitting the danger levels? Something as simple as going for a walk or exploring any new location, never mind applying our Brain Optimization Practices or (BOPs), can help you get the peace of mind needed to mentally address the problem that may be the basis of your stress.

Alpha (8-13 Hz)
Emotion and Fight-or-Flight Control

Alpha is advertised as an instant stress reliever, reducing the impact of our stress response, and it is! It has even shown to help us regulate our emotions and how to best deal with our flight-or-flight response should the need arise. Many studies have focused on the role of alpha in the frontal cortex in the processing and regulation of our emotions. The right frontal region is thought to orchestrate your fight-or-flight response and the left frontal region is associated more with the regulation and alteration of the response. It is differences between the power of alpha in these two regions that mark the difference between chilling or freaking-out.

A Shocking Frontal Lobe Imbalance

The most recent study indicates that when presented with a literally shocking situation, the amount of alpha power in the right or left frontal region determines how we feel and respond to a shock. In the study, during threat of electrocution (just a small shock, we promise!), participants that had the biggest surge in alpha in the left regulatory frontal lobe were as cool as cucumbers and were even less likely to blink while under threat of a zap attack.

However, those that displayed a more striking hemispheric imbalance, with too much alpha in the right fight-or-flight region, were the super stressed heads of the study. Even at rest (we mean when you are not being threatened with electrocution) ratios of left and right hemispheric frontal alpha activity (hemispheric asymmetry) outside of the norm are linked to stress and anxiety disorders. So in our (BOPs) for reducing stress we aim at boosting alpha and inducing alpha balance, as well as control of theta and consequently control of beta. This is the key to how we produce speedy results.

Beta (14-30 Hz)
Beta Burnout

Beta, your brain's gauge for assessing the need for action, and then instigating it, requires a lot of defocusing in those of us that easily succumb to stress. While beta waves get a bad rap they can healthily accompany us throughout our day by providing an alertness booster. In a healthy, relaxing stress free day your average Joe or Jane's brain should generally hum from delta/theta when you wake to alpha/low-beta throughout the day then back to theta/delta when the day is done—not forgetting surges of gamma that heighten your experience and your brain processing speed day and night.

You want just enough beta to get the job done. But the continual swamping of our brains with beta frequencies, particularly the faster kind (~20-30 Hz) runs amuck in stress related disorders. On the flip side, you can certainly put beta to good use in its true environment and reap the brain boosting benefits of elevated beta during exercise.

Gamma (30-80Hz)
Positive vs. Negative = Right vs. Left

While B-eta gets a B-ad rap, G-amma gets a G-ood one, but as you brainiacs know, it's all about when and where brainwaves are applied. Being the fastest brainwaves (save for ultra-fast waves) the processing power of the brain regions experiencing gamma, are supercharged. Yet, how you feel as a result depends on which brain area you are zapping into action. For example, if you are looking at pictures of cute kittens and puppies gamma is associated with parts of the right hemisphere and you might feel all warm and fuzzy inside. If those cute kittens and puppies happened to be in a blender on the other hand, the same regions of the left hemisphere would also be gammafied and would conversely generate negative emotions.

Gamma Boosting to Save the Day

When we begin to worry, overall our brain is gamma boosted, presumably to kick start our brains into finding a solution fast before worrying reaches panic status. But if you are a chronic worrier like those with generalized anxiety disorder (GAD), gamma gets completely out of hand. Those specific regions of the brain that process negative emotions when we see kitties in a blender get supercharged, fueling a whirlwind of emotional worry and anxiety in GAD sufferers. So without further ado, let us get the good out of gamma through all-natural, all-healthy BOPs that intuitively work on boosting the right regions of the brain.

SUMMARY

- The fight-or-flight response is the perfect evolutionary tool to have us ready for action, guns at the ready, to enhance our chance of survival in potentially life threatening situations.
- **Today our fight-or-flight response in our brains and bodies can become chronic by being continually over-activated by many modern stressors which are not important for our immediate survival.**
- Chronic stress has been linked with many physical and mental ailments from headaches and anxiety to heart attacks and panic attacks.
- **Neuroplastic changes induced by chronic stress include frontal lobe and hippocampus degeneration and growth of the amygdalae, making for an easily confused, error-prone and emotional mess.**
- Stress plays a lot on exasperating and altering brainwave hemispheric asymmetries, with alpha and gamma imbalances currently understood best.
- **When stress is out of control theta swamps our hippocampus and struggles to regulate your beta waves.**
- Alpha waves in the left frontal lobe dampen the right frontal lobe's fight-or-flight response. With too much alpha in the right and we activate our fight-or-flight response.
- **Too much continual beta has our brains and bodies ready for action 24-7, which is well-known to lead to burnout.**
- Stress generally cranks up our gamma waves. Left frontal gamma surges might give you the power to find solutions quickly but too much too often leads to over-worrying and anxiety.

Up Next...

All this abstract fight-or-flight stress that is not truly associated with our immediate survival simply piles up, day to day, minute by minute, becoming an integral part of our brains, bodies and lives and can lead to health problems, broken relationships, career and financial problems as well as spiritual dilemmas.

Ultimately, in order to use BOPs to entrain a happy healthy brain we need to utilize them to reduce stress first before we can start building a better brain. Now let's get our hands dirty and start extinguishing your stress!

RAPID DE-STRESSING

BRAIN OPTIMIZATION PRACTICES

De-Stressing Is Always Step 1

If you have experienced prior success with meditation, re-introducing your meditative practice is a great start to de-stressing. If you are pretty new to relaxation practices this section will give you a strong foundation for beginner level meditation and for setting your foot down on the road to complete and utter relaxation. Either way, if daily stressors are bringing you down we *insist* you begin to take time for yourself.

We say insist rather than recommend since recommendations often get met with the same thoughts of "I will if I have time," "I'm just too busy today," yadda yadda yadda. These types of excuses are your overworked beta waves talking. But don't ignore them; see these thoughts as triggers, internal alarm bells that are reminding you to take five. As the old Zen saying goes "you should sit in meditation for 20 minutes a day, unless you're too busy; then you should sit for an hour."

Relaxing Reverses Rough Times

Let us speak on behalf of your alpha waves, for a moment. Relaxing is the key to creating more time for yourself. By relaxing you can reverse the negative effects that stress has on your brain and unleash the power within your own mind/brain to skilfully begin to master your stressors. With practice you and your brain, will automatically return to the knowing of this relaxed and soothing state within and this will increasingly become a positive and life increasing habit that you can count on.

For the first week you might find that you are just exploring which time of the day you can initially set aside for routine practice. Ideally routine relaxation practices are great first thing in the morning and the last thing at night, hijacking the brain boosting transition from the slow waves of sleep to wakefulness and back again. However, any time of day is fine and learning when to use these techniques at anytime to prevent being overwhelmed and stressed is key, although some times may be tougher training for absolute beginners. Even 10 minutes at your desk at work can make the difference between mastering your day with calm confidence or heading for those all too familiar stress circuits of fear, anxiety and adrenaline based waters.

BOP 1: DEEP BREATHING

Deep breathing is the first port of call for all meditation practices and with the body-mind connection (see Chapter 2 to learn more), simply slowing down your breathing instantly affects your brain. Remember then, *to mind your head you need to mind your breathing*. Amazingly, like other meditative practices, mastering something you already do quite capably without thinking—breathing—has profound effects on the brain, brainwaves and neuroplascticity. Mindful based breathing is oh so simple, yet oh so super effective.

1. **Sit comfortably**
Sit comfortably on a chair or on the floor with your back straight, upright, shoulders relaxed. (You can lie down although even relatively experienced meditators can fall asleep in this pose).

2. **Use hands to check breath**
Put one hand on your chest and the other on your stomach. (You can remove this step when you feel comfortable with relaxed breathing).

3. **Breath into your stomach.**
Take deep, long, slow breaths in through your nose and into your

stomach. This may seem like an odd idea at first, but using your hands as guides you should feel the hand on your stomach rise as you breathe in, with the hand on your chest moving very little.

4.   Slowly breathe out
Slowly and gradually breathe out through your mouth. Release as much air as you can while engaging your abdominal muscles to help you control your breath. The hand on your stomach. should move in as you exhale, with the hand on your chest moving very little.

5.   Breathe
Continue breathing in through the nose and out through the mouth paying attention to maintaining long, deep and slow abdominal breathing.

HINTS & TIPS

•   To begin with, your mind may wander very easily and you forget about your breathing. Don't let that deter you, it's natural, just gently refocus your thoughts on your awareness of breath. If you can manage a minute, fantastic! Test yourself by trying to extend the length of time you can focus, just a little more each day.

•   **Routinely using relaxing music and or burning incense or scented candles at the beginning of your practice can develop mental triggers that ease you into a meditative state even before you have officially begun!**

•   When coming out of any meditation it's good practice to wind out gradually, instead of snapping back to a beta brain reality. To accomplish this, simply slowly count from 10 or say a positive mantra such as "My breaths will be deep and my heart will be open," or "May stress and negativity dissolve into happiness." Then, remain still a few more minutes while relaxed and with your eyes open.

BOP 2: MUSCLE RELAXATION

For most of us that are in need of a thorough de-stressing, the second port of call is another meditation practice that works along with your deep breathing to unwind and relax your body from head to toe. When stressed a lot of the tension we experience is felt by our muscles. This can develop into common anxiety related niggles such as back and neck pain. Relaxing your muscles will not only relieve muscle tension but thanks to the mind-body connection this will take you into a deeper state of blissful relaxation.

1. Checking in
Begin with your deep, full, cleansing breaths to open your mind to more slow waves. Take a few minutes to focus and get settled on your breath.

2. Progressive relaxation
It is good mental practice to find a particular order in which to relax your body, although it is not essential. Follow the techniques below as you gradually work your way through each part of your body. The table below contains a common head to toe sequence, you may prefer it in reverse.

Take a moment to acknowledge how the part of your body feels, where are the areas of tension?

With each exhalation feel the tension leave that body part, taking you into a deeper and deeper state of relaxation. Be slow, caring and thorough in your thinking. If you are focusing on your head, remember to relax everything, your nose, ears, mouth, jaw etc. If you are focusing on your right foot, don't forget your toes.

Focus on the tension flowing away and the way it feels as your muscles become limp and loose.

Stay in this relaxed state until you are ready to move onto the next body part. Remember it's not a race; go at your own pace.

1. Head
2. Neck and shoulders
3. Right arm and hand
4. Left arm and hand
5. Chest
6. Stomach
7. Upper back
8. Lower back
9. Hips and buttocks
10. Right thigh
11. Left thigh
12. Right knee
13. Left knee
14. Right foot
15. Left foot

HINTS & TIPS

• If you are left handed you may find it more natural to move through your body from left to right.

• You may find it easier to relax your muscles by visualizing a healing light passing through your body, gradually easing out any muscle tension from head to toe. Or with each breath imagine you inhale healing, relaxing energy and exhale any tension.

BOP 3: INTRODUCTORY LEVEL VISUALIZATION

It is best to go through both breathing and muscle relaxation before going on to visualization practices. This allows you to make the most of your imagination. If your blood is boiling, your mind could cook up a storm if trying to visualize a peaceful, calm, serene beach paradise.

Also bear in mind that the term visualization is an over generalization, as with some visualization routines we engage all of our senses to truly bring the visualization to life within the mind, not just our visual perception. To begin with we offer you a very simple routine for slowing down your brainwaves and to get started with visualization practices. But if you want to fast forward to full immersion, grab a pair of headphones and get tuned in to Releasing Overwhelm's guided visualization BOP.

1. **Checking in**
Take a few minutes to get settled. Begin with your deep, full, cleansing breaths, followed by muscle relaxation to open your mind to more slow waves and iron out any extra tension in your body.

2. **Visualize a clock face**
Visualize a clock face, in any form that feels natural and easiest for you. Be it a stopwatch, grandfather clock or digital sports watch, pay attention to the seconds.

3. **Tick, tock, tick...**
Hear the ticking of the second hand, each sound solidifying the visualization of the moving hand with increasing clarity.

4. **Speed check**
Notice the speed and consistency of the clock ticking.

5. **Slow down**
Gently shift your focus to slowing down the clock, each exhalation slowing down the ticking further and further.

6. **Time stands still**
Now notice the increasing gaps between each tick. As you continue, the ticking slows down at a speed that seems natural to you. As the clock eventually begins to draw to a complete stop, the ticking begins to melt away into pure silence.

7. Enjoy
Enjoy the feelings of inner peace and relaxation.

BOP 4: RELEASING OVERWHELM
BRAIN TRAINING AUDIO

The first in our accelerated success audios is specifically designed to conquer stress, anxiety and burnout that is all too common today. If you are unfortunate enough to feel too stressed to benefit from self-directed relaxation techniques, this therapeutic audio can instantly relieve stress and reset the stress levels in a matter of days, giving you the mental space needed to accept daily relaxation practices into your life. Even if you are sailing through your daily practices, chipping away at your wall of stress one brick at a time, you can boost your results by incorporating Releasing Overwhelm for instantaneous stress release. The audio includes scientifically constructed messages for your subconscious aimed at extending your relaxation throughout your day and leading you into the depths of sound rejuvenating sleep.

This audio is available here:

http://successwaves.com/products/catalog/Releasing_Overwhelm.html

NeuroLogical Brain Training Goals

DE-STRESSING

Notes

_____

_____

_____

_____

_____

_____

_____

_____

_____

Notes

Part II

THE NEW AGE OF SELF-COMPASSION

"You can search throughout the entire universe for someone who is more deserving of your love and affection than you are yourself, and that person is not to be found anywhere. You, yourself, as much as anybody in the entire universe, deserve your love and affection"

~ Prince Gautama Siddharta, the founder of Buddhism, 563-483 B.C.

Caring Is In Our Genes
Protecting the Young

Getting the "warm fuzzies" is PRICELESS. You know, that warm fuzzy feeling when you receive a postcard from an old friend; or when a friend surprises you with your favorite treat, or someone takes the time to bring you soup when you're sick? Feeling cared about is at the essence of a happy human being. It's deeply rooted in what it means to be human. Fish can spawn 1000s of eggs, with hatchlings becoming young adults in just a few short months. So, they don't really need to hang around to see if one little fishy will survive long enough to pass on their genes (although some species do protect their eggs and young!). In this respect humans are definitely not most fish. We rarely have more than one baby at a time and for those of you with kids, you know all too well how long it takes your hatchlings to grow up to be well-rounded, self-sufficient little creatures.

Protecting the Group

From youth to old age someone caring about us can make the difference between happiness and sadness, joy and depression or even life and death. It's vital to be caring and in turn it's imperative to feel cared about. Let's say you're a pre-humanoid ape and you have the "I just don't give a toss if anyone cares about me" genes. Well then you will likely behave like a giant pain in the other pre-humanoid ape's asses, far reducing your chances of survival. Why would they care about you if cannot be trusted to adjust your behavior based on what others think? If you don't care, your behavior could threaten the happiness and survival of every other member of the group. It's no great wonder that we humans care so much about feeling cared about.

The Route to Caring Starts with The Self
Where Did the Caring Go?

In the modern age, life is oh so demanding and has taken its toll on community and family life. Very few of us are like the Walton's, with over a dozen family members supporting us all from under one roof and a whole community that could wander in and out your house as if it was their own. Even in a city surrounded by people and buzzing with life we can all, at times, feel lonely and uncared about. This feeling, can make us less caring towards others and feel crappy and stressed and cause us to act out of our natural caring loving character. It can lead to a vicious cycle. Studies agree that feeling cared about is good for us. It boosts our positive emotions, increases caring for others, fizzles out stress and can have lasting effects on the brain.

Love Thyself

Perhaps the most vital key to truly caring for others and feeling cared about, is valuing and loving *yourself* first and foremost. By loving and caring for yourself you can boost your brain and body and enhance your caring for others. It's quite the opposite of a vicious cycle, it's a positively flourishing cycle! You may be like many of us and find self-compassion a difficult pill to swallow, with those all so silly feelings of unworthiness and self-criticism seeming like an impenetrable wall.

Know this: although the road to self-compassion is a steep one, once you get the pace going, the effects will snowball until compassion for the self and for others opens you to new possibilities borne out of connection, and caring. How can we say this with such certainty? It's simple practice and it's backed by the latest cutting edge research. In true Mind Your Head style, it's not rocket science, it's the latest positive brain science!

Compassionate BOPs and the Brain

Types of Compassionate Meditation

In the past five years we have been able to witness the remarkable effects of compassion on the brain thanks to studies on compassionate (CM) and loving kindness meditation (LKM), as well as non-meditative compassionate imagery on the brain. LKM has a unique focus on cultivating positive emotions and heartfelt unconditional kindness for the self and others. CM aims to cultivate compassion or deep, genuine sympathy for those stricken by misfortune, together with an earnest wish to ease this suffering.

Special Brain Regions for Each Type

All meditation techniques share many attention and well-being associated brain benefits and share developments in the same brain regions. However, each individual flavor seems to have specific parts of the brain that it is particularly good at improving. Even when comparing meditation practices that have many similarities, as with CM and LKM, they have special training centers in the brain that are spatially and functionally distinct.

LKM & Emotional Control

With LKM two gyri (the slimy ridges or folds on the surface of the brain) get special attention. Neuroplasticity fattens these two gyri up; one with specific roles in generating empathy and the other being essential for communication between the cortex and the conjoined hippocampus and amygdalae in the regulation of mood, emotion, self control and motivation. Disorders of the mind such as depression, bipolar disorder and schizophrenia eat away at these gyri. So a little loving and kindness every day can truly keep the psychologist at bay!

CM & Understanding Others

Compassionate meditation on the other hand has its own special gyrus to focus on that gets hyperactivated during meditation. The more active it is the better we are able to infer and understand the thoughts and feelings of others, an ability called theory of mind (ToM) that you will hear more about later. Perhaps more importantly CM trains your brain to allow for feelings of empathy for the misfortunate, without getting overwhelmed and harbor negative emotions, making us more emotionally resilient. Even compassionate imagery without meditation is able to help brain damaged individuals rewire their brain for empathic thinking.

SUMMARY

- Evolutionary speaking, caring is essential to the survival of our species. We need to rear our young over many years, with both ourselves and our young surviving better and having more abundant lives with the support that living in groups provides.
- Being uncaring to yourself is in actuality being uncaring towards others as any behavioral consequences and steps towards mental and physical that are likely to result will affect others in your life.
- LKM cultivates positive feeling towards the self and others, while CM cultivates positive feelings towards someone who is experiencing misfortune and wishing for their suffering to cease.
- As with all BOPs, LKM and CM have specific regions of the brain that are enhanced only from that specific meditative practice:

regions that process empathy and enhance emotional control
(LKM) and those regions that are associated with understanding
other people (CM).

Up Next...

So far it seems that the different flavors of emotion based BOPs all rev
up regions involved in emotional regulation. All of which lead to the enhancement of our ability to relate to others, to understand their feelings and
enhance our selflessness, while keeping our own anxiety and mood in check.
What's more is that both novice and expert meditators experience these lasting changes to their emotional circuitry even outside of meditation. So let's
stop hanging about, and get "BOPing" by spreading some love!

THE NEW AGE OF SELF-COMPASSION
BRAIN OPTIMIZATION PRACTICES

BOP 1: SWEET TALKING

With a little dose of NLP (Neuro Linguistic Programming) know-how, we have found a way to raise your compassion meter even higher and much faster than with compassionate practices alone. As you know NLP deals with the language of the mind which is integral to being compassionate to yourself. We have all experienced a mind lashing from our inner voice, reminding us of our stupidity, ugliness or worthlessness. We are even sarcastic to ourselves within our own minds and can even be a bit of a brain bully. Most of us wouldn't accept too much of that kind of nonsense from other people, but we have got so used to giving ourselves a telling off that most of the time we don't even notice.

Now we will use one of the most simplistic yet powerful aspects of NLP to sweeten the talk between you and well, yourself, which should enhance the sincerity of the following self-compassionate practices.

1.   Recall a time when you have had negative thoughts about yourself.
Really try and be in the moment, engage all your senses in imagining the scene. What is a common phrase you use to tell yourself

off? E.g. failing an exam, being late for work, missing an appointment or meeting with friends etc. What did you say to yourself?

2.   Focus on your inner voice
Now let's take that nagging, whinging, angry or moaning voice and that phrase and play with them a little. Work your way through the list below to transform the voice to a helpful and caring one, no matter what the message.

-Where is the voice located? If it is inside your head move it with your mind to outside of your body? Does this help? Experiment with its location.

-Which way is the voice facing? Most likely a wingy, angry or moaning inner voice is pointing straight at you. Turn the voice to face away from you, how does this make you feel?

-Play with the volume. Turn it up or down and notice the difference.

-Add some funny music. Be warned, singing "I am an idiot" to Beethoven's 5th symphony or Everybody Was Kung Fu Fighting may induce a fit of giggles. If you are alone try singing it out loud. (Your theme tune can be used any time you are stressing at yourself to lighten the mood).

-Change the pace and tone of the voice. Soften and lighten the voice, imagine your speaking to your innocent inner child, see how that makes you feel.

3.   Change any negatives to positives
Write down the phrases you bad-mouthed yourself with and transform it with positive word choice. Turning "I'm such an idiot today" into "My brain could do with a boost today" morph's those feelings of guilt and disappointment into an empowering subconscious message for your brain.

4.   Revisit the scene
Now that you have played with your inner voice let's revisit the scene in your mind that led to that nasty little self-critical phrase. Really try and be in the moment, engage all your senses in imagining the scene. Instead, this time we are going to replace it with your kind, caring voice and positive message, wherever and however that might be. Notice how different you feel and how different you behave as a consequence.

Now you are more aware of the profound effects on feelings and behavior that can arise directly from the different ways in which you speak to yourself. Try on a daily basis to become more aware of your inner voice and when it gets out of hand, tone it down, dampen the volume and transform the words into an empowering message. With this practice, instead of your inner voice stirring up more troubles, you can get a little boost when you feel you have botched something up. It makes more sense to fill yourself with this extra juice than rubbing salt in the wound and making things worse. If you think you may be guilty of overusing a meanie of an inner voice, be good to yourself and focus on incorporating the practice of a new inner voice into your daily BOPing rituals with the help of your NeuroLogical journal.

BOP 2: GIVING AND RECEIVING COMPASSION

Self-Compassion is Selfless

Finding self-compassion is one of the least selfish acts you can perform. By learning to love oneself more, your capacity for growth and change, as well as love and appreciation of others will bloom as you go. Gaining the ability to soothe yourself will also have a huge impact on your confidence and independence.

Focusing on Compassion is Therapeutic

LKM (loving kindness meditation), is a traditional and ancient Buddhist meditation also known by its original Pali language name, metta. Metta literally means "loving compassion." In the past few years CBT (cognitive behavioral therapy) has been developing compassionate meditation practices like LKM. This has lead to evidence-based compassion focused therapy (CFT) and is now used in the clinical treatment of many mental health problems. In fact, it has even recently been shown to enhance recovery from severe trauma.

CFT Guides Growth

You may wonder why anyone went to the bother of developing CFT if LKM and CM can make astonishing upgrades to our grey matter. Well, if you don't have a Buddhist monk buddy or a spare spiritual guru at hand to provide the guidance needed to enhance your understanding and the benefits of compassionate practice, the road to speedy results may be blocked by a few common obstacles. CFT is designed not only for you to feel the effects of focused compassionate thoughts, but also provides the structure for overcoming these obstacles, both of which lead to the development of a deeper understanding of your relationship with yourself. These techniques can help extend your compassionate practices into everyday life and not just during meditation time. Here is a loving kindness based meditation followed by a CFT learning technique that complement each other well in the process of learning to love and appreciate yourself.

First, develop three simple phrases by thinking of positive desires for yourself. Formulate your desires into three or four phrases. For example: may I be healthy in body and mind; may I experience happiness and joy and may I be filled with loving kindness.

Do you have your phrases ready? Great, now you are ready to board the compassion train! Oh, wait! What we find however is that for some individuals who give themselves a particularly hard time, it is easier to pick another person to be the initial focus of loving attention. To ease us all into this exercise gently, think of someone whom, to you, showing love and compassion is second nature and we will start from there.

1.   Breathing & relaxation

Begin with your deep, full, cleansing breaths to open your mind to more slow waves. Take a few minutes to focus and get settled on your breath. If you are feeling in need of it, follow this up with your muscle relaxation BOP for deeper relaxation.

2.   Send desires for your loved one with kind internal voice & visualization

Begin, with your soft and kind internal voice, to repeat the phrases in your mind and with each positive phrase your mind utters, send those loving desires to your loved one along with the positive warm fuzzy feelings that come as part of the parcel. You can also use the power of visualization here and hold an image of your loved one being enveloped in a love-heart shaped frame, glowing brighter and brighter with warmth and love as you repeat your phrases.

3.   How did It feel to give love?

Reflect for a moment about how you felt about sending loving desires.

4.   Receive desires from your loved one with kind internal voice & visualization

Now the person that you have a loving bond with is going to shower you with the same mantras in return. Immerse yourself in their loving kindness and loving energy as you imagine them repeating the phrases back to you.

5.   How did it feel to receive love?

Reflect for a moment about how you felt about receiving loving desires.

6.   Focus loving kindness on yourself

You can now extend this abundance of love and kindness that you have been sent to yourself. Use your experience of both receiving loving-kindness and giving loving-kindness to help guide you. Give love willingly to yourself with the sincerity and ease that you sent love to your loved one. At the same time revive the very recent sensation you had of being open and willing to receive love from your loved one. Ride the wave of love and give yourself the love you deserve.

HINTS & TIPS

- It's not unusual to feel resistance when focusing love on oneself, don't fret. Accept that this is part of the healing process. Any resistance should remind you that you are on the right track to overcoming feelings of self-doubt and negativity.
- Remember this can be practiced anywhere, from crowded, stress-inducing places such as long lines and traffic jams, to when someone is pushing all your wrong buttons. And if you regularly make this part of your BOPing practice, you can grow new neurons to fill out your LKM gyri, enhancing the regulation of your mood, emotional self control and motivation.

BOP 3: GROWING FROM COMPASSION

OK. So you may have found the previous BOP pretty easy first time round or you may have felt a little (or a lot) of resistance to all that positivity and good will. Either way don't be put off as this next CFT technique will allow you to make contact with, build on and develop your inner compassionate self.

Specifically, your feeling and understanding of the intrinsic qualities and behaviors of a compassionate person are a growing practice which, when developed, will continually overflow into your own naturally and instinctively compassionate behavior in the outside world. Imagine living in a new version of your world, able to receive and give and be loving and understanding. What if with some practice, with practice, you were able to trust in the good in the world and the good and loving future you hold for yourself and your community, family and friends?

Keep in mind that you will be using the power of your imagination to see yourself at your compassionate best. It doesn't matter if you don't feel you actually are highly compassionate at the time, but it is important to imagine the qualities of a highly compassionate person and imagine that it is YOU that has these qualities—imagination is key here. We will move through envisioning and embodying three root kinds of compassionate qualities for as little as 30 seconds each. Feel free to add any more that you can think of to expand this BOP even further.

1.   **Checking in**
As usual, begin with your deep, full, cleansing breaths in and out your nose. When you move onto muscle relaxation pay particular attention to relaxing you facial muscles and jaw.

2.   **Smile & relax**
Allow your mouth to turn upwards into a slight, warm, friendly, comfortable smile. Continue with the muscle relaxing routine if you feel it is necessary.

3.   **Growth 1**
Let's begin with the quality of **kindness** and your desires to be a **helpful, supportive** and **compassionate** person that wants to help others to be happy and free from suffering. Hold your smile and using your compassionate, kind voice in your mind, gently and playfully imagine that you have great desires to be helpful. Notice how you feel when you imagine having these desires. Spend 30 seconds -1 min (or longer if you want), eyes closed, imagining.

4.   **Growth 2**
The feeling of **strength** is equally important to being compassionate. Strength comes from **confidence, kind authority** and **maturity**. So holding your smile and kind inner authoritative and confident voice, begin imagining yourself with these qualities. Let those feelings flow into your posture and how you are seeing yourself. Imagine how you would talk to others, move around in the world and see how you would express the confident, mature, authoritative and compassionate you. How does this make you feel? Spend 30 seconds -1min (or longer if you want), eyes closed, imagining.

5.   **Growth 3**
Now focus and imagine yourself having great **wisdom** through

having learned much from your life. Imagine yourself as **open, thoughtful** and **reflective**. Again keep your smiling expression and compassionate internal voice with you as you envision yourself expressing wise, thoughtful insight. How do you interact with others in your mind? How do you feel? Try this for 30 or more seconds.

6. Growth 4
From possessing wisdom, strength and kindness a whole host of other qualities come with it like **generosity, forgiveness, playfulness,** and genuine **concern** and **commitment** towards others. Imagine you are looking at yourself from an outside perspective, notice your motivations and feeling towards yourself as you interact with others. See other people relating to you as a compassionate person. See yourself relating to other people in the ideal compassionate way that you are developing. For the next 30 seconds enjoy watching yourself being a compassionate person in the world and others relating to you as such.

Using the last two BOPs you will begin to further develop your compassionate self. By doing so you will find that activating compassionate ways of thinking about yourself and of others, even your enemies, will become clearer, easier and more natural to you. Accessing and expressing your compassionate qualities will come with ease, even if someone is deliberately pushing your buttons—you can just send them some loving kindness, how infuriating for them! Now, have another go at the previous exercise where you used positive mantras as heartfelt desires for yourself and others—much easier!

HINTS & TIPS

- You may find it much easier or get an added boost from modeling your imagined compassionate self on a real life compassionate person. Whether it's that shop keeper that always takes the time to send love and gratitude every time a customer enters their store, a Buddhist monk, or even Ghandi himself, it's no matter. Imagine yourself in their compassionate shoes, seeing and feeling what they might do and feel, borrowing their compassionate genius and love. You can borrow their skill, amplifying your own compassionate qualities.

BOP 4: AUTHENTIC POWER
BRAIN TRAINING AUDIO

Would you like to have unstoppable inner confidence and to own your best strengths and assets so that you can optimistically achieve what you set your mind to? Authentic Power is specifically designed to help you switch off fear and instantly learn to train your brain, to live with greater ease and certainty by maximizing your confidence and optimizing your mood.

The benefits of being self-loving, insure that—with each listening and use of this audio—you'll be developing the neural patterns of those born with innate unconquerable self-confidence and high self esteem. By listening to this audio daily, you too will re-train your brain to live in instantly life changing "knowing", high energy and wise self confidence that is invaluable in social, business and romantic situations.

This audio is available here:

http://successwaves.com/products/catalog/Authentic_Power.html

NeuroLogical Brain Training Goals

SELF-COMPASSION

Notes

Notes

Part III

BRAND-NEW BELIEFS & HABITS

"If you don't change your beliefs, your life will be like this forever. Is that good news?"

~ W. Somerset Maugham

Beliefs
The Bouncers of Your Dreams and Goals

Earlier in this book we briefly mentioned the role of your beliefs in influencing your thoughts and behavior, which affects how we set our goals and determines whether or not we will actually achieve our dreams. In short, your beliefs are generalizations you make about yourself and everything else in the world around you. Our beliefs and desires affect the way we think and feel; whether the belief is based on experience, or merely a notion and whether it's helpful or a hindrance.

While your beliefs can give you the power to find health, wealth and happiness, they also have the power to prevent you from achieving your goals. The heads and tails of the coin of belief are empowerment and disempowerment. Like bouncers at a nightclub's doors, beliefs have the power to block the way to life's opportunities or open the way to the time of your life. So it's pretty important that we get a solid understanding of our beliefs and their link with our desires or the formation of good or bad habits: bad habits that have us running around in circles or good habits that propel us towards achieving our goals and dreams.

The Power of Beliefs

Let's take a belief you may have formed in school as a kid for an example. Many of us form beliefs about what we are good and not good at pretty early in life. Say your teacher praises you for your frantic finger painting of mummy with "Wow what a great painting, you could be an artist someday." The belief that you are good at painting can help you develop the belief that you enjoy painting and are really quite artistic. Who knows just how far the domino effect of a single positive belief will reach. That one simple belief could manifest the next modern day da Vinci!

Likewise, negative beliefs can be formed in just the same way and lead to unfulfilled goals or a denial of one's worth. For example, negligent parenting could stimulate the formation of a core belief such as 'I'm not wanted' which, in turn could lead to "I'm not nice or lovable." This can play havoc with relationship skills in later life if you don't shake that belief before it lays down its roots. Just the simple belief that you find something difficult can actually make something difficult. Conversely, just the simple belief that you can do something can make doing it so much more easy and enjoyable to achieve. If you try not to cling to an unwavering belief system and instead see it as a garden of beliefs you can take advantage of the power of having a flexible belief system. By pruning and nurturing the growth of the beautiful beliefs and pulling out the weeds, the doors you will open for yourself can be astounding.

Beliefs, Desires and the Brain
What do I believe? Ask ToM

The scientific understanding of the mind's belief system is in its infancy. Presently, there is little certainty about the kinds of brainwaves most impactful upon our beliefs when making decisions in life. While we don't know what kinds of brainwaves have the biggest impact, brain scans do show us which parts of the brain are busy when accessing our beliefs and desires. These scans have identified a network of brain regions that are involved in beliefs in oneself and of others. Specifically, the network identified in the results of the study deals with our theory of mind, or ToM for short. ToM is how we attribute beliefs, desires and intents to ourselves and make inferences about the beliefs of others.

The Will to Want

Beliefs and desires, as mental states, involve similar regions of the ToM network, mainly in the frontal regions of the cortex. Your beliefs also recruit areas at the back of the cortex whose main functions are to plan movement and action but have also been associated with processing feelings of free will. The processing of beliefs in the brain seems to be integral to evaluating our internal thoughts and external events and in influencing our actions. As we grow up we rope in another region of the cortex that dampens our ego and specifically inhibits our own perspective. Instead, that region uses the ToM network to allow us to try to see things from another person's perspective, essential for developing healthy social skills like empathy. (More on this in Chapter 3: Focusing on others).

The Danger of Illogical Beliefs

Funnily enough there is a striking similarity between the brain's belief systems of those fanatically obsessed with the paranormal (those that live, eat and breath ghosties and ghoulies) and of those diagnosed with clinical schizophrenia. Within the ToM network there is a huge over-reliance on the activity in the right hemisphere as opposed to the left when compared to healthy individuals.

This hemispheric asymmetry is thought to favor the acceptance of 'loose' and 'uncommon' associations in bolstering beliefs that logic would deem a tad difficult to believe. Entertaining such beliefs only opens the door to other beliefs loosely formed on fuzzy logic, a potentially dangerous cycle if you want to maintain your sanity. But you don't have to be labeled a looney tune to hold such beliefs. And now that you have Mind Your Head in your hands, weeding out negative beliefs—the little monsters of our minds—and replacing them with little angels is simple to achieve.

From Beliefs to Behavior

How important is this network to our habits and behaviors in the achievement of our goals? Being the essence of beliefs themselves, the ToM network is intricately linked with our day to day habits, behaviors and ability to reach our goals. Having strong beliefs that violate logic and reason not only change the way the brain is working when entertaining wild beliefs but they even influence how the brain works when it's at rest.

Negative Beliefs Encourage Bad Habits and Desires

Perhaps the extent of the influence beliefs can have on our behavior can be seen in individuals burdened with the mother of all habit forming brain bogey-men, OCD. A special kind of belief called a metacognitive belief is particularly important to remain positive for the nurturing of a healthy mind. Metacognitive beliefs or thoughts are your ideas about your ability to monitor and control your own thinking processes.

With OCD, sufferers tend to think that they don't have a lot of control over intrusive compulsive thoughts, which is a highly negative and positivity inhibiting metacognitive belief (like many other can'ts, won'ts, shouldn'ts and couldn'ts). In an experiment just last year such negative metacognitive beliefs were shown to both spark OCD symptoms and also exasperate them. What's more is that those who had the mildest cases of OCD were influenced far less by these intrusive metacognitive beliefs.

Positive Beliefs Encourage Good Habits and Desires

So ultimately having a positive set of beliefs about yourself, your abilities and what you can achieve in life, based on sound logic and reasoning of course (no monsters in the mind please), will boost your brain and bolster your behavior towards positive and happy outcomes. If you reach a standstill with one of your neurological goals and just can't seem to get your behavior to comply then perhaps it's time to take a step back and see if an irrational belief is the fly in the ointment. And the same goes for your desires, the interwoven connectivity between belief and desire networks mean that if you focus on developing a strong positive belief system, your desires will follow.

Habits
Habits and the Brain

The secret ingredient that fuels the formation of habits as they become deeply ingrained and seemingly thoughtless, natural behavior, is neuroplasticity. Recall that neuroplasticity is simply the brain's ability to sever old unused neuronal connections and forge new connections that can be used to reshape and reinforce happy, healthy living. Thank the stars that our brains are malleable! Luckily, through your understanding of how the brain and brain plasticity works, you are in the prime position, with regular practice, to break self-hindering habits and replace them with healthy ones.

Switching Systems

You see, both good and bad habits are examples of super-successful and strong neuroplasticity. And, repetition (ah…the dreaded 'practice' is the key to their success. When, through repetition, we make an action or behavior a habit (anything as seemingly benign as being a bit of a moan, impulse buying or biting your nails to major life disturbing habits such as gambling and addiction) we shift between two systems in the brain. One system methodically deals with actions and their outcomes and the other brain system requires no lengthy decision process, where your repetitive behaviors have become your habits.

A-O to S-R

Initially a new behavior will involve some relatively complex thoughts in thinking about the outcome of your intended actions (called the action-outcome system or A-O system). If I asked you now to pick your nose you might consider many things such as, "is anyone around me I don't want to see this" or "which finger fits best" or even "should I really be doing this!" If you are a serial nose picker however, you are unlikely to have debated about it that much. When a certain behavior becomes a habit, the second system takes over, where little thought is required and the thought or event itself will actually trigger an automatic response (the stimulus-response or S-R system).

The Striatum

Both of these systems involve a specialized structure nestled deep within the forebrain, the striatum. The striatum is super connected to both the cortex and the master organizer, the thalamus. Thus the striatum receives a whole load of information, everything from your senses to your internal state and body movements. It receives this mega upload of information and then processes and sends the signals to brain regions it is well connected with that are involved in learning routine behaviors (habits). This includes behaviors which control voluntary movement and emotions or those that bring you awesome feelings of reward when you achieve your goals.

Neuroplasticity Generates Habits—the Good, the Bad and the Brilliant!

The striatum is highly specialized and comprises a few different modules. One striatum module deals with information for the active thought responses system (A-O), and another deals with the habitual response system (S-R). The latter system tightly weaves your senses and your actions together using sensorimotor regions of the cortex. It is this region where movement is guided by the senses and habitual thinking and not by deliberate thought. It seems that the more behavior is repeated, the more neuroplasticity is activated in the S-R modules of the striatum. This enhanced neuroplasticity causes a snowballing shift from the A-O to the S-R system which truly ingrains a behavior into our brains and bodies.

Take Home Message

Scientists are busy figuring out just how it all goes down, but the take home message is clear. The effect of repeating behaviors on making neuroplastic changes is really strong within the striatum. Therefore unhelpful habitual behaviors may take a little time and intentional action-outcome thinking to de-wire. Using simple repetition and determination we can form brand new happy habitual behaviors to help override the bad ones. As we have been highlighting from the get go, neuroplasticity is a double edged sword. Just keep in mind that now, with this knowledge, it is up to us. We have the choice as to which side of the blade we use. With the promise of happy, positive life affirming, dynamic and creative behaviors becoming your default habits we believe the choice is an easy one.

SUMMARY

- Our beliefs are associated with our desires, dreams and goals and can aid us in the formation of both bad and good bad habits of thinking feeling and doing.
- Beliefs and desires involve the ToM network, particularly parts in the frontal lobe. Your beliefs also recruit areas of the occipital cortex used for planning movement and processing feelings of free will.
- ToM network asymmetries that enhance the right hemispheres activity are associated with those of us with strong illogical beliefs based on loose information.
- Neuroplasticity fuels the change from using action-outcome (A-O) based circuitry to stimulus-response (S-R) based circuitry, making a planned behavior a habitual response by switching modules of the striatum for that behavior.

Up Next...

The fantastic thing about the neuroscience of beliefs and habits is that we can use visualization practices to help develop the ToM network and striatum and any other brain regions involved. By influencing our beliefs and behavior in our inner, imaginary worlds we influence our brains in such a way that it helps us generate the same results in the real world. Using BOPs to practice and experience new behaviors from within your mind will open up doors for you to implement those behaviors in the external world. This, in and of itself, is a BOP that continues to solidify new beliefs or behaviors through real life experience.

BRAND-NEW BELIEFS & HABITS

BRAIN OPTIMIZATION PRACTICES

BOP 1: BREAKING DOWN NEGATIVE BELIEFS

Begin with Visualization

With the goal of creating empowering and restorative beliefs and habits and breaking down the bad, you need to take visualization practices to the next level. Simply visualizing ideas and situations in your mind, haphazardly and without learning to enhance visualization is less likely to prove effective in getting the desired results: long lasting changes in beliefs, behaviors and habits, whether they are habits of thought, your emotions or your actions. In this regard, it is important to understand how we paint the details of our inner worlds. Just like you can train your perception in the external world you can train your perception in your inner world.

Inner Use of Limiting Beliefs

Let us begin with examining your inner belief systems, so that we can maximize the effectiveness of the BOPs used to change your negative beliefs. You already know, from the section prior to this one on self-compassion, the importance of paying attention to your inner voice. You will use that knowledge as a primer for the following techniques. Beliefs which limit us are powerfully dangerous thoughts. Yet sadly it is rare to meet an untrained mind that doesn't have such limiting beliefs. They come in many forms, from limiting beliefs about other people's behavior ("blondes are always more fun" or "brunettes are always more dull"), to personal and self-esteem related beliefs, including metacognitive beliefs. Remember? Thoughts about how you believe you think.

Since we are focusing on ourselves let's start out with a personal belief. Anything from "I don't deal well with 'X' kind of people" to "I can't make a diet work, I don't have the control" or "It's impossible for me to be truly happy" or "I don't truly deserve love."

1.   Recall a limiting belief
Recall a limiting belief that you currently have about yourself and that you would like to change.

2.   To begin with let's just answer a few simple questions
This will help increase your powers of perception regarding how you hold this belief in your mind. If you don't know the answer, visualize the belief again with that question in mind. For most people, personal limiting beliefs are usually heard as 'noise' in our heads—you hear a voice telling you that you aren't this, that or the other. Others sometimes "see" the noise, rather than hear it. For these people, they may see the words or a representative scene or image and it likely induces strong negative or limiting feelings.

- Where is it located?
Whether you see it or hear it in your head, try and determine where the position of the voice, image or feeling is coming from. For some people strong negative beliefs have a habit of looming over them and making them feel like they are completely under a large umbrella of negativity. Who knows, you may find the feeling is in your big toe! Regardless of its ultimate location, try and have fun with pinpointing it.

- Get down to the details?
Perhaps you have a very clear, vivid bright picture in mind or your inner voice is booming over you at a fast pace in an angry tone.

- **Pay attention to how you feel**

What emotions does the belief bring about? Guilt, fear, anger or confusion? Where inside or even outside of your body do you locate this feeling? Also, are there any physical sensations? Discerning the difference between a negative emotion and the unpleasant physical sensations that occur is a vital and useful skill for achieving progress with many BOPs and learning to recognize and master control of your emotions.

3.   Recall a dispelled belief

Now that you have a feel for the details let's pay attention to a belief that you used to hold but now believe is completely and utterly untrue to you. Perhaps, in the past you believed you would never be able to drive, but now you have the driving skills of family Schumacher. Or maybe there is something that feels ridiculous to believe in now, such as Santa Claus or the Easter bunny. Or it may even be something so radical that you clearly know it is a silly, non-evidence based belief about yourself such as "I am an alien" or "at night I grow wings."

Think that thought again but this time pay attention to what is going on in your inner world as you think it.

-**Where is the thought coming from?**

Where is the tooth fairy floating about around you or where is the sound of that once believable negative mantra, are they close? Or maybe it seems as if they are coming from far away?

-**What are the visible or audible details?**

E.g. what color is it? What shape is it? What texture is it? How loud or soft is it?)

-What feelings and sensations are evoked?

What emotions does the belief bring about? Perhaps you feel amusement and silliness regarding your nonsensical belief? What about any physical sensations?

4.   Reflect

Did you notice the differences between a belief you are clinging on to that affects you in the here and now compared with a belief that you don't really hold true anymore? Good, you are getting the hang of paying attention to the details.

5.   Give your limiting belief the qualities of the old belief

Now you have the tools to play dress-up and disguise your limiting belief as a belief that you no longer value and can therefore no longer affect you. If your old belief made you feel silly, was a quiet voice and sounded like it was in the distance, then your limiting belief should be given the same attributes. "It's impossible for me to ever be happy" is unlikely to have the same affect if instead of looming over you in an accusative voice the voice comes from a far and is riddled with happiness and mirth.

HINTS & TIPS

- Use all of your focus to think of your limiting belief and morph the picture, noise, feelings and sensations that it generates to have the same qualities as your old disregarded belief from the past. Beginning the technique after your breathing and relaxation practices might help calm your mind for focus.
- **Explore all the possible attributes and details that you may have in your mind about the belief. The more details you can swap the more depth your new visualization can have and the easier it is to dampen the effects of your limiting belief, to help erase it and make room for some new ones.**

BOP 2: CREATING POSITIVE BELIEFS

There is an equally effective technique for creating new empowering beliefs. For example, if previously you thought that you didn't deserve love, the goal with this exercise is to create the belief in your ToM network that you do deserve love. This time instead of focusing on limiting and untrue beliefs we will focus on encouraging beliefs and true beliefs.

1. Establish your new positive belief
2. Recall a true belief

Now, think of another belief that you do possess and know to be absolutely true about yourself, or some other non-personal belief that is certain. For example, something as concrete as "when the sun comes up there will be light."

3.   Explore the true beliefs details
Now let's really envision and bring the true belief to life, check the attributes table to see if you can expand on the details. What kind of picture/sound does this kind of belief paint for you? Where is it located? How does it make you feel emotionally and physically?

4.   Make your new positive belief become true
Finally let's take your new desired positive belief and give it the same attributes as the true belief you just examined. Again, the more detail the better.

HINTS & TIPS

•   You can use your NeuroLogical goals journal to assist in forging new, positive beliefs. Just a 5-10 minute slot of BOPing time every day can help with letting go of old beliefs and creating new, useful positive ones.

•   **As we mentioned earlier some of us, may not even be aware that we have certain beliefs that prevent us from changing bad habits or achieving our goals. When you can't seem to change a habit or some magical force seems to be preventing you from achieving your goals it's time to probe deep and see if you can tweak a belief that is the underlying cause of the difficulties, using the same techniques as described above and below.**

BOP 3: THE SWISH TECHNIQUE
Behaviors Paint a More Visual Picture

When we deal with visualization of behaviors (and by extension our habits) as opposed to beliefs, our imaginings are more scenic and situational and we tend to have a lot more mental details that we can work with to paint a vivid picture—particularly handy for the Swish technique but not essential. There are many behaviors that aren't healthy for us that most of us would like to replace with more useful ones. For example, you might get overemotional during confrontational situations or maybe you criticize others (with thoughts or with words) when you feel a pang of jealousy for example.

Put Your Finger on the Trigger

The theory behind the Swish technique is to make use of the mental pathways that allows for your negative behavior or habit in order to create the new desired one. Another key aspect of the Swish technique is that to perform it we need to find out the trigger or context that causes you to behave that way. It may be an environmental or indeed internal mental trigger that sets of the behavior you would like to change. For example, perhaps when you are criticized by your partner when they use a certain tone, this may be the trigger that makes you lose your emotional control. In this case the criticism and tone are the triggers that set off your negative emotion. So it is this situational trigger that you would focus on.

As with all the techniques in this section, the Swish technique is very adaptable and you can use it to influence any of your emotions, behaviors, thoughts and beliefs. Follow these steps:

1. **Recall using the unwanted behavior**
Eyes closed, imagine a window or a photo frame in front of you. Paint the scene in your mind within this window as vividly as you can, fill in the details and then hit the play button.

2. **Identify the trigger**
Identify the trigger that sets off your unwanted behavior. Make an associated picture or a mental movie of the situation that causes the bad behavior.

3.　Pay attention to the details

Notice the attributes the visualization has. What does it look, feel, taste, sound, or smell like? Where is it located? How clear is the image, is it sharp as a pin or a bit fuzzy? How does it make you feel physically and emotionally? If you feel your emotions are becoming too intense, come back to focusing on your breath. Take a little time to play with and explore the image.

4.　Reset

Now wipe the visualization board in your mind clean. Stretching, standing up and moving about or giving yourself a good shake will do fine.

5.　Painting the positive picture

Now let's have some fun in painting the desired image, where you experience the trigger and instead you behave as you would like to behave in the situation. Create an image or situation where you respond appropriately and are extremely proud of yourself. If you are not sure how to behave you can model someone else, fictional or real, that would respond to the trigger in a beneficial way and pretend it's your behavior. Play around, have fun, it is a learning process, and you may modify the behavior even more with time and experience of using it in the real world.

6.　Enhance the details and positivity

Really focus on enhancing the details of this image. The trigger should now promote positive feelings of some kind.

7.　Shrink the positive image

Now, make this image small in your mind; lovingly shrink it to the size of a postage stamp or even smaller. Place this mental image in the bottom corner of the unwanted behavior picture.

8.　Swish and replace the negative scene with the new positive one

Now here is where the Swishing comes in. You want to take the small wanted image and expand it so it replaces the old image, while simultaneously shrinking the old negative picture and letting it shoot off into the distance and disappearing. Imagine a swishing sound as you do this. Notice the changing of the attributes and emotions. Enhance these details and enhance those positive feelings, make them overpower your mind and body, try to truly experience the desired result. If the image is very colorful and vivid, make the colors more bright and even more vivid than you thought physically possible.

9. Reset
Now clear your mind again. Hold your breath or count your fingers, anything to clear the visualization from the mind.

10. Repeat
Repeat steps 4-9 five to seven times until you find it difficult to hold the unwanted image in your mind. To begin with, it might take 5-10 seconds to swish the pictures. Each time you repeat you will find that you can swish much faster, possibly within a second.

NeuroLogical Brain Training Goals

BELIEFS & HABITS

Notes

Notes

CHAPTER II:
FOCUSING ON HEALTH

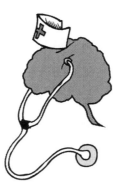

"Health is a state of complete harmony of the body, mind and spirit. When one is free from physical disabilities and mental distractions, the gates of the soul open."

~B.K.S. Iyengar

PART I

MAXIMIZING THE MIND-BODY CONNECTION

"The root of all health is in the brain. The trunk of it is in emotion. The branches and leaves are the body. The flower of health blooms when all parts work together."

~ Kurdish folk wisdom

What We Knew Then
An Ancient Past

F or thousands and thousands of years, from the dawn of our recorded history, cultures have intuitively been aware of the power of the mind and body connection. Throughout history, the relationship between body and mind has been described in countless ideologies, cultures and religions. Sumerian and Egyptian cultures whose writings originated 30th century BCE were well aware of the mind-body relationship.

While our understanding of Sumerian culture hints at meditative and yoga practices, we have a much better understanding of the Egyptians' mind-body practices, since it is they whom have been thoroughly poked and prodded by archaeologists, historians and enthusiasts alike.

Ancient Egyptians Knew About It

Over 5000 years ago ancient Egyptian physicians believed that diseases of the body can stem from causes of the spirit, physical body or mind. OK so the Egyptians weren't exactly accurate about what generates the mind within the body. They skewered out and flung away the brain during the embalming process, thinking it had little purpose and that the mind could be found in the heart. I wonder if there are a bunch of brainless Pharaohs wandering around up there in the afterlife dazed and confused! In either case Egyptians quite rightly believed that feelings and thoughts can influence the health of the body. For example they likened depression to a "fever of the heart."

Ancient Cultures All Around The World Knew Too!

The ancient histories of India and China are infamous with regards to meditative practice and ancient systems of medicine in which the mind-body connection is paramount. The ancient Greeks were also in on the mind-body connection and meditative practices too. Philosophers such as Plato were well-known for singing the praises of bodily exercise as a key for developing the mind. While the Greek father of western medicine, Hippocrates, believed that good health depends on a balance of mind, body, and environment.

What We Know Now
A Juvenile Re-beginning

Despite an exceedingly ancient conception of the relationship between the mind and body, modern society is only just using scientific tools to unearth the roots of the connection and get a clearer understanding. As early as the 1920s the mind-body connection was scientifically proven through studies revealing the processes involved in the fight-or-flight response: where one's mind, in response to external environmental changes, causes hormone production that sets your reflexes on fire and prepares your body for action when your mind perceives something in the environment as a threat. If you don't think there is a threat (MIND) then you don't respond (BODY)—an irrefutable connection.

The Relaxation Response

After practicing the de-stressing techniques described in the last chapter, you will personally experience the "relaxation response" (the antithesis of the "fight-or-flight"). In the "relaxation response" brainwave changes cause your heart rate and breathing rate to lower while enhancing muscle relaxation and happy hormone production. Relaxation response training allows patients to monitor the state of their bodies' muscle relaxation on a screen (a form of biofeedback) as they consciously try to induce, increase and sustain the re-laxation response. This biofeedback technique has been used to treat both chronic and acute pain and body ailments, everything from arthritis to menopause.

Mindfulness Switches Your Genes

In a 2013 study, investigators found a whole host of genes that get acti-vated when you practice the relaxation response. Using mindfulness based practices such as meditation, yoga, deep-breathing and prayer produces im-mediate changes in the expression of genes involved in immune function and how our bodies regulate energy and hormone levels. Amazingly, but not sur-prisingly, genes that were suppressed or switched off have prominent roles in inflammation, stress, trauma and cancer. Relaxing, as with stressing, causes fundamental changes to how our bodies work by harnessing the power of the mind, which influences our brain to positively affect our bodies, all the way down to our genes.

Mind-Immune System Connection
Psychoneuroimmunology

But the connection between your brain and mind with the health of your body goes even deeper than as we just described. In the 1980s various laboratories were discovering just how intimate the connection between your brain state and the health of your body is. They revealed that we have neurons that directly contact glands and cells of the immune system, coining a new branch of scientific research called psychoneuroimmunology (PNI), linking the mind (psycho), neurons (neuro) and health (immunology).

Since then, hundreds of scientific studies have broadened our understanding of the mind-body connection. They have highlighted the deep interdependence between your mind and your emotions with your immune system and the ability to fight disease. It gives a whole new meaning to the expression 'they died of a broken heart' or 'good health brings happiness'.

Sadness in the Mind Depresses Your Body

Medical experts have found that those of us that get sick and are hospitalized are at high risk of dealing with mood disorders. Why? Because it's part of the body's natural reaction to illness. The flip side of the emotion-immune system (mind-body) connection has been studied in individuals with depression, anxiety and autism. In these conditions unhealthy brainwave patterns and low levels of serotonin not only mess up the mind and your emotions, they mess up the body too. If you have ever dealt with depression or anxiety you are perfectly aware that it seems far too easy to succumb to illness during depressed states. Depression can make you more susceptible to all types of illnesses, from autoimmune diseases such as irritable bowel syndrome to constantly harboring the common cold.

Happy Hormones Make for a Healthy Body

Hormones and Immune Systems Talk

Hormones coming from the brain and direct neuron-to-immune system connections are central to health and disease. Let's take serotonin, one of your happy hormones, for example. Serotonin, sometimes called THE happy hormone, is manufactured in the brain and not only regulates our emotions; it's also involved in pretty much everything from mood, memory and sleep, to appetite, social behavior and sexual desire. It is also the key player in keeping our immune system up to speed with our feelings.

Changing Your Behavior to Improve Health

For example, if you are sick and your immune system is fighting disease, your serotonin levels are lowered, you're likely to feel less social and you may slow-down to conserve your energy. From an evolutionary standpoint, this phenomenon is pretty handy for getting healthy quickly by slowing down and preventing the spread of disease by feeling less social. If you are happy on the other hand, your serotonin levels are high, which boosts your immune system. Happiness and physical health go hand in hand.

SUMMARY

- Humanity has been aware of the mind-body connection since the beginning of our recorded history, it is only in recent history that we realize that the brain is the middle man in this relationship.
- **The fight-or-flight response is the initial scientific investigation that linked how we think with how our bodies' status is: perceive threat and get the body ready for action.**
- The relaxation response is the opposite of the stress based fight-or-flight response, which can be induced through BOPs so that the workings of your mind relax your body, even at the genetic level, protecting you from ill health and disease.
- **Psychoneuroimmunology is the study of how your mind influences how your neural systems and your immune system interact.**

- Depression, anxiety and other negative emotional states impair your immunity making you more prone to illnesses. Conversely, being happy, enhances your immune system.

Up Next...

Thankfully the founders of PNI have not only studied what happens when the mind-body connection all goes to pot, they have identified ways to rebalance your mind-body relationship and reclaim a healthy immune system. Guess what the magical treatment is? Grade-A BOPs of course!

MAXIMIZING THE MIND-BODY CONNECTION
BRAIN OPTIMIZATION PRACTICES

BOP 1: RELAXING YOUR BODY IMAGE
Your Body Image Influences Your Life

First and foremost, engendering a healthy body image in your mind will help you greatly in your efforts to make use of the mind-body connection. Studies have shown that having a negative and distorted self body image has a negative impact on your self-esteem, eating habits, emotions, chances of depression and eating disorders and your general physical health. The image you have of yourself is not only integral to your mind-body connection, it also influences our path in life, from the people we speak to (or don't speak to), the activities we get involved in (or avoid), the career choices we make (or discourage), to how we behave towards ourselves and others.

Loving Your Body with Compassion

Even if you feel you have a pretty healthy representation of yourself now, learning these tools can help you maintain that healthy image and be prepared for and recognize the signs which may cause it to falter. Thanks to your compassion training you have been experiencing with increasing ease how compassion for yourself and others can positively influence how you view both yourself and others. However, to truly and utterly love the skin that you're in will allow you to care for your health more.

Caring Provides Motivation

If you don't like your body why would you truly care about it? Why would you feel motivated to put down the calorific double bacon burger with extra cheese, fries and coke, switch off the TV and go skipping off out the door for a workout? Or get to that doctors appointment you have been avoiding, all in the name of taking care of your blessed body? If you believe that your nose IS too big and crooked, hair IS weird, wrinkles ARE worse, I AM too fat, muscles ARE too small or teeth ARE too crooked, it impacts your desire to take good care of yourself. In short, these kind of negative ISs and AREs and AMs get us nowhere fast.

Don't Love Your Body? Then Say Hello Again to Failure

Men and women alike suffer from poor self-image. If you are one of those that have a bad body image and your being a bit of a brain bully you might consider how you are making things harder for yourself. You can really be a spanner in your own works. You may be one of the many that feels like they have tried everything or are constantly battling to maintain a healthy body that meets the high standards we place on ourselves.

The alkaline diet, the belly fat cure, the carb lovers diet, the detox diets, the fruit flush diet, the protein power diet, the grapefruit diet, the hormone diet, the blood type diet...there are more diets than there are hot dinners! Joining the gym, buying workout DVDs, gadgets and outfits and trying new diets can all be futile if at your core you don't possess a positive love for and desire to care for your body. Serial dieters know this all too well. You try the latest thing out, it works for a while, you gain/lose weight, start feeling good about your progress and then for the umpteenth time you find yourself back at square one.

Love Your Body and Say Hello to Success

If we are going to make long lasting progress we need to get down to the crux of the matter: our beliefs and behaviors that keep us stuck in a negative body image bubble. If we can burst that negative body image bubble by recognizing our limiting beliefs and bad behaviors—it's a job well started. If we can then replace them with empowering beliefs and good behaviors then there is absolutely nothing holding you back from making use of your mind-body connection in an eternal upward spiral of health and happiness—it's a job well done.

By now, you have experience with relaxation, visualization, compassion and belief and behavior BOPs. If you are feeling comfortable using these BOPs now they will serve you well for dealing with body image. If you feel you still need a little practice, feel free to deepen your experience and understanding of your current repertoire with our favorite friend, repetition. Either way you can learn a lot from trying these CBT, NLP and mindfulness based BOPs.

1.　**Checking in**
Begin with your deep, full, cleansing breaths. Take a few minutes to focus and get settled on your breath. Employ a relaxation technique of your choice, be it muscle relaxation or the slowing down of time or any other that you prefer.

2.　**Focus on your body image**
Do you have a picture in your mind of what your body looks like? Close your eyes and bring to mind the details of your body from head to toe. Take notice of how you feel when you recall this image, let the feelings flow good and bad. All that is important here is that you are aware of how you feel and what you are thinking.

3.　**Focus on the good bits**
Now let's focus on the good bits. Relax a little more with some deep cleansing breathes. Are there any parts of your body that you love? At least like? Or are comfortable in accepting? Even your eyebrows, your nails or your eyelashes? If not use the power of

imagination and imagine that one part of you no matter how small, you really quite like. Make these feelings stronger, into feelings of love, comfort and acceptance. Make the body part glow in your mind if this suits you. Revel in these positive feelings.

4.   Spread the love
Start to spread this feeling (and glow) around your body at which ever speed feels comfortable. With each new part of your body that is enveloped in positivity feel the feelings magnify and get stronger, bit by bit, until your entire body is immersed in positivity.

BOP 2: POSITIVE BODY IMAGE AFFIRMATIONS

Were you able to feel positive about one, two or maybe even your whole body within your mind? In any case daily positive affirmations will help you consolidate and improve on this day by day. Feel free to pick from, modify and own these positive body image affirmations, practice them and then repeat steps 2-4. Did you notice any differences? Positive affirmations followed by steps 2-4 make for one heck of a daily BOP. Try repeating each one in your confident, compassionate inner voice three times or more. Remember that each of these affirmations are actually true, even if they don't feel that way to you just yet.

I accept the beautiful body that I am in.

My body is a functioning whole.

There is no such thing as a flaw, we are all just unique.

My body is beautiful and exudes happiness and health.

BOP 3: RECOGNIZING YOUR BELIEFS AND HABITS

From the body image technique you may now be more aware of some negative beliefs and thoughts about your body that you have, "I should be thinner" for example. The next technique will allow you to explore those beliefs and behaviors further, then we can focus on replacing them with good ones!

1. Checking in
Begin with your deep, full, cleansing breaths. Take a few minutes to focus and get settled on your breath. Employ a relaxation technique of your choice.

2. Recall a bad body image moment
Recall a time when you were aware of your negative body image causing you stress. Before a big date or meeting? In front of the mirror? Try and heighten the details in the image, colors brighter, sounds louder, thoughts clearer. What are you saying or thinking? What is your inner voice saying? How is its bedside manner?

3. Record
In a notebook or in your NeuroLogical journal keep a note of the triggers, details, behaviors, feelings and thoughts. (Also in a notebook or in your NeuroLogical journal keep the same kind of notes for when you have extreme dissatisfaction with your body in the real world.)

4. Analyze
Take note of any common triggers, behaviors and thought patterns that are emerging. These are your new alarm bells.

BOP 4: CHANGING YOUR BELIEFS AND HABITS

You can use the swish to deal with your behavior in these situations and because you are now more aware of how you get into these situations (triggers, environment, thoughts, actions) you can use positive affirmations and visualizations (above) to still your mind before your negative thinking gets out of hand. However, it is wise before you go rushing off and changing your behaviors to first investigate your beliefs. If you don't want them to double up as progress blockers that is! Here is a short and simple technique for investigating your beliefs.

1. Observe your feelings
Recall one of those feelings you had when you were feeling bad about your body. Use your powers of visualization to bring the situation to life and really focus on your emotions at the time.

2. Observe your thoughts
What thoughts were connected with this feeling. Let's take "My nose is too big" as an example.

3. Investigate beliefs
Let's investigate the beliefs behind this thought by exploring the answers to a few simple questions and write them down in your journal:

-What is the meaning of this thought?

-That I want my nose to be smaller as I consider it too big.

-Why does this thought bother me?

-Because if my nose was smaller I think I would look nicer to other people, people don't like ugly people.

-What would be so bad if this thought were true?

-That other people would think I am unattractive.

-What core belief might this reflect?

-That other people think that you have to have a certain size of nose to be considered attractive.

-That I cannot be attractive unless I meet some unknown standards.

-That I have to look a certain way to be liked.

When it's all written out like that it's much easier to see the flaws in the arguments of the mind. We are so wrapped up in our emotions that it is difficult sometimes to see when negative thoughts and emotions are triggered, that a funky smelling belief can be causing the stink.

BOP 5: MINDFUL EATING
In a Nutshell

Mindful eating is likely what you suspect it is. Using the art of mindfulness, you aim to be present when eating, which is a surprisingly rare event. Most of us get so distracted or are too engaged in other activities to even notice that we have scoffed a whole chocolate bar (or other favorite treat) without even noticing! Mindful eating is used clinically to help people cope with modern eating problems. It's definitely not a diet as there are no menus or food restrictions.

It is all about developing a new mindset around food that engenders healthy eating. All sorts of eating disorders, from anorexia to bulimia and binge eating, are staved off and brought under control by mindful eating. Mindful eating has been the focal point of many studies that have found that it can help you to reduce overeating and binge eating, lose fat and lower your Body Mass Index (BMI), reduce anxious thoughts about food and your body and even improve the symptoms of type 2 diabetes.

The Take Home Message

Mindful eating practices will help you balance out any overeating, over restriction or unhealthy bingeing that results from imbalances and miscommunication between your body and mind. You will become more aware of the cues your body leaves you in order to signal when and when not to eat and even what and what not to eat. You can also utilize mindfulness' powers of relaxation and emotional control to surpass those moments when emotion can influence unhealthy food choices. Instead, you can be aware of those thoughts and feeling without overreacting. This allows us to experience these thoughts and feelings, yet instead of succumbing to them, you respond healthily and appropriately.

1. Checking in
First pay attention to how your body and mind feels before you start to eat? E.g. Low energy? Stomach rumbling? Empty? Guilty?

2. Make a mindful investigation
Take a small piece of your meal (or just a small piece of food for practice such as a nut or raisin) to be the focus of your attention. Go through the following points, exploring all the details to enhance your awareness of your food: texture, hardness, density, shape, color and odor.

3. Take a mindful bite
Now take a small bite out of the small piece of food that you have and take care to be fully aware of the sensory experience of chewing, tasting and swallowing. Closing your eyes will help sharpen

your awareness. Notice the changes in texture and flavor as you eat.

4. Repeat

Repeat for the second bite of the small piece.

5. Continue

Try and maintain a slow, steady and mindful pace of eating throughout your meal.

6. Checking out

When you are finished eating pay attention again to how your body and mind feels? E.g. Full? Satisfied? Sore? Guilty? Proud?

A regular exercise like the one above is only part of the parcel with rewiring your mind-body connection, but is a great place to start. Combined with all our other Mind Your Head BOPs, mindful eating will really pack a punch. The next chapter's exercises on emotional control are prime BOPs that can be utilized for healthy eating practices.

BOP 6: QUANTUM WEIGHT RELEASE
BRAIN TRAINING AUDIO

Are you a chronic dieter, having tried every diet and yet continue to struggle with weight? Would you like the new science of losing weight and seeing yourself slim and healthy in the shortest amount of time? Starting today you can instantly train your brain to control your hunger, and release your weight. Quantum Weight Release was developed after working at a weight loss clinic and is designed to remove the most difficult issues, self talk and problems with weight loss identity and beliefs that occur after many failed diets.

Using the latest cutting edge research in neuroscience, you can train your brain with the most immediately effective BOP to stop emotional eating, end the stress circuit that has you reaching for food and begin to act and eat like a thin person, dropping the weight and those extra pounds for good. Your pounds, fear and self-struggle removed.

This audio is available here:
http://successwaves.com/products/catalog/Quantum_Weight_Release.html

NeuroLogical Brain Training Goals

MIND-BODY CONNECTION

Notes

Notes

Part II

FIT BODY, FIT MIND

"To keep the body in good health is a duty...otherwise we shall not be able to keep our mind strong and clear."

~ Prince Gautama Siddharta, the founder of Buddhism, 563-483 B.C.

Exercise Based Brain Basics
A Healthy Body Makes For a Healthy Mind

In the first section we focused on how generating a healthy or unhealthy mind can lead to a healthy or unhealthy body. Now we will approach the reverse, how increasing the fitness of your body can increase the fitness of your mind. We have a slightly better understanding of how maintaining a healthy and fit body is equally as beneficial a BOP as is the reverse. You have likely heard before that a fit body leads to a fit mind? Well it's pretty remarkable how profoundly your brain can change for the better in children, adults and the elderly, simply from exercising the body. On the surface of it all a clear benefit of exercise is that it gets your blood pumping, changes the flow of your blood and growth of blood vessels and helps your brain to breath a bit better and get better access to nutrients.

NAA Thanks
Exercise Enhances NAA Levels

Yet the benefits to your brain that exercising provides goes much deeper than enhanced blood flow. The scientific community have reported that the better your lungs and heart can work to get oxygen to your muscles without exploding (cardiovascular fitness) the more your neurons make a very special substance called N-acetylaspartic acid (NAA). NAA is the second most abundant chemical compound that is found in the brain, and there is a reason there is so much of it—it's vital! NAA is to a neuron what a neuron is to the brain. Its multiple roles are integral to how well your neurons work and ultimately, how well your brain works and how well you perform. Exercise of all varieties has been shown to boost NAA levels and hence boost your brain.

NAA Enhances Neurons

You may want to take a peek at the neuron diagram (Fig.1) again to refresh your memory as we tell you how phenomenal nano-sized NAA truly is. One main function is that it helps keep all your neurons hydrated. Without water balance in the brain not only would those electrical messages have trouble being passed along, the cells would have trouble staying alive! What's more is that it is involved in generating energy for the neurons and helps other brain cells (a type of glial cell) to coat their axon with myelin, the stuff that increases the speed of the electrical messages. It also helps form one of the most important neurotransmitters in the brain (the chemical part of the message that is passed across the synapse).

What We Know Now Is Just the Beginning

This one little molecule can help maintain water balance, speed up the electrical message, provide energy and is involved in generating chemical messages to boot. It's the fix all compound of the brain. Researchers found that the more fit your body is, the more NAA you have in your neurons and the better your working memory is (short-term memory for learning on the spot information like a phone number that may take repetition to commit to long-term memory). They also suspect that exercise induced NAA increases in the brain could boost it in ways that haven't been tested just yet and there may even be other NAA-like fix all compounds waiting to be discovered!

Exercise Boosts Neuroplasticity
It's a Matter of Increasing Matter

There is one important key which can enhance the aforementioned mechanisms as well as other neuroplastic changes to improve learning, memory, attention and behavior, and which prevents cognitive decline across your lifespan and even enhances recovery after brain injury? EXERCISE!!! In the past years, evidence from both human and animal studies has suggested that physical activity and physical exercise have a facilitating effect on neuroplasticity, which in turn boosts our mental performance. Increases in both grey matter (and white matter) have been found in the frontal lobe, temporal lobe and hippocampus; your decision making, information processing/filing and long-term memory systems respectively. It goes on to follow that all this enhanced neuroplasticity comes in hand with influencing the connectivity and communication between brain areas.

Exercise Re-wires Neural Networks
Enhancing Error Prediction

Fittingly, exercise based neuroplasticity influences the reshaping of neural networks and functional activity of the brain. A prime example is how the hippocampus (long-term memory) and an area of the cortex called the anterior cingulate cortex (ACC, part of the DMN and ToM network) are more intricately connected through exercise. The ACC is involved in blood pressure and heart rate regulation and is more active when we exercise. It is also involved in error detection, monitoring conflict and decision making outside of exercise. However, for those that exercise regularly than compared with those that don't, the ACC's activity is actually lower during an error prediction exercise, while error prediction success rates are higher. This suggests that the enhanced connectivity between the ACC and the memory associated hippocampus helps the brain in handling conflict better, with more efficient error detection and in turn better decision making.

Certainty in Losing Weight

Another fantastic example of re-wiring networks is how exercise can make changes to your brain that make you better at losing weight! We have heard it time and time again, but have only just now in 2013 been presented with the proof that exercise makes changes in the brain that influence the regulation of food intake and related behaviors. If you can recall, the DMN network is active when you reflect in internal thought, normally a dangerous space to be in for someone struggling with losing weight and trying to control hunger pangs. Well there is a core to this self-referential network, the seat of self reflective awareness (where it is also thought that we process our body image), an area of the cortex called the precuneus. In an experiment with obese individuals, exercise caused a reduction in precuneus activity. This reduced activity was associated with defocusing that self-reflective little food monkey in their brains that can play havoc with one's self-compassion, motivation and will power when you have issues with healthy eating. What's more is that the greater the reduction in activity the greater the fat loss and reduction in hunger ratings!

Exercise Boosts Brain Functions

So the brain is juiced up and rewires itself in response to exercise, but to what end? In what other ways do exercise-based BOPs change how we tick? How do they change our cognitive functions? So far scientists have found compelling evidence that exercise positively influences a whole load of brain functions: it prevents memory decline as we age and boosts our memory in general, improves emotional control, improves our attention and speed of processing, helps protect from and alleviate the symptoms of brain altering conditions like Alzheimer's, dementia and Parkinson's in the elderly and in young people with developmental disabilities and even improves our children's test scores. More and more positive discoveries are being made as the investigation goes deeper.

Mix Up Your Exercise Styles

Interestingly, different kinds of exercise are thought to influence different neural networks, with different functions. For example, one study has shown that cardiovascular training that really gets the heart rate going improves your episodic memory in middle aged adults—that's the memory that forms the movie of your life, the scenes of times and places and their associated emotions, going's on and knowledge. While on the other hand some more gentle exercise involving stretches and coordinated movement enhances our powers of attention.

It makes sense that as different forms of exercise will require the use of different skills that make use of both overlapping and distinct parts of the brain, that they will influence different as well as shared neural networks to different extents. This indicates that when it comes to exercise—as in most things in life—embracing the new and trying many different forms of exercise is the best thing for you.

Stay Away From the Dark Side

One theory is that exercise provides the boost needed to assist in neuroplasticity. But it is your actions, tasks, habits, social interactions and even the general environment that provides a more direct and targeted way of homing in on particular brain regions and harnessing the neuroplasticity boost. As with all things brain related, the potential exists to reveal the dark side of neuroplasticity boosting and as such, you should look before you leap.

Imagine all of your other routines and habits in your daily life (outside of exercise) are bad BOPs, ones that encourage rage, anxiety, fear and other emotional and social nasties. If you are creating new brain cells and enhancing connections via exercise-based neuroplasticity then you can reinforce the bad brain states and connections as well as the good. It's all about balance. As you yourself are consciously aiming for positivity producing brain changes, you can safely use exercise to beef up your brain and make room for behavioral growth, learning and acquiring new skills.

Tried and Tested

Many certified geniuses steered away from the dark side and made use of this link between physical fitness, balanced lifestyles and beneficial BOPs to boost their performance. Leonardo Davinci was well-known for his physical prowess, as well as producing masterful pieces of art and being a successful scientist, engineer, mathematician, sculptor, botanist, musician and writer. Basically the man was a friggin mastermind! He was said to be so physically strong that he could even bend horseshoes with his bare hands (and I caught a fish that was thiiiis big!).

A little more recent than 15th century BC (and hence more of a believable modern legend) is an amazing example of a genius that used exercise to feed his brain. Dr. Garret Lisi is a modern day surfer bum physics genius. Yes that's right you heard it, surfer bum, living in a van by the beach, physics genius. And this genius just happened to come up with a potential theory of everything, a mathematical theory that attempts to explain and link together all known physical phenomena that exist in the universe!

Exercise Nurtures Optimal Living

Both Leonardo and Garret lived very balanced and highly optimized lives, with exercise being an integral part of their lives and their success. New studies even suggest that to maintain these higher brain states, we must also maintain our physical fitness. If fitness of the body gets lowered it influences the capabilities of the brain. You might be thinking that these guys were just born geniuses: that they exercised because they were geniuses, not that they were geniuses because they exercised. Well you would be surprised. A report a few years back provides data that suggests that lifestyle factors (e.g. exercising) were more influential than heredity (the genes we inherit from our parents) in explaining the relation between physical fitness and brain function—more simply put, nurture trumps nature.

Exercise BOPs Transcends the Womb

Astonishingly this exercise based nurturing of the brain begins even before we leave the safe comfort of our mother's womb. Beginning by assessing the brains of new born babies we can already see the benefits of their mothers exercising during pregnancy. From just 5 days old it was possible to tell the difference between babies with Moms who had exercised and those that had settled for the couch. These babies were smarter when it came to baby intelligence. Then at one year old these same smart cookies have been shown to have better conscious control of their movement. The positive effects from exercising during pregnancy even carries through till five years of age where these kiddie-winks scored best for general intelligence and in oral language.

Awaiting Results from Latest Study

Who knows how far in life Momma made exercise BOPs can benefit us and what specific changes are made to the baby brain? We are eagerly awaiting published results from researchers at the University of Montreal on an intriguing investigation of 60 pregnant women. One half of the women volunteered to stop exercising throughout the remaining weeks of their pregnancy and the other half are working out 3 times a week for 20-90 minutes and at a minimum of 50% of their maximum possible intensity—that is relatively rigorous exercise. The soon to be born babies will be whisked into mini-EEG caps to give us a sneak peek into how their mother's exercise during pregnancy influences their brainwaves in these early stages of life.

Exercise Boosting Brainwaves
Sleeping Soundly

Now, getting back to the world of brainwaves, this time we are addressing the question of how they are influenced by exercise and in turn how this influences how we function. Let's begin with something we all are very aware of: exercising your booty off helps you sleep like a baby! "Oh I had an amazing sleep, must have been all that sweaty work and fresh air."

A hard days physical work leading to a sound sleep is something we all know from experience and don't need science to help us believe, but science does help us find out what is really going on inside our skulls. When we are in the land of nod, the more we have exercised, the longer we spend in slow delta wave sleep and the less time we spend in lighter, theta based REM sleep. The end result is that these changes in our sleep pattern are related to having greater skill in employing positive coping strategies for dealing with life's problems is even thought to be linked with enhancing our level of curiosity.

Dealing with Depression

Exercising also lowers many depression related symptoms. One example is how it can calm down your somatosensory brain regions, which tend to be over activated in hypochondriacs and in people with depression and anxiety, where we pay far too much attention to sensations within the body, especially negative ones. A study on depression in the elderly showed that exercise caused alpha wave hemispheric asymmetry to be ironed out and the right hemisphere calmed down a little by alpha waves, causing depression symptoms to slink away.

Beating Executive Burnout

Yoga is a form of exercise that has long been known to have balancing effects on the brain. Yoga was really put to the test in the modern age by seeing how it affects the brainwaves of business executives. These high flying corporate executives weren't just any kind of business men or women, they were from giant oil and natural gas corporations, one of the most fast paced and highly stressful executive positions imaginable. These guys are in a never-ending race against, time, technology and targets. This never ending fight-or-flight race creates unimaginable tension and psychological pressure with mental and emotional drain hampering 'executive efficiency' and leading to that well-known 'executive burnout'.

These corporate executives tested out a yoga system based on brainwave coherence called SMET, or Self Management of Excessive Tension, which can provide astonishing brain balancing results from non-strenuous exercise and in a very short amount of time. In this experiment the effects of 20-30 minutes of SMET Yoga every day for 6 days were just brilliant. The results revealed a 19% increase in delta, 5% increase in theta, 15% increase in alpha, 19% increase in gamma and 2% decrease in beta strengths throughout the brain. Even this rudimentary analysis shows that just 6 days of a yoga based and super simple, non-sweaty BOP enhanced the slow waves which are lacking in stress heads, decreased beta a little which is excessive in stress-heads and gave the brain an extra kick with enhanced gamma waves helping the executives be mindfully rooted in the here and now stay at the top of their game.

Ignoring Irritating Sounds

Have you ever wondered how some people manage to stay calm and collected when bombarded with annoying sounds, be it a constantly nagging boss or a horde of screaming children? Some people stay as cool as cucumbers while others are left clawing at their ears. Well, low intensity exercise can make a huge difference as to how well you can cope with annoying noises. One experiment has shown that your chilled out alpha waves go down about 20% when listening to annoying noises or are performing mental arithmetic. But if you have exercised for 20 minutes beforehand, then you get roughly 30% more alpha (particularly lower frequency alpha) than if you hadn't exercised. This holds true for theta too. So exercise can enhance your slow waves allowing you to remain calm in mentally complex or in mentally unnerving situations. Bonus!

Coping with Confinement

One unnerving situation is being sent to Mars! In the MARS-500 mission astronauts spent 520 days in confinement in a Mars flight simulator. The effects of exercise on their brain activity during the mission were assessed using EEG. Exercise caused a reduction of hyperactivity in their frontal lobes which was essential in maintaining the quick thinking and decision making skills needed to survive such a flight. It kept their brains running smooth despite serious sensory deprivation.

While this study didn't get down to the brainwaves involved in making these changes the evidence suggest that this depends on the type and intensity of the exercise. One study indicates that alpha activity calms down the emotional areas of your brain when moderate exercise is new to you, but if you are doing your usual routine, alpha waves occupy the somatosensory brain areas calms down your sense of body awareness. This is true for moderate intensity exercise. For high intensity exercise both alpha and beta change significantly, where reductions in frontal beta are thought to really balance out our emotions. So you can get better at keeping cool in stressful situations by mixing up your exercise regime, trying new things and modifying exercise intensity—variety really is that extra added spice in life.

SUMMARY

- Exercise gets your blood pumping, changes the flow of your blood and growth of blood vessels that helps your brain get better access to oxygen and nutrients.
- **Exercise increases neuronal NAA levels which keeps neurons hydrated, helps speed up the passage of the electrical signal down the axon, provides them with energy and is also a building block for the formation of neurotransmitters.**
- Exercise induced increases in both grey matter (and white matter) have been found in the frontal lobe, temporal lobe and hippocampus; your decision making, information processing/filing and long-term memory systems respectively.
- **Exercise re-wires the connectivity between brain regions, such as in the DMN where connectivity changes can result in positive changes in our abilities and behaviors, such as having a healthier relationship with food or having better control of our emotions or improving our memory.**
- Different forms of exercise that require the use of different as well as overlapping parts of the brain, influence different as well as shared neural networks, resulting in both general and exercise specific improvements in brain function.
- **We may find that exercise provides the fuel for neuroplasticity but it is our life's actions, tasks, habits and social interactions that utilize neuroplasticity to mold neural networks.**
- Exercise increases the time spent in slow wave delta sleep, re-balances extreme hemispheric asymmetries in those who are depressed, enhances resting state slow waves and associated calm states even in irritating situations, boosts gamma waves and our focus and attention and reduces frontal lobe beta to aid relaxation.

Up Next...

Let's get ready to get our blood pumping, boost our NAA levels and cultivate improved brainwave states, mental abilities and behaviors. Just a little bit of exercise everyday will have you sprinting towards a healthy mind

FIT BODY, FIT MIND
BRAIN OPTIMIZATION PRACTICES

BOP 1: MOTIVATION FOR EXERCISE

We can talk and talk and talk about exercise but really it's all about action. So firstly in order to perform an action, we need some motivation. Here are some CBT based techniques for developing motivation for exercise.

1.   It's all too easy to commit self-sabotage by taking on too much all at once. So perhaps start with something that you know that you can do; a 10 minute walk, or a 5 minute jog to help build your confidence first. Record in your journal when you exercise, for how long and how easy or challenging it was to clearly map your progress.

2.   Before you exercise pay attention to your thoughts, feelings and behavior at the time. You may identify unhelpful thoughts and underlying limiting beliefs that are causing the motivational issues. If so you can use the techniques in Chapter 1 on changing beliefs and habits to help you out.

3.   Mentally rehearse your exercise routines, either on the bus, before practice, during BOP time or even before you sleep. Practice visualizing your next planned exercise as successful, enjoyable and

rewarding. As usual when visualizing, engage all the senses, maximize those positive sensations and embellish your positive thinking. Be as specific and detailed as possible.

BOP 2: WALKING MEDITATION

Committing yourself to daily exercise is an easy thing to say, but not an easy thing to do, even if you are aware of motivation boosting practices. Sometimes you are too stressed/ anxious/ bummed out/ pushed for time and then on goes the guilt when you realize that you failed in maintaining your daily exercise commitments. Well to avoid the negativity spiral and still have a well-deserved sense of achievement when an exercise session just seems impossible to you (it happens to even the most balanced of us all) try this simple walking meditation exercise. The latest study has shown that mindful walking reduced stress symptoms and enhanced quality of life in adults with high levels of psychological distress. It can be done practically anywhere and last anytime although best done outdoors for at least 10-20 mins.

1. Preparation
Before you set off, spend a little moment in stillness, and check in with your breathing relaxation technique. Being aware of your breath, try and expand this awareness to your entire body.

2. Beginning
At a fairly relaxed, slow, regular pace pay attention to your bodily sensations as you walk. While the sights around you or random thoughts may start to take over your attention, keep returning your focus to your body, how it feels, what parts are moving, which are relatively stationary? Pay attention, from your bobbing head to your swinging arms and all the way to the feeling of the ground and shoes on your feet. Use your body scanning technique from muscle relaxation if it helps you.

3. Release tension
You should pay special attention to any tension felt in the body and respond appropriately with a conscious effort to relax that body part. Allow all of your body to become relaxed as you walk, fluidly, tension and stress-free.

BOP 3: SMET YOGA

Now we are going to go through with you the super simple and gentle positions and movements of the body that were shown to recharge the minds of high flying business executives. They are painfully simple, even more so for you as you have been practicing being mindful of your body and in practicing relaxation. While these yoga *asanas* (body positions) are simple and require no special level of physical fitness, we encourage you to explore yoga styles or other stretching based exercises when aiming for a positively reinforced relationship between body and mind. Here is a short, 5-10 minute, easy routine you can practice anytime anywhere. The techniques that require lying or kneeling on the floor can easily be modified for sitting at your desk to be more easily incorporated into your working day.

PART I-Checking in

1. If you have the floor space come down to the floor and sit with your legs extended in front of you. Sit on your knees with your buttocks resting on your feet. If you have knee problems or this is uncomfortable for you try sitting cross legged, whichever is most comfortable for you. If you don't have floor space stay seated and continue with steps 2-4 only and move to part II.
2. **Begin to take notice of your deep cleansing breathing.**
3. Rest your hands on your knees, and on an in breath feel your back elongating, gently lengthening and straightening.

4. Stay seated for one minute, paying attention to your breath. Mindfulness practice is perfect for yoga positions that are held for any length of time although one should aim for their entire yoga routine to be a mindful based practice (which is what focusing on the breath enables you to do).

5. Slowly move your hands behind your back clasping one wrist in the opposite hand.

6. On the in breath, keeping your back comfortably straight and extended, start bending forwards at the waist and gently rest your forehead on the ground.

7. Stay in this position for one minute. Keep mindful focused attention on your body and breath, be aware of the changes in body sensations. A modified version of this asana (position) is to release your wrist and let your hands drop behind you, palms facing up, feel free to try.

8. With your hands behind your back, come up on an inhalation and slowly release your hands and then return your arms to rest on your upper legs.

PART II-Instant Relaxation Technique (IRT)

1. If you have floor space, move from your seated position to a lying down position: extend your legs in front of you, support yourself with your hands if needed and lower yourself to lie down on your back. If you don't have room or are stuck at your desk, get comfortably seated, with your arms resting on your thighs and with no tension in the body.

2. Close your eyes. This is your fully relaxed position. If you are lying down you should have your arms at your sides palms open, soft and facing upwards. Your legs should be apart, with knees and feet relaxed and legs comfortably apart (1-2 ft).

3. Now join your legs together and place your arms to your side. Now you are going to tighten all your muscles, the exact opposite of the muscle relaxation technique you have been practicing. On a long deep slow in breath, start tightening your muscles with your toes and then also tighten your heels. Then add tightened calve muscles and allow this tightening to progress up your body, to your kneecaps, thighs, buttocks and hips. When the tightening reaches

you're the hip area (before reaching the abdomen), exhale completely while maintaining tightness in your lower limbs.

4.   Tighten the stomach as you fully inhale and hold the breath, tighten the chest, back, arms, neck, face. Hold the tightening, hold your breath and then instantly release all that tension from your head to your toes. Come back to your fully relaxed position. Relax for 20-30 seconds and focus on your breath.

5.   Repeat steps 3 and 4 three times.

6. *Slowly turn onto your side. Relax with your head on your hand a few moments if you like. When you are ready slowly and gently come to standing.*

PART III-Awareness

1.   Stand upright with your feet an inch or two apart. Lift and spread your toes and the balls of your feet and settle into the floor. Keep a gentle and straight posture, chin and head supported yet relaxed. Your arms should rest comfortably at your sides. Maintain a gentle smile throughout.

2.   **Now begin to sway your body gently from right to left and left to right. Feel the weight shift between the left and right foot, be aware of the sensations in your body with this gentle movement. Move from left to right 4-5 times maintaining relaxed, natural, steady breathing.**

3.   Now sway gently from front to back, steadily and slowly feeling the weight shift from being on your toes to being centered, to your heels and back again. Repeat 4-5 times while maintaining relaxed, natural steady, breathing.

4.   Next, on an in breath, allow your right arm to slowly rise up and out to the side of you, directly in line with your body, palm facing upwards. When your arms is 90° out from your body, rotate your palm to face upwards and exhale fully. On the next in breath continue raising your arm upwards until it is extended straight above your head.

5.   Exhale. Maximize the stretch from your right foot to right hand by breathing in and extending the arm all the way up, pulling the hand upwards, arm brushing your ear.

6.   Exhale and bend over sideways to the left to extend the stretch further. Maximize the stretch to a point where you can comfortably maintain it. As you stretch pay attention to the stretch in the right side of the body and maintain for 5-10 natural, calm, breaths.

7.   When you inhale return to stand upright, arm directly upright position.

8.   On the next exhalation bring your arm down to 90°, palm facing upwards.

9.   Rotate your palm to face downwards, inhale fully and then exhale while bringing your arm down to rest at your side.

10. Now feel the blood rushing to your palm and perhaps a tingling sensation. In fact you should have a lot more awareness of the right hand side of your body, and it should feel much more energetic. Pay attention to your awareness. Be mindful for a few moments.

11. Now repeat steps 4-10 for the opposite side of the body, the left side.

PART IV-Checking out

1.   Repeat steps 1-4 (if you are sitting in a chair) or steps 1-9 (if you can comfortably sit on the floor) of Part I, Checking in.

HINTS & TIPS

•   For floor positions use a couple of cushions, towels, blankets or other comfortable material to sit on.

•   As you have been practicing breathing techniques, you have a head start for practicing steady and fluid coordinated breathing and movement. Keep both breathing and moving smooth. This may feel like too much to concentrate on to begin with, yet with practice and patience and calming any frustrations it will become automatic pretty quickly.

•   As different forms of exercise have both mutual brain benefits and benefits specific for that particular kind of exercise, mix it up as much as you can. Try new things, why not Tai Chi or hockey or roller derby or climbing. See what free coupons you can find to try out a new class or have a search on Youtube for free routines and exercises. Variety is the spice of life.

- There are many styles and ways of teaching yoga, some intensely cardiovascular, others less so. Try a few different classes at your local gym and find out which style you prefer.

NeuroLogical Brain Training Goals

FIT BODY, FIT MIND

Notes

Notes

Part III

PAIN AND PLEASURE

"The secret of success is learning how to use pain and pleasure instead of having pain and pleasure use you. If you do that, you're in control of your life. If you don't, life controls you."

~ Tony Robbins

The Pain-Pleasure Relationship
A Common Neurobiology

With all this talk of exercise, gentle or otherwise, some of you may be experiencing pain that limits how much pleasure you can get from such physical experiences. Why do we know this? Because pain and pleasure share a common neurobiology and are inextricably linked within the brain—relationship status: it's complicated!

One reason that studying their relationship is wrought with complexities is that pain and pleasure are highly subjective, depending on the individual (your neurobiology) and the context (the who, what, where, why, when). If you have ever stubbed your toe on a table leg while chillaxing at home you were likely to curse the world as you clung to your throbbing digit. Yet if you are used to playing in competitive sports you could have broken your toe and not even have noticed a thing until the game is over and your state of mind changes. We have all heard those human superhero stories, 'Man With Broken Legs Saves Child' or 'Super nanny braves third degree burns to save baby'. Why? As a survival mechanism we have been hardwired so that the pain or pleasure that we experience is highly influenced by the 'meaning' behind it.

It's All About Context

If you stub your toe while being chased by an angry mob, would it be a good survival tactic to drop everything you are doing and succumb to the pain? No, you probably wouldn't even feel the pain. And on the flip side if you knew that something tastes irresistibly yummy but is laced with poison, or previously had rats crawling all over it would you eat it? No, in that context that tasty treat may even look repulsive to you. In both cases, in order to survive, your brain interprets pain and pleasure differently depending on the context. As such, pain and pleasure are influenced by our past experience, our memories and our emotions including the influence of cultural and social factors, the environmental input from our senses and our current state of mind.

Homeostasis

With so many factors at play, there is a delicate balance between seeking pleasure and avoiding pain that is all about homeostasis, or in other words, keeping your bodily systems balanced. Take a simple example like hunger: when you are 'starving' (far from equilibrium) the taste of food and the pleasure you get from eating it is phenomenal compared to when you aren't that hungry (close to equilibrium) and can even induce pain and displeasure if you are already full (the opposite end of the scale). It is all about keeping the balance.

Pleasure Reduces Pain
Pleasure Brings the Balance Back

Pain takes us away from homeostasis and pleasure brings us back. This is why pleasure in itself is enough to relieve pain. Many experiments have found that smelling pleasant odors, viewing attractive images, listening to pleasurable music and the enjoyment that comes with sexual behavior can all be used to relieve pain. Even just expecting the simple reward of pain relief, is enough to reduce pain, it's part of the wonders of the placebo effect. Give someone a sugar pill and convince them it is a miracle pain cure and a surprising number will be cured by the placebo effect, where the body miraculously heals itself.

Just Expecting Pleasure Is Enough

The placebo effect is pretty effective when it comes to neurological conditions like pain, epilepsy and depression. Yet if you get a pain remedy that is scientifically proven to relieve pain and you don't know that you have taken it, the pain relief experienced is significantly less than when you knowingly take the pain medication—as found in experiments where sneaky nurses injected pain relieving medication without the patients knowledge. Just the pleasure of expecting a reward (in this case pain relief) is enough to kick the brain into action and make more of the experience.

Pain Reduces Pleasure

The reverse of pleasure reducing pain is also true, pain can also reduce pleasure. It makes evolutionary sense. What if there is something more important than the reward at hand when you look at the bigger picture? Perhaps if you can hold your horses a little you will get an even greater reward or maybe taking the initial reward will put you at even greater risk later—don't accept candy from strangers kids! This tends to make the initial 'reward' seem less pleasant and we have less motivation to seek out that particular reward.

Too Much Pleasure & Too Much Pain— Both Are Bad For the Brain

Pain's ability to reduce pleasure is one of the reasons why chronic pain and depression tend to come hand in hand. Chronic pain sufferers tend to also suffer from anhedonia, the reduction in pleasure felt in life's day to day activities. The influence of pain on pleasure is a vicious cycle making the pain feel worse and displeasure and depression grow. The reverse of this is also true. Too much pleasure can result in addictive tendencies and can lead to conditions like drug addiction or obesity where you numb yourself to the true experience of pleasure. This overload of pleasure intensifies emotional and physical pain and displeasure when you are without the addictive stimulus be it drugs, foods or even emotions.

So all in all, our experiences of pleasure and pain are created through our bodies' built-in desire for balance, in the seeking of rewards and pleasure and avoidance of punishment and pain. With the ability to influence the experience of one another, pain and pleasure, and the seeking of reward and avoidance of punishment, are part of the same whole, the same interwoven systems and networks within the brain.

Looking Inside the Brain
Motivation is Dope

The motivation to seek pleasure or avoid pain within the brain is different to the actual experience of pain and pleasure. Two different neurotransmitters (the chemical message part of synaptic communication) are involved, one for motivation and the other for the experience of pain and pleasure. Each neurotransmitter affects a neural network of neurons that have specialized receptors at their synapses to read that specific chemical message (the neurotransmitter). Dopamine is the neurotransmitter that affects the motivational aspect of pleasure seeking and pain avoidance. If you have ever been a 'doped-up' hippy and smoked a bit of marijuana before you may have experienced the dopamine rush that gets you 'high' (euphoric), with a motivational boost fueling you to seek out pleasurable experiences. This might include devouring six packets of biscuits, three cakes, two sandwiches and five and a half packets of chips—a dangerously waist expanding condition more commonly known as the 'munchies'. Dopamine's actions also indirectly cause changes in the second system that deals with the actual experience of pain and pleasure.

Our Internal Pain Killing System

The second neurotransmitter sensitive network for the experience of pain and pleasure is the opioid neurotransmitter system. This is why the drug opium (an opioid that influences the opioid neurotransmitter system in the brain) is considered a pleasure inducing pain killer and is taken recreationally to experience pleasure as well as to relieve pain. However it can also cause problems with our motivation as it also indirectly influences the dopamine-based motivation influencingnetwork., but also can cause problems with our motivation. An abundance or lack of opioids in the brain is needed in order for you to like or dislike something due to the pain or pleasure experienced. But it is having higher levels of dopamine that motivates you to go for it.

From Pain to Brain and Back Again

OUCH! You stubbed your toe! Nerves in your skin rapidly send a message to you spinal cord, which shoots up your spine and into the primal part of your brain (the brainstem and cerebellum) and onto the thalamus, where the pain signal is relayed to the pain related regions of the forebrain. This system, called the afferent pain system (afferent meaning moving towards a center, the brain) dictates how we feel pain.

Yet many parts of the afferent pain system are part of another closely related system in the brain, called the descending modulation system, which does what it says on the tin: the message travels down to the body from the brain (descending) and helps us alter our pain (modulation). Neuronal messages in this system start up within the cortex and are sent down through the spinal cord to the sight of pain to either enhance the pain message that returns back up to the brain, or much more preferably, inhibit the pain. The trick is how to hijack this system to reduce the experience of pain, the best drug-free and freely available solution being BOPs.

Brain Atlas of Pleasure and Pain

Pain, pleasure and indeed the motivation to seek and avoid them are highly overlapping when it comes to areas of the brain at work. Neurons in regions all over the brain including the somatosensory parts of your brain that deal with bodily sensations, the frontal cortex (decision making) and the limbic system (emotion) are excited or inhibited in the control of the central pain relieving neuronal pathway that runs through the grey matter within your spinal cord to influence the pain and pleasure felt in the body.

The main thing to notice is that while there is a part of your brain dealing with the physical sensation of pain, a large part of pain and indeed pleasure is based in emotion and attention, with BOPs that aid our emotional and attentional control also helping us to control our experience of pain. Have you heard of the urban legend (which is actually urban fact!) where someone chops of their finger while preparing dinner and doesn't notice until they see their finger staring back up at them in the salad bowl? Their attention was somewhere else and so their experience of pain wasn't even registered. Gruesome! Cue finger salad joke.

Integrated Pain and Pleasure Networks

Being literally all over the place within the brain, this large pain-pleasure network overlaps extensively with many other networks in the brain including the DMN. An experiment hot off the press has demonstrated that the overlapping nature of this large spacious pleasure and pain network is what contributes to the subjective experience of pleasure and pain. Being so complex, with potential for many variations in network and sub-network activity, allows for the flexible nature of our perception of pleasure and pain. If the networks were more simple, pain may always be pain and pleasure always pleasure, irrespective of the context.

Pain and Pleasure Hotspots

What is more is that within the separate structures within this network a pattern is emerging, where the functional modules of neurons within these structures have specialized roles. For example, different groups of neurons within the amygdalae encode the negative and positive aspects of pain and pleasure when presented with a situation that may result in a reward or punishment. These pain and pleasure hotspots tend to be found right next to one another which likely explains how pain can decrease pleasure and pleasure can reduce pain, as they are found to exist side by side quite literally within the brain.

A Painful Look at Brainwaves
Alpha Synchronicity Enhances Pleasure
More Alpha in the Pain Network=Less Pain

With regards to the pain-pleasure network, one brainwave in particular has stolen the limelight, alpha. More specifically, it seems that the more alpha waves desynchronize, the more intensely we experience pain. In a recent experiment where participants were exposed to enough laser heat to cause them pain, alpha wave activity was being recorded while scanning the brain to find out which areas where active. They found that the intensity of the response of the pain network to pain was controlled by the amount of alpha power in the system. The stronger the alpha signal, the less the intense the pain was with less connectivity being found between these distant areas in the pain network via other brainwaves.

Alpha in Advance=Less Pain

What they also found was that before inflicting pain when the volunteers were at rest, the stronger the communication was between regions of DMN that overlap with the pain-pleasure network, influences how intense you will feel the pain when it is applied. Basically, if your DMN is hyperactive and lacking in alpha before pain comes your way don't be surprised if pain intensity is high. If you are already super chilled and alpha reigns supreme your better able to take the pain.

Alpha Desynchronization Tunes You in to Pain

Another recent study on alpha waves focused more on two primary locations of the cortex where this pain causing alpha desynchronization occurs: the sensorimotor and occipital regions. What they found was that alpha desychronization occurred in these two areas to awaken two different parts of the brain. The one that is based on connecting your senses to your body and movement, is the sensorimotor region. The other is related to getting information from the pain causing event so that you know what the heck is happening to you. This is the occipital region where vision is processed. Together this makes us more tuned in to what is causing the pain and how our body feels in response to the event.

Don't Forget Beta

While most other brainwaves haven't been similarly studied, there is a study or two that mention increases in beta when experiencing pain. It seems that with individuals that are more sensitive to pain, they have selected beta wave enhancements. As far as we can tell no studies have started to explore the alpha/beta relationship when we talk of pain and pleasure but there are rumors of research results soon to come.

Theta, Pain and Memory

There are also a few rare pain related studies on theta waves. If you have ever experienced chronic pain or even moderate to light pain for extended periods of time you will be familiar with pain interfering with your working memory and attention skills. Just have someone beat you repeatedly with a stick while you try and remember your weekly shopping list if you don't believe us.

As you know, theta (and delta and alpha) brain waves tend to be involved in many memory related brain processes. For working memory to function well theta links up a part of your frontal lobe, the prefrontal cortex, and the hippocampus with working memory functioning at its best when theta is strongest. When you are experiencing pain however, this theta based connectivity is impaired. Only when the theta waves can break through the pain and stay synchronized will your memory serve you well.

Go Go Gamma!

Gamma waves have also had a mention in the pain based literature. One study has shed light on the situation, pinpointing at least one of gamma's roles in pain perception. Again the mad scientists used lasers to zap participants, who this time had to press a button when they perceived the pain. They found that changes in beta activity, delta/theta and gamma were directly related to how quickly you respond to pain. The beta activity booms after you press the button which may be involved in the stress response. The evidence suggests that the transformation of feelings of pain into a seemingly instantaneous motor response (in this instance pressing a button), more likely involves gamma waves, seeing as they surge right before you press the button. It would make sense that the fastest brainwaves take over while inhibitory and relaxation inducing alpha waves subside, to give you the fastest reactions possible as pain is associated with a threat to your survival.

Pleasure on the Brain
Complex Networks Equal Complex Outcomes

Where do pleasure associated brainwaves fit in with all these studies focusing on the pain related side of the system? As previously mentioned, it seems that the number of different inhibition and excitation patterns for the pain-pleasure circuitry result in the broad variation in how the same pain or pleasure causing action can be perceived differently. One simple prod or poke can produce a whole range of different experiences, even for the same person, depending on the context of course. To produce differing experiences of pain or pleasure some areas of the brain are typically more inhibited when experiencing pain and others more so when experiencing pleasure. How we generally perceive pleasure and pain, from person to person, reflects some parts of the network being stronger and able to communicate messages more efficiently, others weaker, or the inclusion or exclusion of certain regions, or network components if you will, all together.

Pleasure Is Clear with Alpha Waves

When it comes to how much pleasure one gets from an activity or experience—whether it's tasting food, watching TV commercials or children playing games—one can easily see which of two QEEG brain images display a brain experiencing the most pleasure. Frontal alpha activity is a clear giveaway. If you have more alpha desynchronization in your left frontal lobe and more alpha synchronization in the right frontal lobe then you find the event quite pleasant. While if you have more alpha desynchronization in your right frontal lobe and more alpha synchronization on the left frontal lobe then this signals an unpleasant experience.

Turning Pain into Pleasure

While no study has truly mingled pain into the pleasure equation another study changed the context and turned pain into pleasure! Again zapping away at participants, scientists first gave them a random series of either a moderately painful heat shock or a non-painful warm sensation and took a look at what parts of the brain are active. Then they took that same moderately painful heat and changed the alternative from a non-painful sensation to an intensely painful sensation. In the second round the moderate pain had actually become a pleasurable experience and looked more like a brain experiencing the non-painful sensation in the first round. As predicted, some expected regions of the system gained some activity and others lost activity. When followed up with some further study, including EEG studies, we will know more about the various routes to pain and pleasure within this large intermingled system.

SUMMARY

- Pain and pleasure are influenced by our past experience, our memories and our emotions including the influence of cultural and social factors, the environmental input from our senses and our current state of mind which reflects broadly dispersed pain and pleasure circuits in the brain—context is key with how we variably experience both pleasure and pain.

- **Generally speaking, pain reduces the experience of pleasure and pleasure reduces the experience of pain, their close-knit association is reflected in the shared activation of brain regions and the partitioning of brain regions into having discrete areas specific to pleasure and specific to pain.**

- When we experience pain in the body, it is signaled via the nerves and spinal cord to the brainstem and cerebellum and on to the thalamus where the message is relayed to specific regions of the forebrain. We then modulate the pain through the descending pathway, where messages originating in the cortex are passed back down to the location of pain in the body.

- **Frontal lobe alpha wave asymmetries are a clear giveaway as to whether an experience is painful or unpleasant (more alpha on the left) or pleasurable (more alpha on the right).**
- We can utilize BOPs to hijack the descending pathway by altering our emotional and attentional states.

Up Next...

Now let's get modulating our pain pathways and tip the balance towards pleasure. Use these next BOPs to make use of both the emotion and attention related networks within the brain to alter how you experience pain. What's great is that even if you are not in pain these are valuable BOPs to add to your toolkit with benefits that reach beyond relieving pain.

PAIN AND PLEASURE

BRAIN OPTIMIZATION PRACTICES

BOP 1: LAUGH THROUGH THE PAIN

Where Does It Come From

In animal laughter studies chimps, dogs and even rats enjoy a good giggle every now and then. For all species, this ancient signal of social communication, laughter, makes us feel good. It doesn't matter who you are or where you come from or what language you speak, we all understand laughter, it's inbuilt. Tickling laughter is thought to be the most evolutionary ancient forms of laughter that we even share with our animal friends. It's more of a reflex-like behavior that encourages playfulness and social behavior.

The laughter reaction to tickling is seen as the primitive building block from which all other forms of humor have developed, from Richard Pryor to Louis C.K. However, such complex social laughter has developed to communicate so many different things and can be used consciously to influence the happiness and even cause sadness in others around you. Laughter communicates things like "everything is fine", "that's stupid", "there is nothing to worry about here". It also signifies that "we get along", "we are one" without using any words. Also, being highly contagious, laughing aloud makes others laugh along with you, allowing them to share the physical and mental benefits of laughter too.

The Evolution of Laughter

How would communicating with laugher, "Everything is good", "That's funny" etc be useful if you were a caveman with limited speech capabilities. Imagine a scenario where you are out hunting deer with your fellow cavemen. Leading the group, like a panther you creep through the long grass. Hearing the crack of a twig, your eyes are drawn to the white tipped tail of a deer flashing out of sight as it disappears round a grassy knoll. Heart rate quickening, you follow your prey, loping towards the grassy outcrop.

As you veer the hill, you let out a blood curdling scream at the sight before you: a huge, looming shape, towering high above, with bright glowing menacing eyes. "Ahhhhhhhhhh BEEEAR!!!" You're heart feels ready to explode as adrenaline crashes through your body. Time seems to slow down to a near stand still. You just about hear the muted cries of your concerned companions, you bring your arms over your head to protect yourself from the inevitable fatal blow... and then you do a double take. "Wait a minute, it is a, a Haaaaaahahahahaaaa!" Your friends burst round the corner and see you double over laughing and immediately follow suit, chuckling, snorting and guffawing their bodies and minds back to a happy and relaxed state. "It's a bush! Nothing more than a thorny bit of shrubbery! " Simply laughing reset the fight-or-flight systems of an entire group, preventing a whole load of fuss over nothing!

Laughter Is Good For Your Health

The evolutionary "We're all alright" social purpose of laughter applies to making your own body and mind feel alright too. Whether you are laughing at something funny, laughing because of a tickly bodily sensation or making yourself laugh, all these forms of laughter have one thing in common, it is good for our bodies and good for our minds. It's so good for us there is even a word for the study of the effects of laughter, gelotology.

Laughter in its various forms has been shown in 1000s of scientific gelotology studies to help treat and prevent a myriad of physical and mental health problems. From improving immune system strength in cancer patients undergoing chemotherapy; reducing stress hormones and anxiety, depression and even schizophrenia symptoms; improving the quality of breast milk; reducing blood pressure, improving vascular health and protecting from cardiovascular disease; hindering the progression of diabetic kidney disease and the list truly does just go on and on and on.

Laughter on the Brain

Laughter, whether you force yourself to laugh or are tickled, involves the activation of many similar parts of the brain. Clearly the motor cortex is activated in regions that relate to movement of the tongue, larynx and diaphragm (all needed for laughter). It can also involve parts of the frontal lobe, that include the prefrontal cortex and ACC, that are part of the ToM and DMN networks, involved in mentalizing and determining the mind and intentions of someone trying to make you laugh.

Perhaps the most important therapeutic activity in the brain when we laugh is activity in the limbic system. This activity is thought to release a whole bunch of hormones, including endorphins, which help with pain relief and are associated with exercise, happiness, health and excitement. Although currently unknown, the likely long-term effects that regular laughter has on your neural wiring, will be the key to fully understanding how laughter has therapeutic value. Expect brainwave and neuroplasticity based geotology research that will begin to answer the laughter riddle very soon.

Laughter in Pleasure and Pain

Laughter is part of the parcel when it comes to happiness. It is a form of pleasure and as such it activates parts of the brain associated with pleasure, including specific regions of the frontal cortex such as the prefrontal cortex and ACC, the limbic system and cerebellum. As you already know, these are regions involved in modulating our experience of pain. It fits perfectly. If laughter activates pleasure brain regions, it also has the power to alter how we perceive pain.

Simulated laughter, yogic laughter and laughter therapy are all much the same. They are therapeutic practices where one takes part in a laughter session and have all been shown to help alleviate pain, even the chronic kind. Laughter therapy has been show in many studies to relieve chronic pain. In one study a 55% reduction in the pain was felt by individuals with chronic muscle pain, as well as a 50% reduction in depression symptoms and a 42% reduction in anxiety symptoms from only 8 laughter therapy sessions. Collectively, not even a full day's work and chronic pain can be cut in half! The power of laughter is immeasurable. Laughter truly is the worlds cheapest, easiest, freeist medicine!

1.   **Checking in**
Feel free to focus on your breathing or perform any other short relaxation technique if you feel you need to. However, you can go straight to the fun in step 2.

2.   **Start laughing**
If you want to think of something funny to start you off, go ahead. But it is not necessary as you will find. Literally just start laughing out loud and don't let it stop, force it out if you need to. Let the laughter build up and take over. 2 minutes of continual laughter is a good starting point.

3.   **Stop, relax and focus on your breathing**
If you still feel some fits of laughter bubbling out of you, don't resist it, in a mindful way let the sensation pass through your body as you continue to deepen your mindful relaxation. Acknowledge any thoughts or feelings that come to you, but pay them little attention, let them float on by in your awareness. Matching the length of time spent laughing with the time spent in quiet focus is good practice but not essential.

HINTS & TIPS

•   The ultimate tip for laughter meditation practices is to practice with others. As laughter is contagious, practicing with others will reinforce your laughing practice and have you laughing harder and longer than if you were on your own.

•   **If you are practicing laughter meditation with a video call to a new friend in our community or offline you may want to close your** eyes before you begin, to lower your inhibitions and help the laughter flow free.

• Use a timer to start increasing the length of time you are in laughter for. If you can manage 10 solid minutes of laughter a day, we guarantee you will positively glow!

BOP 2: OBJECT FOCUSED METITATION

While all meditative practices have been shown to be helpful in the management of pain here is one that should allow you to focus your awareness outside of the body. Sometimes we are so focused on our internal pain that we mentally make our pain worse, making it all the more difficult to obtain relief from pain.

1. **Pick an object and place it in front of you**
It doesn't matter which object you use to focus your attention just as long as it's not too big and not too small so that it is easy enough to inspect visually. Some like to use a lit candle or flower or picture of a deity although it can be absolutely anything.

2. **Checking in**
Close your eyes and focus on your breath and perform any other relaxation technique of your choice to get your mind and body settled.

3. **Observe the object**
Open your eyes and study the object in detail, noticing all details of the object without over thinking them, just notice the details. The color, the shape, the texture, how it interacts with light. Refrain from making any judgments, simply observe. Begin with 5-10 minutes or longer if you feel you can.

BOP 3: LETTING GO OF PAIN
BRAIN TRAINING AUDIO

If you are challenged with chronic pain or discomfort, the profound relief found in Letting Go of Pain will instantly help your mind-body connection to 'turn' off your pain circuits and bathe you in well-being and bliss. Based on the latest scientifically proven research from leading Universities and practices on how our brains and bodies can be soothed and trained to mitigate pain. Letting Go of Pain's profound healing, and comfort and four practices, will provide you the gateway to a new experience of freedom from suffering, with deep emotional, and physical healing.

This audio is available here:

http://successwaves.com/products/catalog/Letting_Go_of_Pain.html

NeuroLogical Brain Training Goals

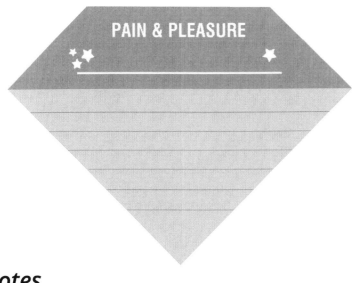

PAIN & PLEASURE

Notes

Notes

CHAPTER III:
FOCUSING ON OTHERS

"It is very easy to overestimate the importance of our own achievements in comparison with what we owe others."

~Dietrich Bonhoeffer

Part I

TWO BRAINS ARE BETTER THAN ONE

"If civilization is to survive, we must cultivate the science of human relationships – the ability of all peoples, of all kinds, to live together, in the same world at peace."

~ Franklin D. Roosevelt

Living with Ubuntu
Other People Are Integral To Your Life

Socializing with fellow humans is essential to our lives, in all cultures, in all four corners of the world. In Africa, the Bantu word, *ubuntu*, means that a person only becomes a person through other people. And resoundingly so. Every aspect of our lives, from birth to death, is intertwined with others. Just imagine for a second that you are the only human in existence. Would you know how to obtain food? Diagnose and cure yourself of disease? Purify your water? Build a stable shelter in a storm? Maybe you're a bit of a survival expert? In that case, you would have an increased chance of survival. But chances are even if Bear Grylls is your uncle life would simply be about survival, not living, just a lonely day to day struggle for your life.

Modern Life Relies on More People

In today's modern society, good luck if you expect to proudly live a life without relying on others. In short, it's darn near impossible not to depend on others. Even if you choose to become a crazy cat lady/man, you need others to live up to your crazy title. You can draw the curtains and have the doors plastered with locks and bolts in a bid to keep intruders at bay. But who made the locks to barricade your house like Fort Knox? Who made the cat food that feeds your feline friends? At times you may rightfully need a bit of solitude, but social isolation and the chronic survival brain of 'going it alone' is no longer valid. We can't get away from the fact that we need others not just to survive, but to live, experience, share, grow and learn.

The Evolving Social Brain
Social Brain Theory

In fact we think that the whole reason we are humans at all, and have evolved beyond chimps, comes down to our need to socialize. Science's most prominent theory is that the drive for humans developing such large brains is mainly because of our evolving and increasingly complex social skills and the life benefits that they engender. This is true now, and has been true form the beginning—from the guttural 'uga ug ug' and hand-waving of our cave dwelling ancestors, to the eloquent, diverse and ever evolving social skills we are capable of today (twerking not included).

The Bigger the Group the Better the Brain

A recent highly acclaimed study found that the larger in size that a monkey's social group is, the larger and denser its grey matter is. In humans, another report has shown that even the number of Facebook friends you have is linked to the number of neurons you have in your cortex. We aren't saying that by sending a million friend requests that your brain will get boosted—ha ha, nice try—but don't be disheartened. Thanks to neuroplasticity, by practicing the mastering of social skills, you can boost your grey matter and be loved by so many that your Facebook friends list rolls straight out of the door.

The Social Brain Is the Key to Health and Happiness

Social interaction is so vital to our brains, bodies and lives that without it our cognitive skills and health are put at risk. Decades of research and literally 100s of studies have unveiled a strong connection between positive emotions, social interactions and the strength and healthiness of your entire nervous system and body. Developing strong social skills in your younger years, and more importantly, maintaining an active social life in your elderly years, is vital for keeping mental and physical health in peak condition and maintaining a healthy immune system. Studies even suggest that those of us that maintain a bountiful social life and nurture close friendships live longer than those of us who are isolated from others. What's more is that a mega-analysis of 148 studies (representing more than 300,000 individuals) suggests that not regularly interacting with others can be as bad for you as smoking 15 cigarettes a day!

The Upward Positivity Spiral
Happy, Healthy and Social

The latest article hot of the press has identified a self-propelling upward spiral of increased happiness, health and well-being, with social interaction being integral to our progression up that spiral. The experiment highlighted that participants that willfully boosted their emotions with LKM (and thereby improved the strength of their social connections) felt more in tune and close to those they talked with, as opposed to those participants without the LKM positivity boost. By becoming more positive, the changes that occur in your brain give room for your social life to bloom, which in turn enhances your brain.

How is Your Vagal Tone?

Sharpening the brain's social related skills involves the vagus nerve; one of the 12 types of nerves (a dense collection of neurons that transmit the same information). The vagus nerve, like all nerves in the brain, is akin to information highways that transmit information between the neurons in the brain and the spinal cord (the central nervous system) and the neurons throughout your body (the peripheral nervous system). In particular, the vagus nerve regulates the resting state of the majority of the body's internal organ systems and operates on a largely subconscious level. As with your biceps, the tone or tension in the nerve—vagal tone—is a good indicator of general health.

Social Skills Strengthen the Route to Happiness and Health

A healthy body is not the only benefit we get from having good vagal tone, it is also central to our social engagement system and hence, it's functioning also influences our social skills, including empathy, and the ability to connect with other people. When we spend all day staring at our phones, televisions, laptops, tablets and other gizmo's and gadgets instead of looking around and engaging in human contact, our biological ability to connect diminishes—and so does our vagal tone.

Increased vagal tone also boosts your overall health and social abilities. And, as we know, a healthy body and mind is happiness' playground and the key to a positive upward spiral of overall happiness and health. Without life's ups and downs we would all be in an eternal spiral of happiness, health and wealth. But that's life: always presenting us with challenges that present a chance to grow and evolve. Armed with this knowledge we can utilize the power of neuroplasticity to enhance our social skills, have a positive effect on our vagal tone and easily get back on route to happiness no matter how many times life tries to throw us off.

Neuroplasticity in the Social Brain

It is said that social influences are among the most powerful factors in inducing neuroplastic changes in brain structure and function. What's more is that it appears that the higher we are positioned on the animal intelligence ladder, the more profound social influences are on the brain. Which fits quite nicely with the social brain evolution hypothesis don't you think? The more significant social influences have been on the evolution of the species and their brains, the more their brains can be molded by changes to their social life.

Negative Social Influences and Neuroplasticity

The evidence is pretty clear that in all animals, especially us humans, neuroplasticity in some parts of the brain may deteriorate due to negative social stresses, while other parts are actually enhanced by such stressors. Experiments have found in many animals (from birds, to rats, to humans), that negative social interactions such as an intruder invading the home, hinders neurogenesis and causes the death of dendrites (the ears of neurons) in the hippocampus and parts of the frontal lobe.

Conversely, this same stress actually causes specific parts of the amygdalae (which is central in generating feelings of fear) to gain neuronal mass, they grow, giving your primitive emotional centers extra potential processing power. These neuroplastic changes to the amygdalae are both anxiety and aggression promoting. They are not very pretty. The degeneration of the hippocampus is associated with low self-esteem and impulsiveness, while the frontal lobe changes are associated with poor executive functioning. The effects of the foregoing often result in a person who is angry, anxious, impulsive and poorer at planning, problem solving, reasoning, attention and self-control. Wow what a lovely sounding character that is! Studies have shown that similar changes to the limbic reward system in response to social defeat promotes drug taking in all animals, even mice!

Positive Social Influences and Neuroplasticity

Luckily, the negative social influences on neuroplasticity are largely reversible the sooner one begins retraining their brain, with aging being known to influence the rate of recovery. Positivity, social engagement and good physical health are the best means to reverse these negative effects and create vigorous and strong social brain circuitry. With proper neuroplasticity training and practice, the amygdalae shrink and hippocampus and frontal lobe are greatly enhanced.

And if you maintain a healthy social circuitry, you could be chatting away, sharp as a pin and fit as a fiddle, all the way through to ripe old age. Our social experiences, good or bad, shape our emotion and reward circuits. This shaping can trigger emotional and behavioral flexibility in tough situations or result in emotional and behavioral rigidity, or even a stubborn unwillingness to adapt, in even slightly testy situations.

SUMMARY

- Social brain hypothesis: that animals in large social groups have bigger brains due to increasingly complex social skills and the life benefits that they engender.
- **Having a bountiful social life is highly correlated with positive emotions and healthy immune and nervous systems that promote good mental and physical health and longevity.**
- Practicing positivity or social skills directly influences a positive upward spiral of happiness, socialness and good health.
- **Good vagal tone is a sign of good health and is affected by our general positivity and social life.**
- Social stress can cause growth of the amygdalae and inhibition of neuroplasticity in parts of the frontal lobe and hippocampus which promotes acting like a cocktail parties' social monster nightmare!
- Positive social interaction can reverse these negative brain changes that create well-balanced disposition through increased relaxation, positivity, calm and calculated decision making, sound reasoning, increased attention and self-control.

Up Next...

As you now know, practicing the enhancement of your positivity or social skills directly influences a positive upward spiral of happiness, socialness and good health supported by enhancement of your vagal tone and re-wiring of emotion related networks. On the flip side we need to prevent the downward spiral through dealing with negativity appropriately. Last, but by no means least we will turn to a mindfulness BOP to neuroplasticaly mold networks in the sculpting of a super social brain.

TWO BRAINS ARE BETTER THAN ONE
BRAIN OPTIMIZATION PRACTICES

BOP 1: NOTICING POSITIVITY

Here is a simple technique for recognizing and acknowledging positivity in your life to kick that brain optimizing upward spiral into action. Used daily this simple, yet highly effective technique can realign your thinking to the positive and highlight aspects of your life that are bursting with or could do with an injection of positivity.

Although you can use any diary, notebook or piece of paper, or electronic document, this exercise is perfect for your NeuroLogical goals web journal. If you're not in the mood to write things down, why not arrange with one of your BOP buddies for a preferably daily (or weekly) session to discuss positive things that have happened to you both? Talking about positivity WHILE being social, now that is the ultimate upward spiral booster! At the end of your day (or whenever you have arranged for your positivity date), settle down to reflect on the amazingly positive things that have happened. if you have been in beta brain mode you may not have had the time to truly appreciate it, now is the time!

1. **Checking in**
If you are feeling a little funky use your preferred relaxation technique to get you in the mood.

2. **Write down/talk about 3 kind things you have done today/this week.**

You may take for granted some of the many kind things you do which you may feel are just expected of you. Don't sell your positive actions short.

3. **Write down/talk about 3 funny things you experienced today/this week.**

If you have been letting stress take over, these previous moments may have passed you by. Focus now to take notice of that funny remark you may have ignored, being busy at work or that cute thing the dog/child did at an 'inconvenient' moment of stress.

4. **Write down/talk about 3 good things that happened to you today/this week.**

From the small to the grandiose; a stranger smiling at you or holding open a door, to success with your BOPs, fun with friends or even simply enjoying the weather. Good things tend to be happening all around us if we are in the state of mind to notice them.

BOP 2: DEALING WITH NEGATIVITY

We can talk about positivity until it comes out of our ears but that won't help us when negative thoughts or the urge to enact a behavior that isn't good for us creeps into our heads. Guilt, fear, worry, anxiety and other emotional nasties tend to follow suit. Sometimes we can't see the bountiful forest of positivity surrounding us for the negativity weeds in our front garden that invade our neuronal circuits and mold our minds for the worse.

While there are many strategies for dealing with negative thoughts and the emotion spiral that results, here is a simple one. You can practice this next technique throughout your daily living, but you can also use it when you have any intrusive thinking and feeling disturbing your Zen during your BOP sessions—it happens to the best of us. What we love about this technique is that you can also train yourself to deal with negativity even if you are in a perfectly pleasant state of mind. All you have do to is use the power of your imagination to visualize a negative experience and deal with it appropriately. Include the first two visualization steps for your BOP practice but skip straight to riding the negativity wave (step 3) if your already caught in the tide.

1. **Recall**

    Recall a recent event where you felt upset, embarrassed, worried, afraid, nervous or panicky—any negative emotional state. Visualize the scene and really focus in on the details, bring the scene to life with all your inner world senses. Were you able to notice the trigger that set off the negativity?

2. **Pay attention to the details**

    Notice the worrying and disconcerting thoughts. Now focus on how you felt at the time. Notice the physical effects the emotional state has on your body (tightness, blood pressure, breathing rate etc). Let your negative emotional state reach about half way on your negativity scale.

3. **Notice the wave**

    Imagine that your negative thoughts, as well as their associated emotions and physical sensations, are all a wave of negativity. Feel reassured in the knowledge that the wave builds up momentum and rises, but what goes up must come down. The negativity wave will eventually fall and fizzle out calmly on the shore.

4. **Ride the wave**

    Close your eyes (if you can, please don't attempt that if your trigger occurs while driving) and imagine you are like a surfer on top and riding the wave in your mind. It may start out tall and feel like the wave is rising, but make sure to pay close attention as it levels off and begins to diminish in size. Ride the wave all the way back down, until it fizzles out, leaving you calm and steady on the shore.

5. **Congratulations**

Mentally congratulate yourself for riding the wave and know that when new worries, fears and urges come, or in fact with any negative emotion you wish to surpass, that you have the tools to deal with them.

6.   **Check out**

Breathe deeply for a couple of minutes, feel free to use a relaxation technique of your choice if you should feel the need to iron out any stresses. Or the exercise may have also highlighted to you some niggling beliefs or habits that are worth investigating further.

HINTS & TIPS

•   Through your BOPs, you may by now be well aware of some of your triggers that set of negativity or worried thoughts. Be vigilant. If you notice your trigger setting you off and a simple counting back from 5 or focused breathing won't help you, prepare yourself to ride the wave. Responses to well used triggers can be near instantaneous. Even when they are not, you may still get caught by the emotional current. This is why it is helpful to remind yourself as often as you can throughout your day that you have the skills tools and knowledge equipped to deal with any negativity that comes your way, big or small. Why can we say this with such certainty? Because if you have been making use of our BOPs so far, you undoubtedly ARE!

BOP 3: MINDFULNESS MEDITATION
If You Can Recall...

If you can recall, the pinnacle of mindfulness is to achieve calm awareness of all sensations in the present moment although not being consumed by any of them. To be aware of your senses, thoughts and feelings in a non-judgmental way and so instead of being overwhelmed by them, we learn to manage them better. Mindfulness mediation is particularly useful for de-syncing of brainwaves in specific parts of the DMN, reducing our focus upon mental self-reference and autobiographical memories and obtaining greater control of our emotions and fear response. An increase in alpha waves within the DMN from meditative practice is also known to support better emotional control. Meditation, like positive social interactions, can reverse the negative effects of the neuroplastic grey matter changes in the amygdalae and parts of the frontal lobe and hippocampus which promotes acting like a total jerk-off!

Balancing Implicit Bias

We understand how greater emotional control and being less of a self-obsessed jackass can improve your social performance and generally make you a nicer person to be around. But just how much does meditative practice alter our ability to interact with others? One recent study shows that meditation has the power to radically alter your social behavior. Have you ever heard of implicit bias? Implicit or hidden bias is the biased view we have of something without even being aware of it. For example, you may consciously think that it's terrible to treat homeless people different (that could be you one day!). However, have you ever even stopped to have a chat with 'that homeless guy' you walk over every day and occasionally give some spare change to? No?

Have you ever seen a spit-spot lady/gentleman squatting next to the 'that homeless guy', deeply engaged in what appears to be a meaningful, heartfelt conversation and wondered why does that scare me? Why don't I stop to scratch the surface and get to know this man I walk over every single day? Well it may be that your hidden negatively biased views about people that are homeless are holding you back. And despite our better conscious judgments most of us suffer from this problem.

The mediation experiment revealed that with just 6 weeks of LKM practice you can reduce these hidden, negative, biased views against homeless people and likely other socially stigmatized groups. Just 6 weeks of practice can even alter social concepts and behaviors we don't even realize that we have!!! This may indeed be an LKM specific change, although generally our social skills are influenced by all forms of meditation.

Meditation is Social Work

Being a focused and attentive listener, readily showing compassion and empathy, being relaxed and open, with self-love and the confidence that comes with it and showing clarity and thoughtfulness in what we say during conversations are all examples of social skills that meditation can help us with. Many studies over the years have shown that those of us that work in 'social' jobs, that tend to have a hefty stress tag, such as being a psychologist, social worker or nurse are not only less stressed by using meditation, they also find that their social skills and job performance are similarly improved—win, win and win!

Building Up To Mindfulness

Mindfulness meditation dominates the scientific research on mediation BOPs both in and out of studies on social skills and our working worlds. However, a mindfulness meditation session can initially be a tough cookie to crack. For newbies, frustrations arising from the first shot at it, can even put them off for good. Luckily for you and what you may or may not have noticed is that almost all of your BOPs so far are in fact mindfulness based in some respect and are shining therapeutic examples of BOPs that have you fully equipped to ease gracefully into a bona fide mindfulness meditation session. Starting with a simple, short, 5-10 minute mindfulness session, and with the help of your NeuroLogical journal, see if you can extend your practice day by day. So, sit down, relax and be mindful as your body bathes in the benefits, your DMN gets to re-wring and your amygdalae shrink and hippocampus grow!

1. **Checking in**

Find a comfortable quiet place to sit, whether on the floor, in the garden or in a chair. Somewhere you can be left in peace for your practice. Sit with soft tall and extended posture, proud and comfortably. Focus on your breath and then use a short relaxation technique if needed to settle your mind. As your skill develops you may want to experiment with meditating in more distracting environments.

2. Deepen relaxation

Focusing now entirely on your breathing, feel your mind unwinding further with every breath. Begin to feel your breath deepening and slowing down, breathing in and out deeply and slowly through your stomach.

3. Realigning focus

As thoughts and emotions come to you be aware of them and gently and kindly let them pass you by. When you notice that you have gotten so caught up in thoughts that you have forgotten that you're sitting there meditating, just gently bring yourself back to your breath. Like clouds, let intrusive thoughts and sensations gently float away.

4. Expanding sensory perception

Be aware of all the sensations in your body, the rising and falling of your chest, the feeling of the chair or cushion or grass or floor beneath you, any sounds in the room and the tastes and smells around you. Open up your senses while maintaining calm, steady breathing and awareness. Again return to step 3 whenever thoughts, feelings and sensations take over your focus.

HINTS & TIPS

•   DISTRACTIONS: Being distracted by your default thinking patterns that have been integrated into your DMN, is totally and utterly expected and should be taken advantage of! The moment you become aware of intrusive thinking, is the perfect and perhaps most important brain training aspect of brain training, life changing mindfulness meditation—have fun with it! Just playfully and softly bring yourself back to mindfulness. If you never got distracted you wouldn't have much reason to meditate and calm your mind now would you? Please, no scolding of one's self. See the advantage it presents you: the chance to train your brain.

• EXCITEMENT: Being excited about your success in attaining mindfulness is another common form of distraction. When this occurs, notice the excitement and acknowledge the pleasure before letting it melt away as with other thoughts and feelings. As with all emotions you know about riding the emotion wave; feel the emotion of excitement diminish just as you would with any negative emotions.

• POSTURE: Play with posture when it comes to mindfulness. This is how you can incorporate meditation into parts of your day which you thought were null and void. Even a 5 minute walk can become a time for mindfulness practice. You can stand still, sit cross legged, in the lotus position, lie down, walk and even bungee jump while being mindful. Don't forget to acknowledge and let go of any new sensations in your body when you experiment with posture. The longer you are able to mediate as you improve your practice, the more posture becomes important.

• GAZE: To begin with, you can do your BOP with your eyes closed. You may prefer to meditate with eyes open but for most people this can be quite distracting to begin with. The gaze should be at a comfortable downward angle. Your eyes should be open, but not staring, and your gaze soft.

• TIME: Continue this state of awareness for 5 minutes at first. Then aim to extend this by a couple of minutes each session, at a rate that feels natural and achievable to you. Imagine you are a scientist that is objectively following your progress and adjusting the times accordingly. Use your NeuroLogical goals journal to record your progress and see if you can achieve 45 minutes to an hour of mindfulness. Perhaps have the ultimate aim of carrying this across to all day to day activities outside of formal meditation practice and be mindful for life?!

NeuroLogical Brain Training Goals

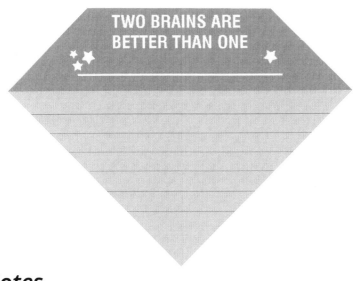

TWO BRAINS ARE
BETTER THAN ONE

Notes

Notes

Part II

LOVE, FRIENDSHIP & FAMILY

"We're born alone, we live alone, we die alone. Only through our love and friendship can we create the illusion for the moment that we're not alone."

~ Orson Wells

Emotion in Social Connections
Importance of Emotions

S o far we have learned that to be more social we can practice the stress management and the maintenance of a positive and open outlook. Now we are focusing on communication with lovers, friends and family. So, it's time that we address where emotions come into our social world. Our emotional state is integral to our behavior and attitude during communication and perhaps may be considered the force that directs and shapes social interactions. When we lack emotional responsiveness or the inability to control our emotions effectively there is a negative impact on our social skills and decision making. This often results in making us pretty difficult and disagreeable individuals. This is all the more true when we suffer from diseases which exasperate our ability to interact, whether suffering from depression, or dealing with the challenges that autism brings. Emotional awareness provides you the tools needed for understanding both yourself and other people (from friends to enemies), as well as the true messages they are communicating to you.

Emotion Detection—Our Sixth Sense

Emotions are our sixth sense. To be more precise, the conveying and the detection of emotions is, in a manner of speaking, our sixth sense. Emotional detection can involve both modes of communication, auditory and visual. Someone's body language, particularly facial expressions (and in many cultures hand gestures), are of high emotional content. Speech, is the other obvious conveyor of emotion. Being able to successfully detect emotions is like having a wireless brain scanner that is giving you a window into an individual's mind to see how they feel.

If you are out of touch with your own feelings, and don't understand how you feel or why you feel a certain way, you'll have a hard time communicating your feelings and needs to others. It is a well-established fact, both in the real world and in the laboratory, that being better at emotional detection as well as control of one's own emotions generally makes you a more likable and popular person. So, developing our emotional sixth sense and having control of our emotions is integral to a healthy social life.

Different Detection Systems for Different Types of Emotion

Both humans and other mammals have a basic emotional system that is pretty essential for evolutionary survival. We have, arguably, six basic emotions: happiness, sadness, surprise, anger, fear and disgust. Recognizing these basic emotions primarily involves the amygdalae and other areas of the limbic system. Outside of our basic emotions lie social and moral emotions, including pride, curiosity, sympathy, generosity, guilt, shame and embarrassment. These moral and social emotions tend to be more associated with activation of parts of the frontal lobe and temporal lobe of the cortex, with varying degrees of activation of the more primitive limbic system.

Cultural Differences in Emoticon Detection!

Even emoticons (you know the typable little faces we make to easily convey emotion online) can be misinterpreted across cultures. In the United States the emoticons :) and : -) denote a happy face, whereas the emoticons :(or : - (a sad face. In Japan however, the symbol (^_^) denotes a happy face, and (;_;) a sad face. Americans may struggle to determine which is a happy or sad Japanese emoticon as they tend to focus more on the mouth, which doesn't change between happy and sad Japanese emoticons.

Japanese people on the other hand have similar struggles as they tend to look to the eyes to determine the difference between happy and sad faces, which doesn't change between the American emoticons. However, once someone explains the difference between a happy or sad face such cultural differences disappear. As such, cultural differences really boil down to collective differences in experience between groups of individuals which can, through experience, be overcome.

Emotional Contagion

Having emotional self-control is just as important as being able to accurately detect the emotions of other people. Why? Because emotions are contagious! So choose your company wisely! Have you ever bumped into a friend who is bouncing off the walls with enthusiasm and excitement and after you bump into them, they magically take you along for the ride? Or when someone is being a negative stick in the mud, they can really stink up a room with their attitude. It is thought that when people unconsciously mimic their companions' expressions of emotion, they come to feel reflections of their partner's emotions. Is it any wonder that if one has angry, aggressive parents that you may have a tendency to become aggressive towards your peers? The infectious nature of emotions can be found at the roots of the empathy tree and ToM network, that allows us to disobey the laws of physics and experience life as if in another person's shoes.

Love on the Brain
Emotions are Central to Close Connections

Feelings and emotions are the glue that holds us all together—they are central and integral to our close relationships. As you know from the first section of this chapter, having positive emotional relationships are important for your mental and physical health. Through creating positive social interactions and strong relationships your vagal tone is increased making you fitter and healthier. What's more is that the resulting influence on neuroplasticity in the amygdalae, hippocampus and frontal lobe, creates a stronger, more balanced emotion system, enhancing your emotional control and emotional responsiveness.

How another person makes us feel and how we make them feel is central to our relationships. But what activity goes on in the brain that produces these signs of positive emotional connections in the brain? How does the brain react towards different people, even our loved ones? What is going on in the brain that separates your love for your child, sibling, lover or friend? What impact do these different relationships have on how our brain functions?

The Complexities of Love

Love, be it for your best friend, close family and especially for your romantic partner, is one of the most profound, intense and impactful emotions in our lives. As with all emotions, love is routed in the brain. Love's activation patterns share similarities and clear differences with other emotions, such as anger or joy. I'm sure you will all agree (as does neuroscience), that love is complex. Your love for your family pet is completely different than that for your brother, your significant other or child. What's more is that the love you feel, and by extension the love related brain activation patterns, for every individual changes with time.

This variation in this over generalized emotion we call love, and the subsequent variations in our behavior that results, is reflected in the differences between neural depictions of love in the brain. Put more explicitly, there are differences in the activation and deactivation of emotion, reward and motivation related networks between the various types of loving relationships. Similarly the brain activation pattern that a friend stimulates in your brain on day 1 of meeting them is unlikely to be the same on day 7300 (20 years later). It's as if every individual person that is close to you elicits a special signature of love that is dependent on the type of relationship and how the relationship grows and develops.

Love Is Evolution Baby

Romantic, head over heels love can make us behave giddy, irrational and even behave pretty ridiculously. Are you fueled with energy? Unable to sleep? Having obsessive thoughts that intrude into daily tasks no matter how important? Are you unusually happy, merry and gay? Do you think the sun shines out of that special someone's ass? Well as crazy as it all sounds, those feelings are a perfectly normal and universal phenomenon that is integral to the evolution of our species.

It is so common that millions and quite easily billions of people are experiencing these feelings this very moment. Romantic love is also clearly different than lust, attraction and the forming of attachments, as well as love for a friend, child or other family member. All of these relationships have interrelated emotion-motivation systems in the brain. Such systems have evolved for survival in groups and the perpetuation of the species in mating, reproduction, and parenting.

Do It for the Kids

The influence that we have as parents on the malleable minds of the young is profound. You have heard that a mother exercising, even before a child is born and is in the womb, is a baby BOP. Well the buck does not stop there. Parental influences (both maternal and paternal) on the development of a child's brain and physical health have received a fair bit of attention in the literature. Having a good, strong, positive, relationship with our own children (or even a niece, nephew or younger sibling, as well as the children of others) is something we should take great pride and responsibility in.

A Negative Head Start

The negative influences of unhealthy or absent social interactions (we discussed in the first section) are quite striking in children institutionalized in orphanages. In a study of 38 children who had become orphaned at the age of 8 or 9, there was a clearly observable difference between the size of their amygdalae—some were more anxious and stressed and had larger amygdalae—than those less stressed and possessing smaller amygdalae. What set the children apart? How long they were without parents was the determining factor! Those that were adopted earlier had more balanced brains than those adopted later.

A similar affect can be found between children of the same age, where one group is exposed to depressed parents and one group is not. Those that were exposed to parental depressive symptoms since birth had much larger amygdalae than those with happy parents. These differences in emotional circuitry are akin to the differences found in autistic children. The resulting differences suggest strong implications for emotion regulation, detection and well-being. While we are also socially responsibly for influencing the brains of other adults in our lives, the drastic impact we can have on our children's social and emotional circuitry is not to be taken lightly.

A Loving Head Start

Scientists have found that even if a baby is born without full development of its hippocampal volume due to the impact of prenatal risk factors (disease, depression, alcohol, drugs, smoking, diet etc.), it can, nonetheless, be improved solely through social support, such as the care from their parents. In another experiment in rats, it was found that just receiving a good licking and grooming for the first week of life outside the womb seemed to enhance the circuitry associated with formation of episodic memories. Simply put, positive interactions with their parents are "hardwired" into the brain and put down roots. Collectively, current findings suggest that there are protective effects of creating a nurturing environment for our children. But be warned—don't wrap them up in cotton wool! Exposure to mild stress early in life enhances their mental resilience and combined with healthy social influences, they develop good coping skills for dealing with stressful situations later on in life.

Imaging Brains in Love

A few brave research groups have spent over a decade researching the ins and outs of love. Their research runs the full gamut of relationships, including comparing romantic love to friendships and maternal love, as well as looking at couples that are still madly in love after 20 years and not forgetting those who have just been bitten by the love bug. Here is a summary of some of their warm and fuzzy findings.

Loving Your Lover vs. Loving Your Friend versus Loving Your Child

There are clear differences when comparing intense romantic love to the love of your friends, even when those relationships cover the same time period. When viewing images of a romantic partner some parts of the brain become more active and others less so than when viewing images of friends. Many of these areas overlap with maternal feelings of love for one's child, indicative of the close similarities between the two types of loving relationships.

Nonetheless, the types of love projected are marked by significant differences in activation patterns.. Generally areas that were more active were associated with the reward and motivation system, while deactivated regions centered on promoting happiness and inhibiting social judgment. In separate studies simply holding your loved ones hand was enough to trigger similar networks, dampening our neural response to stressful situations and pain.

ACC Activation

The ACC is part of the cingulate cortex, the region of the cortex that is sandwiched between the brain's hemispheres. With maternal love a specific region of the ACC is activated, neighboring an area activated by sadness and anxiety, which is thought to foster a mother's empathic feelings for their little tyke. Both maternal and romantic love activates another region of the ACC that is associated with pleasant and happy feelings. This area of the brain is right next to a spot that's active when we feel socially excluded. However, the sweet spot in question is thought to do just the opposite, generate pleasant feelings of social inclusion, belonging and attachment to our loved ones.

Shared Insula Activation

Deep within the cortex, a region called the insula lights up for both maternal and romantic love and has both emotion and reward associated connections. An activated insula is associated with generating our 'gut feelings', as well as sensations of 'emotional touch' that enhance the pleasure of loving skin to skin contact. The specific part of the insula that becomes activated when viewing our children and partner is right next to the area of the insula that, when it is activated, influences our 'gut-feelings' when checking out attractive, yet unknown people. Another area of the insula, even further away would light up if you have negative feelings about the person. Which particular part of the insula that is activated when dealing with others is clearly important for defining how we feel about someone; with loved ones having their own special home in the insula.

Shared Striatum Activation

The striatum, as you know has modules that deal separately with different types of information: one module for the active thought responses system (A-O), and another module which deals with the habitual response system (S-R). The striatum also contains neurons that respond to food and drink rewards, as well as money related motivations. Researchers think that striatum activation is another reason why investing time in love for one's partners feels rewarding and becomes habitual pretty easily.

Romance Specific Hypothalamic Activation

There is one saucy thing that clearly makes romantic love special and that is sexual attraction. Activations were found in a specific region of the hypothalamus that is also active when registering sexual cues, such as unveiling sexy lingerie or any other verbal of visual sexual innuendos. Funnily enough this region is also active when you are lusting after someone and falling in love is not the intention.

Activation Specific to Motherly Love

Activity entirely specific to maternal love is found within the orbitofrontal cortex in the frontal lobe. This area of the brain is also correlated with decision making and expectation (particularly expected rewards and punishments). This is unsurprising considering parents are expected to make daily decisions regarding rewarding or punishing their child's good and bad behavior.

Another maternal specific brain region is a subcortical part of the forebrain called the PAG (periaqueductal gray). PAG has been shown to have roles in humans in modulating pain and in defensive behavior, while in rodents it affects maternal behavior. Having a high concentration of oxytocin receptors—one of your body's natural love drugs—PAG activation is likely associated with maternal behavior in us humans too.

One last region that is active only in loving mothers when viewing their children (not even other people's children) is a gyrus (the ridge of a brain wrinkle) called the fusiform gyrus. As part of our facial recognition machinery the researchers suggest that its heightened activity allows mother's to better judge the facial expressions of babies and children, who rely less heavily on verbal communication and whose faces are changing rapidly with age.

Deactivations

Cortical and subcortical brain regions are also deactivated when we focus on the object of our affections, with striking overlap between maternal and romantic love deactivation patterns. Parts of the frontal, parietal and temporal lobe and the amygdalae that are associated with depression and negative feelings and social and emotional judgment shut down, helping create that giddy, happiness and 'love is blind' attitude that the bitter and twisted find oh so sickening.

Love Is a Drug
A Drug Cocktail

Like any other emotion, love is regulated by hormones. Love is a hormone cocktail that includes dopamine, oxytocin and vasopressin, as well as serotonin and cortisol and other stress hormones to name a few. Moreover, many of the areas of the brain that are activated by love have high densities of receptors that can interpret these hormones, making them super sensitive to these hormones which influences our behavior.

Trust, Addiction and Motivation

Oxytocin for example is associated with reducing panic and pain and is also known as the 'trust hormone.' It is therefore likely to be important for the 'getting to know you' phase of love. Vasopressin on the other hand is more associated with the forming of attachment to your romantic interest. At the same time, heightened dopamine release is why love can feel like an addiction, adding that 'feel-good' factor that makes love a rewarding experience and has you wanting more.

Obsession

Serotonin on the other hand is reduced in early stages of love. Although it has been labeled as one of life's happy hormones it has a whole host of roles. With love, it is thought that changes in serotonin levels are involved in the obsessive part of love. In fact, the love related brain areas are the same areas that light up when people take cocaine! It's a wonder that we don't overdose with such an intense cocktail of love drugs!

Take Home Message

The take home message is that emotion-reward related neuronal circuitry is at the center of our strong emotional relationships in all their flavors. However, the variations between the activation and deactivation patterns and structures involved are what influence the changes our relationships have on our social behavior. People that we are closely involved with truly affect both our neuronal circuitry and behavior. Reciprocally, our own presence influences their brains and behavior, and by extension influences their happiness and well-being.

What's more is that many of the same brain structures are involved in representing all of humanity in our minds—the good, the bad and the ugly—but there are sweet spots within those structures that are specific to different kinds of relationships. There is clearly a fine balance of brain activity that needs to be lovingly and carefully maintained to nurture and maintain healthy relationships. By creating and maintaining close, loving relationships that encourage positive emotions we also promote neuroplastic changes that protect us from the other face of the coin, negative feelings and depression. Love truly is the best medicine.

Brainwaves
Pioneering Studies

As the foundations have been laid for understanding the activation patterns in the brain the next logical step is to look at how brainwaves fit into all this. To date, only two recent papers have been released that pave the way for understanding any brainwaves' involvement. These experiments involved recording participants' brainwave activity while looking at images of strangers, appreciated friends and their romantic partners.

The Waves of Love

Frontal and parietal beta is higher for anonymous faces and is related to how familiar we are with a face. The less familiar we are with a face, the more of a threat they could pose, which sharpens our attention and has us ready for action should the need arise. Occipital delta and alpha and temporal theta waves are part of the face detection process. They don't change much between different kinds of faces.

However, the strength of both delta and theta waves in the frontal lobe is what highlights the differences between stranger, appreciated friend and lover. Between known and unknown faces, frontal theta is much higher for known faces and is likely associated with episodic and semantic memories that are associated with the relationship with the individual person being viewed. Frontal delta on the other hand is greater the more love is involved. Appreciated people in our lives have a higher response than unknown people but it is the loved ones that really shine through here. Romantic partners clearly boosted frontal delta.

Take Home Message

While all oscillations are involved in recognizing faces and the brain activity other people induce in us, it is the increases and decreases in strength and synchronicity in different regions that make the difference between, stranger, friend, family and lover. Our sources say, that when EEG and brain scanning technologies are used in the same experiment, allowing us to more accurately pinpoint the structures that are being affected by various brainwaves, we will develop a far deeper understanding of loving relationships, or any other kind of relationship for that matter.

SUMMARY

- Emotion detection and emotional control are the ultimate social skills.
- **Recognizing basic emotions involves the limbic system, whereas social and moral emotions more heavily involve the cortex.**
- Cultural differences exist between our emotion systems in the brain, although our brains can adapt to these differences.
- **The better we are at detecting another person's emotions the more easily we can feel the emotions they feel—as emotions can be contagious.**
- Differences in the activation and deactivation of emotion, reward and motivation related networks help define the different relationships in our lives.
- **All of these relationships have interrelated emotion-motivation systems in the brain that have evolved for survival in groups and the perpetuation of the species in mating, reproduction, and parenting.**
- Loving and nurturing relationships with children is pivotal for the development of their emotion-reward systems and well-being throughout life.
- **Different kinds of relationship have similarities in their activation patterns in the brain: romantic love and maternal love both share activity in regions of the ACC for empathy and happiness, the insula for emotional touch and reward and the striatum for habit formation and reward.**
- Certain regions are active only for certain kinds of relationship: the hypothalamus activation in romantic relationship's sexual attraction and in maternal relationships, the orbitofrontal cortex, PAG and the fusiform gyrus are active for reward and punishment, defensive behavior and facial expression recognition respectively.

- In loving relationships there are deactivations of regions active in non-loving relationships such as deactivations in the frontal, parietal and temporal lobes and amygdalae, turning off negative feelings and social and emotional judgment
- Love is a drug as it involves the release of hormone cocktails that include, dopamine, oxytocin, vasopressin and serotonin for trust, attachment, feeling good and obsession respectively.
- The variations in the activation and deactivation patterns in our brains as a result of different social experiences is what defines our relationships.
- Differences in delta and theta waves strength in the frontal lobe are what highlights the difference between stranger, appreciated friend and lover.

Up Next...

Emotion detection and awareness and emotion control techniques shall now take the spotlight as these skills are at the foundations of our meaningful connections. These BOPs will hone your emotional circuitry to have you tuned in to your loved ones and in the emotional driver's seat. We also include and advanced LKM BOP so that you can give your love related neural networks a boost to benefit your loved ones. These techniques are all about emotion detection and control.

LOVE, FAMILY & FRIENDSHIP
BRAIN OPTIMIZATION PRACTICES

BOP 1: EMOTION DETECTION
Empathy

A huge part of being emotionally aware involves empathy—to tune in to the emotional state of others, which involves your ToM and emotional networks (as you have learned). By truly understanding others and directing your thoughts outside yourself during social interactions, we re-wire the ToM network to be less self-absorbed and thus less prone to destructive thinking about how things relate to yourself and your life—an irritating habit of some self proclaimed 'good listeners'.

Over Empathic?

If you are a nurse, doctor, support worker, psychologist or anyone working in the health and care industry you will be well aware of the flip side of empathy. When it is your job to interact with people in situations that easily harbor negativity, being overly empathic and taking on daily doses of negativity can, if one is not prepared, begin to re-wire your own neural networks for negativity.

When being empathic towards someone who has just one the lottery, you can ride their high. Being empathic when someone is in pain, both physical and emotional, can result in the empathic individual truly experience the negativity in their own brain. In order to avoid this, we need to transform empathy into compassion, where we may feel pity and hold warm caring emotions and intentions for someone in distress but do not experience the negativity ourselves.

Empathy Protection

Bearing the negative side of empathy in mind we suggest that you only practice emotional detection and empathy related BOPs when you already feel you have made sufficient progress with all the other previous BOPs. This way, you are comfortably de-stressed, have enough love for yourself and your body, can deal with negative thinking, beliefs and habits and have guided emotional networks towards positivity.

Most importantly, we have had you practicing BOPs that de-wire self-referential processing. This means that if you develop your empathy skills you won't be overwhelmed by them and dredge up past or future pains should someone be communicating negative emotions you yourself have experienced. This way if a stranger, lover, family member or friend comes to you in a time of need, you have the emotional stability to be a knight in shining armor.

Make a conscious effort (NeuroLogical diary alert!!!) to have at least one social interaction a day, no matter how short, that you are designating as a BOP. This will be a time to focus on building your empathy skills. You can also modify this technique for imagined situations, using your visualization skills to create a virtual playground for empathy building rehearsals.

1.   Focus
Provide the speaker with your undivided attention.

2.   Dampen judgment
Never minimize or trivialize what is said. Just as you have dampened your mental focus on intrusive thoughts and feelings in mindfulness practices, dampen your judgments now.

3.   Emotion detection
What emotions do the words the speaker uses convey? Is the speaker happy, angry, curious, frustrated, bored or playful? Prepare to respond to the emotion with appropriate tonality and body language as well your choice of words.

4.   Hush
Don't feel you must have an immediate reply. Often if you allow for some quiet after a pause in speech, they themselves will break the silence.

5.   Make reflections
Assure that you understand clearly by asking clarifying questions and restate what you perceive the speaker to be saying. Make use of their use of words, phrases and gestures to help build rapport.

BOP 2: EMOTION CONTROL

All forms of meditation influence emotional control, in both shared and distinctive ways. Now that you have oiled the gears through various meditative practices, let's get them turning and start practicing your emotional control. There are many ways to go about this, but first we will give you a short exercise about exploring your emotions and then we will give you an emotion control technique with two situational variations.

1.   Recall a recent time that you lost control of your emotions
Take the time to use your visualization skills and really paint the picture with as much sensory detail as you can.

2.   Explore yourself when you lose control
Notice any sensations in your body as the emotion overcomes you. For example fear is closely associated with squirmy feelings in your gut and a rapid heartbeat or sadness tends to weigh down heavily on our chest and make you feel lethargic. It is very important the you can distinguish the bodily sensations from your actual emotion and how it makes you think and behave. Many of us, through unwitting practice are easily consumed by emotional bodily sensations, which heightens the intensity of negative emotions, making you feel them even stronger, from numbing depression to

hyperventilating panic and everything in between. Being able to acknowledge your emotion and the associated emotions separately is a valuable skill.

3.   Understand the root causes of your emotion

Whatever the negative emotion is, be it anxiety, panic, fear, sadness, guilt, anger or any other, understand that emotions do not simply arise out of thin air. Granted that with the rapid speed with which they can take over our minds and bodies they can sure as hell feel like they ambush us out of nowhere. Negative emotions may also stem from unhelpful thoughts. When an emotion seems to really come from nowhere this may indicate that you may have a more deeply rooted belief or habit that has you set on emotional auto-pilot at the first whiff of your trigger.

If you suspect a core belief is involved, here is a short list of some of the many common examples of misplaced emotional beliefs that can cause us bother. You will definitely benefit from logically reasoning out why the following common limiting beliefs are false and unhelpful in surpassing a stressful situation. You know what to do with such cumbersome beliefs if you happen to own any of these bad boys don't you? Head on back to the changing beliefs and habits techniques from Chapter 1.

"I/it must be perfect in all respects in order to be worth it."

"I must be loved and thought highly of by everyone or I'm worthless"

"Something in my past controlled my life then so it must control me now and in the future."

"It is disastrous when things do not go to plan."

"Feeling depressed comes from outside forces which I can't do very much to change."

"I can be happy from simply doing nothing, enjoying myself and taking life as it comes."

4.   Explore controlling yourself when you lose control

There are many alternative ways in which you can react to any overly emotional situation. Use the power of your inner world to explore different situations. How would it feel if you bottled up your reaction to your trigger and didn't show your emotions? Or, how would it feel if you just found a simple, polite way to remove yourself from a situation? Or how about if you caught yourself before you became consumed and counted calmly down from 5 or rode the negativity wave to relax? How does the situation progress? Is the result better or worse? Explore your options and seek solutions that have the best outcome. This provides great alternative courses of action for when it happens in the real world.

5.   Own your emotion control
Whichever alternative solution to losing control of your emotions worked best, bring it to life. Expand on the details, enhance the colors, brighten the picture in your mind and enhance the positive feelings this solution brings you. How does your body feel now? Enhance any positive feelings you get from your alternative solution.

HINTS & TIPS
•   Try and remember to reflect similarly if this happens in real-time, outside of BOP practice—once you have calmed down that is. Build up a repertoire of knowledge about your emotions. Us humans are pretty good at tricking ourselves (disguising fear as anger being a choice example) so pay close attention to your body and mind.
•   Still losing it on the odd occasion despite much practice? Well how about real world simulations instead of inner world simulations? You can use TV shows and movies that you know will trigger the kinds of emotions that you are having trouble controlling. Perhaps political discussions can really get your blood boiling. If so, watch a political debate and try and control your anger using the above technique. Or, if fear keeps rising to the surface then why not have a stab at controlling yourself with the latest scary movie on and the lights off?

BOP 3: ADVANCED LKM BOP

Brain Benefits

LKM, as we previously mentioned, promotes the neuroplastic fattening of two gyri of the cortex thought to improve our empathy abilities and regulation of our emotions control. In stark contrast, disorders of the mind such as depression, bipolar disorder and schizophrenia eat away at these gyri. So keep the psychologist at bay as well as master your emotions and feed your relationships with a little bit of love each day!

Researchers who were similarly peeking into the brains of male LKM experts noticed that their brains' response to upset looking people is indeed a pretty picture. Their brains set emotional contagion apart from feelings of compassion, thus preventing being overwhelmed from too much empathy and taking on negative emotions. Another study of LKM, this time in women only, has even indicated that LKM may help decelerate the aging process! LKM makes the protective caps that prevent the ends of your DNA from being chewed up, which keeps your DNA fitter and stronger for longer! Loving makes you live longer!

LKL Level II

In Chapter 1 you familiarized yourself with LKM when learning about self-compassion. Now that we have a better understanding of just how important others are in shaping our brains and lives and you have been developing emotional detection, empathy and compassion, let's take your LKM to the next level.

In your initial LKM based BOP you got familiarized with giving and receiving love to and from a loved one as well as to and from yourself. Now let's try and extend your loving-kindness meditation practices to include someone you don't know well enough to have any strong feelings about, like a store-clerk or your postman. Then we will move onto someone you dislike or that gets on your nerves. Then someone you (at present) feel you resent or have a great deal of animosity towards. Having extended loving-kindness spanning the full spectrum of love-to-hate the BOP comes to a climax in the extension of loving-kindness to all in the world.

Can you remember the three simple phrases you developed for your last LKM. You can use these or formulate new desires if you like. It is the same meditation as before and we will again start with generating feelings of loving-kindness towards someone with whom it feels natural and easy, just to get the ball rolling. Then it's all aboard the compassion train to the final destination: love for all beings.

1.   Breathing & relaxation
Begin with your deep, full, cleansing breaths to open your mind to more slow waves. Take a few minutes to focus and get settled on your breath. If you are feeling in need of it, follow this up with your muscle relaxation BOP for deeper relaxation.

2.   Send desires for your loved one with a kind internal voice & visualization
Begin, with your soft and kind internal voice, to repeat the phrases in your mind and with each positive phrase your mind utters, send those loving desires to your loved one along with the positive warm fuzzy feelings that come as part of the parcel. You can also use the power of visualization here and hold an image of your loved one being enveloped in a love-heart shaped frame, glowing brighter and brighter with warmth and love as you repeat your phrases.

3.   Reflect—how did it feel to give love?
Reflect for a short moment about how you felt about sending loving desires.

4.   Receive desires from your loved one with kind internal voice & visualization
Now the person that you have a loving bond with is going to shower you with the same mantras in return. Immerse yourself in their loving kindness and loving energy as you imagine them repeating the phrases back to you.

5. How did it feel to receive love?
Reflect for a short moment about how you felt about receiving loving desires.

6. Repeat for different kinds of people
Repeat steps 2 to 5 for different categories of people in the following order:

-yourself
-a neutral person
-a disliked or annoying person
-a severely disliked person
-all beings on Earth

HINTS & TIPS

•   As before uncomfortable or unhelpful feelings and bodily sensations may arise. If this occurs, let them be present and don't try to resist it. Just accept the feeling and sensations for what they are, momentary feelings and sensation and ride the wave.

•   **If after many attempts you see little improvement with someone who has become the focus of your love and kindness, explore your feelings and thoughts and see if there are perhaps some limiting beliefs or unnoticed habits that are foiling your good intentions.**

NeuroLogical Brain Training Goals

LOVE, FRIENDS, FAMILY

Notes

Notes

PART III

YOUR BEST COMMUNICATING BRAIN

"Communication is a skill that you can learn. It's like riding a bicycle or typing. If you're willing to work at it, you can rapidly improve the quality of every part of your life."

~ Brian Tracy

Social Neuroscience

Since the 1990s, social neuroscience has clearly broken away from the neuroscience traditionalists who considered the nervous system an isolated entity. We now understand that social interactions have a huge impact on our health and behavior, with our brain central to this relationship. Our brains are far from isolated.

While we might think that we are all alone upstairs, our brains are not only tuning into our environments, but we can also tune into other people's brains too, through social interaction. In essence, social interaction is the communication of information between two or more people and includes two main aspects: one is perceived visually as body language and the other is perceived as sound in speech. The foundations of understanding communication between your brain and that of your acquaintances, loved ones and even enemies lives in the brain of the individual –that's you!

Our Inner Worlds

We all have an inner world tucked away inside our minds where we have mental simulations of everything we know and have experienced. It allows us to make predictions about what might happen next in our environment, a simple example being predicting the chances of a car being on the road from sights and sounds. Your inner world also allows you to visualize anything your mind can muster without there being any physical representation around you. Emerging from birth, and perhaps even in the womb, our inner worlds are formed through repetition, where an action that we perform will become automatically associated with the expected sensory consequences.

Action-Perception Loops

Let's take something simple for example, that plucking a guitar string is associated with the sound of a particular note. A certain action causes you to perceive something predictable, the sound. This also works in reverse. Hearing that same note tells you that you have successfully plucked that particular guitar string. An action, or any stimulus that you perceive with your senses, allows you to predict the events to follow.

Scientists call this an action-perception loop, a real-time loop of information formed between our brains and our environment that allows us to interact with and learn from our environments. The information flow goes as follows: the environment emits sensory signals>sensory systems detect environmental signals (sights, smells, sounds, tastes and physical sensations)>multi-sensory signals are processed to generate our perception (perception: making sense of the signals)>decision and reaction processes occur>motor system response (action: instigates movement of body)>interaction with the environment...and back around again. In short that is: environment > sensory system > information processing > motor system > environ…you get the picture.

Time and Space Travel

Although action-perception loops basics are pretty simple—perceive signal-perform action—these loops form the basis of your dynamic and complex inner world based on your interactions with the real world. Your inner world is magnificent and in some respects your brain views your inner world to be just as real as the real world. If you imagine being chased by a pink elephant riding a donkey, the sensory motor regions of your brain light up just as if you truly were being chased by a pink elephant riding a donkey.

Your inner world also includes simulations of other people, their bodies, beliefs and intentions – an internal soap opera with you in the director's chair. Communication is the conduit for transferring our inner worlds to another person and for others to shape and color our inner worlds with their experiences, without having to experience it yourself. You could say that communication, or at least effective communication is like a teleportation and time travel device all wrapped in one, without the hefty price tag.

Sharing Our Inner Worlds
Inter-Personal Action-Perception Loops

For the formation of our own personal inner world our sensory and motor systems are linked up with our external environment. When we are imagining and envisioning, our sensory and motor systems are linked up with our internal environment. But what happens when more than one brain is involved in the equation and they are communicating with one another?

Well from here on in the knowledge is a little sci-fi in flavor but that's just how amazing our communication skills are. We form a new information based action-perception loop between the motor system of the person conveying the message (action) and the sensory system of the person receiving the message (perception). It is the changes in the environment that are the signals used to transfer the message; either changes in sound (speech) or light (body movement). But in this example the immediate surrounding environment is just a conduit for information. It's not the environment that you are learning about in the conversation, it's the speaker's inner world that is being experienced through your questions and interactions with the speaker.

Let's imagine that you are listening to a story being told by your friend about their recent holiday in Guatemala. You have never been to Guatemala but your friend describes to you their adventures stored up there in their inner world. Your friend's motor system works away to create the speech and body language (action) needed to convey to your senses the hot tamales they had in Guatemala City (environment). Your sensory systems eat up and process this information (perception), which may lead to you asking a question like, 'The guy put the tamales where?!' to interact with and learn more about your friend's inner Guatemalan environment. So instead of the stimulus in the action-perception loop being an inanimate object in your physical environment it comes from the inner world of another brain—mind boggling!

Wireless Communication

It is kind of like a wireless internet system. In such a system, information from the World Wide Web is transformed by the router into radio waves that are picked up by your computer's wireless receiver revealing the information on your screen. Similarly, information from the sender's brain (the World Wide Web) is transformed by their brain's motor systems via their bodies into sound and light waves (the router), which is picked up by the receiver's sensory system (the wireless receiver) to reveal the information within the messenger's mind. Basically, the transmission of information between the brains of two individuals is similar to the transmission of information between two areas of a single brain, the two separate inner world systems become one.

Meaning

The better the communication, the more the activation patterns of one brain is synced up to match the activation patterns in the other brain. However, there are two aspects that will clearly affect how the information is regarded and interpreted and hence how in sync two brains are. The first, which is the crux of and starting point for all communication, is a shared understanding of what is being communicated. For example, if you start waving the American V for victory hand sign about in a Scottish pub your likely to be greeted with a small Glasgow kiss; that is, a swift and unexpected head butt to the face! Believe it or not V for victory is the same as giving the middle finger in the UK—a shared meaning is clearly needed to avoid confusion and a potential black eye.

Context

The second factor that affects how information is interpreted is context. For example, if you were to say 'I'm on fire' in a curry house, you likely mean that the hot and spicy food is tingling away at your taste buds. On the other hand if you were screaming 'I'm on fire' while being, well, on fire, the meaning is likely to be more literal. With a shared understanding and communication in context, it is truly phenomenal how our brains are so intricately linked with one another, sharing experiences, thoughts, feelings, ideas and even our brainwaves, across space and time.

Brain-Brain Synchronization

In brief, two brains couple and share information through inter-personal action-perception loops formed during communication. When this happens our brains make use of brainwaves to sync up their brainwaves to the same beat, influencing equivalent neural networks. What's more is that the more two brains are in tune with one another the better a message is transmitted, the better the communication and the more the activation patterns of one brain is synced up to match the activation patterns in the other brain. To get a clearer picture we have broken down communication into its two main parts, verbal and non-verbal, and explain what we know about what is going on in the brains of two communicating individuals.

Body Language

Body language is the most common form of unspoken face to face (or indeed body to body) communication. From your general posture to hand gestures and facial expressions, this typically subconscious behavior we call body language is like its own form of sign language. Through body language we are able to convey a considerable amount of information, with as little as the flutter of an eyelid or slightest wave of your hand. From an evolutionary perspective body language is the principal form of communication, one that has been advancing our socialization even before we evolved the powers of speech.

Eye Gaze and Facial Expression

One of the most important aspects of body language is a mutual meeting of eyes and facial expressions. The eye gaze not only connects people together and invites joint social attention, but also conveys a whole host of information about a person's attention, interest and intentions. When you ask your neighbor why they are elbow deep picking through trash and they say 'I love the smell of garbage first thing in the morning', a sarcastic glance is more than enough to suggest 'this is a joke, I really don't want to be doing this, it's better you don't ask'. We can get all of that and more from a second or two of glancing at your neighbor's face. Without observing your neighbor's eye movements and facial expression, as well as gestures and body posture, you might begin to believe your neighbor has truly lost their marbles and actually does love the smell of garbage to kick start their day.

Mirroring
Communication Is a Charade

The perfect example of what goes on in the brain when communicating via hand gestures can be found in an experiment based on a game of charades. You know the game? Charades, fun to some and perpetually annoying to others. It's a game in which the players act out and pantomime a word. It is often broken out in awkward social situations in an attempt to get the socializing ball rolling or when power cuts leave us petrified and alone without our household TV.

In the experiment, the charade signaler was hooked up to an EEG while their hands acted out non-verbal clues designed to help the observer guess the correct word. The observer was later hooked up to an EEG and shown a video recording of the hand signals. Using some fancy mathematics the scientists were able to determine that the EEG signals of the two people playing charades were related. So closely related in fact that the charade signaler's brainwaves could, like a weather forecast, predict the response in the observer's brain!

The clue giver and clue receiver had formed an inter-personal action-perception loop that conveyed the signaler's inner world message. Two networks in the charade observer were coupled and synced up by brainwaves to the signaler's motor cortex that controls the signalers hand gestures. One is called the mirror neuron system or MNS in this case found within the observer's motor cortex. While the other network you already know of from chapter one's section on beliefs and habits, it is the ToM or theory of mind network. Without these two networks it would be nearly impossible to communicate and our inner worlds and brains themselves would be very isolated indeed.

What is the MNS?

Studies on Macaque monkeys in the early 1990s uncovered miraculous mirror neurons. Today, scientists believe that "mirror neurons will do for psychology what DNA did for biology"—completely revolutionize and broaden our knowledge and capabilities, marking a new dawn of understanding. These neurons not only fired up when a monkey performed a specific action, such as picking their nose, but also when it observed one of the scientists, who was also picking their nose. Mirror neurons also fire when you know an action is being performed but can't see it. For example you can hear your colleague picking his nose, but can't see through the office cubicle walls. You can't see it physically, but your brain can, lucky you!

Are you one of those people that find nose picking a squeamish thought and it totally grosses you out? You're probably hoping that we change the subject pretty quickly as the firing of your mirror neurons is making the experience seem all too real, you might even feel a little queasy. Apologies!

Where is the MNS?

Not so long ago the MNS was thought to be in parts of the frontal and parietal lobes. However, a recent study pulled together the results from 100s of mirror neuron experiments and revealed that mirror neurons are found all over the brain, from the hippocampus to the cortex to the cerebellum and back. We don't as yet have a solid understanding of the MNS but we are working on it.

Parts of the MNS Are Action Specific

One very clear message from studying the MNS is how activation and firing of specific neurons within the MNS is highly action specific. For example, specific sets of neurons that are related to tongue muscles fire when you hear someone make an 'rrr' sound as opposed to hearing an 'fff' sound. With help from your MNS, you know subconsciously that the speaker had to use their tongue muscles to make that specific 'rrr' sound. Another example is that turning an object around will fire a different set of neurons than those fired when simply picking up an object. The MNS allows for the correct perception of another person's actions by re-enacting them within your own brain.

The MNS and ToM Work Together

We have only recently discovered that the MNS works closely with the ToM network. As you may recall, the ToM network is responsible for attributing beliefs, desires and intents to our own life and making experience based inferences and predictions about the actions, thoughts and desires of others. Working together, the ToM network is thought to truly provide depth and meaning to an accurately perceived and understood action or behavior or emotion picked up by the MNS. While the MNS perceives and categorizes the action, the ToM network figures out the why someone is doing or saying something. If your ToM network goes down, how would you tell the difference between a slap on the back being a friendly part of communication or a conflict provoking act? It is when these networks perform optimally and in synchrony that allows for super effective social interactions.

Two Brains Truly Are Better Than One

There are many examples of situations that require super effective social interaction that primarily involves body language, such as operating a sailing boat, functioning as a team to win in a sporting event, exquisitely coordinated dancing and playing in an awe-inspiring band or orchestra. The amazing thing is that even though these actions can be performed when someone is all on their lonesome, simply performing the actions with others enhances accuracy and success. For example when two pianists synchronize their playing during a duet, the accuracy level exceeds the playing of only two hands coming from a single musician. This is all thanks to their brains' remarkable ability to sync up with other people's brains, to have them performing as one better, faster and stronger brain. Syncing up brainwaves allows for fast and precise information exchange in real-time, both within and between brains.

Brainwaves and Body Language in the Future

So far only a few studies have taken simultaneous recordings of multiple interacting individuals. Brainwave synchronization between individuals has been tested for many different forms of human interaction. Experiments—including comparing brains of people imitating one another, playing a computer game or card game together, playing musical instruments together and even flying a plane together—have all found that we perform better as individuals when our brains sync up with one another.

A very recent EEG experiment of people playing a guitar duet has hinted that lower frequency brainwaves such as delta are much stronger for inter-brain communication within a super, duel-brain network (the two brains behaving as one). While the faster brainwaves like theta on the other hand, are higher in strength within a single brain part of the dual-brain network. However, brainwave synchronization has been found at all frequencies. So this early finding will need to be investigated much further so we can make some clear sense of it all.

Verbal Communication
Theta, the Speed of Speech

All languages go up and down in volume and intensity and have a standard rate for how many syllables we fit into a minute of chatter. For example when it comes to speech, Spaniards are considered to be sprinting as opposed to Chinese people whose syllable rate tends to be more of a stroll. In all cases the changes in volume, intensity and syllable rate all have a frequency of 3-8 Hz, which is the same frequency as the brainwave that is in the verbal communication spotlight, theta. The speech rhythm of the speaker and the theta rhythm in the auditory cortex of the listener sync up.

Out of Sync with Motor-Mouths

Interestingly, when we get over excited or stressed out and speak faster than 8 Hz this actually decreases how well the auditory cortex can sync up with the speech. Have you ever had a colleague, friend or other less likable creature come storming into the situation, rapidly waving their hands and speaking at 10 million miles an hour? You might get the general idea of what is going on—"BOSS...Frak!!...PROJECT... WAN&$! ... HAD ENOUGH OF THIS $#%!"—but the communication systems are being overloaded and your brains are much less likely to sync up. Or, perhaps you have experienced when someone is giving a speech and due to nerves they start off speaking so rapidly it is as if their lives depended on it? If you can recall such a time you will remember that it was difficult to follow the start of the talk, but as the speaker relaxed and the pace of speech became more reasonable it was far clearer to understand and even enjoy.

Upgrading to a High Definition Radio

It also seems that the better you are at listening, the more adapted your brain is to syncing up with the speaker, allowing you to remember more facts and details of stories that you are told. A highly sought after cocktail party skill. In this scenario the speaker is much like a radio station that, using their mouth, is broadcasting an FM show at a station whose frequency is theta. The theta speech waves are picked up by listeners' antennae, their ears. As the listener has pre-tuned into the station, using theta brain waves and matched the frequency of theta speech waves, the speech signal is amplified for better listening.

To further amplify the signal, especially in noisy environments, our brains also sync up to the mouth movements of the other person to help extract more meaningful information from the fuzzy speech signal. What's more is that the more familiar you are with interacting with a person, the easier and quicker it becomes for two 'people' to sync up their brains. And, as always, practice makes perfect. Neuroplastic changes upgrade the signal receiving system in the brain to make us better at listening. Who doesn't like a good listener?

Alpha for Effortless Listening

If you can recall all the way back to the introduction, we mentioned that alpha and theta play tag during verbal communication. Faster brain rhythms in the alpha range (8-13Hz) are also involved in understanding speech. However, the harder it is to understand someone, the more theta waves take over. It seems that alpha waves are activated when listening is effortless. For example if you struggle to hear what is being said and alpha just isn't doing the trick, more theta waves will come to your aid to help your brain hear better.

Anticipation, the Poor Man's Telepathy

There are even parts of the brain that fire up before you hear what is said, that help you predict the speaker's next words. And the more extensive the coupling between a speaker's brain and a listener's anticipatory brain regions, the better we are at understanding what is being said—it's a primitive form of telepathy one might say! Combined with the fact that brain to brain coupling allows us to transmit information through time and space, the human communication system is our own personal superhuman technology.

SUMMARY

- Our brains are at the center of executing and detecting communication in body language and speech.
- An action-perception loop is a real-time loop of information formed between our brains and our environment that allows us to interact with and learn from our environments: environment>sensory system>information processing> motor system>environ...
- Our inner worlds are enriched with real world action-perception loops, allowing our imaginings to literally simulate reality within our brains and minds.
- Communication allows us to form inter-personal action-perception loops where the stimulus in the action-perception loop comes from the inner world of the brain communicating the message.

- Effective communication occurs when the information that is being communicated has a shared meaning between the individuals, is in context and the two individuals brain's activity is synced up.
- **The MNS is a system of specialized neurons that fire both when we perform an action and observe an action being performed by another, allowing for the correct perception of another person's actions by re-enacting them within your own brain.**
- The MNS and ToM network have been shown to sync up to the motor system of an individual conveying a message, in order to detect and apply meaning to the other person's actions.
- Although inter-personal brainwave synchronization has been found at all frequencies, elementary evidence suggests that lower frequency brainwaves such as delta are much stronger for inter-brain communication within a super, duel-brain network, while faster brainwaves are higher in strength for the within a single brain part of the network.
- In speech, changes in volume, intensity and syllable rate all have a frequency of 3-8 Hz.
- **In listening, having the same frequency as speech characteristics, theta brainwaves in the auditory cortex sync up to the speech rhythm of the speaker.**
- The better the auditory cortex-speech rhythm synchronization the more successful the listening is.
- **Alpha waves are stronger the more effortless the listening is. The less detail there is to hear, the more alpha is inhibited and the more theta is amplified to help us make better sense of the message.**
- Inter-personal brain synchronization occurs even before we hear the sound being communicated, the better the synchronization the better we are at understanding the message to come.

Up Next...

It's finally time to teach you the secret for gaining access to other peoples inner worlds. This will strengthen your relationships, boost your brain, health, support and opportunities. Not just with those people you already sync up brainwaves with naturally but even those you don't see eye to eye with. After practicing these BOPs you may see more eye to eye (or brain to brain) than you would ever have thought possible. These BOPs can open up many new doors of opportunity that through miscommunication would otherwise have remained closed to you.

YOUR BEST COMMUNICATING BRAIN
BRAIN OPTIMIZATION PRACTICES

Inner World Communication
Effective Communication

Have you ever instantly gelled with someone that you only just met? You seemed to just hit it off and are on the same wavelength? Well that's because you were! Your brains, and hence your body language and speech were dancing with one another to the same step. When this occurs you are communicating your inner worlds to one another and feel that your inner worlds are being understood.

Ineffective Communication

On other occasions, maybe even with someone you have communicated well within the past, you may somehow get off on the wrong foot, despite mutual kind intentions. The mood gets awkward, something grates someone the wrong way and you just don't seem to get one another. The conversation may ungraciously fizzle out or alternatively might get a touch heated and go out with a bang. Well again, that's because you really did set off on the wrong foot. The way in which your inner worlds were transmitted through body language and speech wasn't effective and so your brains were out of step with one another.

Responses
Golden Nuggets of Opportunity

No matter how someone responds to what you have said, whether your words rang true to them or they awoke the beast, a response is ALWAYS useful feedback. Like we have said with regards to any form of failure, responses in a conversation, both good and bad, are priceless. These juicy chunks of information can reveal how best to respond back if you know how to listen.

Responses in All Shapes and Sizes

Imagine that every time you go to reply to someone the response comes out of your mouth as a colorful plastic shape. You see a response has attributes and features that alter what shape comes out of your mouth such as the speed, tone or word choice and the body language used. Different combinations of attributes make for different shaped responses. It is like our heads have many different shaped holes in them like a small child's shape sorter toy. However, when we are in a particular mood or mode some holes are open, others are closed.

When a response to someone comes from you in a shape that doesn't fit, the information contained in the response will either bounce off completely or have to be squeezed in their heads by force, quite literally rubbing them the wrong way. What if you left all your communication channels open, were able to receive any response and effectively figure out its meaning and finally, generate responses that are eaten up by those you communicate with. This doesn't mean that you always have to agree with other people. The key is that when you disagree, your response sails through the listener's shape sorting holes (or information filters) without even touching the sides!

Our Recipe for Mastering Communication

So how do we learn to keep the communication channels open, well-oiled and flowing without a hitch? To leave every interaction feeling like you have gotten you message across no matter how tricky the customer or testy the situation is? And how do we be that person that gets along with people from all walks of life with ease: " Her/Him! Yeh, he/she is great right? They really listen to you and are always so thoughtful/funny/on the ball/chilled out". Through using BOPs of course:

1. **LEARNING ABOUT RESPONSES**
    To recognize the language used in peoples inner worlds, to hear how they are thinking at the time.

2. **PLAYING WITH RESPONSES**
    To practice using different inner world languages.

3. **MATCHING RESPONSES**
    To match a speaker's body language and inner world language, opening up the channels of communication and getting on the same wavelength.

This is a simple recipe for learning to be a master of communication that translates to face to face interactions as well as written communication, be it a letter, text or email to strangers, friends family and even colleagues in the workplace.

BOP 1: GET IN THEIR HEADS

How We Describe Our Inner Worlds

First things first let's teach you how to recognize the language used in peoples inner worlds. Through picking up both visual and verbal clues you can gleam information about someone's way of thinking at the time. This a key tool for figuring out the best way to communicate effectively and specifically tailor your response to the minds of those you are talking with.

The everyday language we use contains clues as to how we are representing our inner worlds and how we are thinking about the subject matter at hand in our minds. The trick is to get a feel for the three main ways people commonly represent their thoughts in their minds. These three main ways are the three predominant ways we tend to explore the real world with our senses.

See No Evil, Hear No Evil, Feel No Evil

We see, hear and feel (and let's not forget taste and smell) our way through life. As we use sights, sounds and sensations (not forgetting tastes and smells) to gain information about the world and subsequently use the same classes of information to describe our inner worlds, as well as to stimulate the simulation of sights, sounds, sensations, tastes and smells in the minds of those we are communicating out inner world to.

Just as you tend to rely more on some senses that others in the real world (although your BOPs have been training you in using all your senses), we do the same in our inner worlds. You may be more heavily representing your thoughts in pictures and use visual words and phrases in speech; or focus more on sounds and use auditory words and phrases; or focus on your sense of touch and bodily sensations and use kinesthetic words (literally words related to the sensations by which bodily position, weight, muscle tension, and movement are perceived).

It's Not Black and White

While olfactory and gustatory words are also used to convey a message, it is uncommon that someone predominantly perceives and describes the world through taste or smell, with the exception of professional wine tasters and perfumers that is. See the table below for examples of these different kinds of words. While you may lean more heavily on one way of representing your thoughts, it normally involves a combination to varying degrees and can change from situation to situation. So try not to pigeonhole people too much or we may be unwittingly wearing blinders that prevent us from seeing when their style changes.

VISUAL

- Focus
- Vision
- An eyeful
- Appears to me
- Catch a glimpse of

- Clear cut
- Get a scope on
- Hazy idea
- In light of
- In person
- In view of
- Looks like
- Mental picture
- Mind's eye
- Paint a picture
- See to it
- Short sighted
- Sight for sore eyes
- Staring off into space
- Take a peek

AUDITORY

- Ask
- Discuss
- Blabbermouth
- Clear as a bell
- Earful
- Give me your ear
- Heard voices
- Hidden message
- Hold your tongue
- Inquire into
- Loud and clear
- Manner of speaking
- Power of speech
- Purrs like a kitten
- Tattle-tale
- Tongue-tied
- Tuned in/tuned out
- Unheard of
- Utterly
- Word for word

KINESTHETIC

- Grasp
- Exciting
- Boils down to
- Come to grips with
- Cool/calm/collected
- Get a handle on
- Get a load of this
- Get in touch with
- Get the drift of
- Hand in hand
- Hang in there
- Hold on!
- Hothead
- Pain in the neck
- Pull some strings
- Sharp as a tack
- Slipped my mind
- Start from scratch
- Stiff upper lip
- Topsy-turvy

Rationally, the second port of call is to improve our listening skills. To be able to focus on both the what, as well as the how someone is saying something. Thankfully you have been fostering greater powers of attention since you started using our BOPs, which will be of great help here. Once you are familiar with the different styles we use to communicate our inner worlds (see below), then get practicing listening to how people you know tend to communicate their inner worlds using the following BOP.

First try this questionnaire on yourself and then use the following simple BOP to train your listening skills and investigate how others are thinking, perceiving and sharing their experiences. Overtime you will really develop a solid intuitive feel about which combination of communication styles will be most effective for communication with that person.

1. **My first memory is of:**
   a) looking at something
   b) being spoken to
   c) doing something

2. **I feel especially connected to other people because of:**
   a) how they look
   b) what they say to me
   c) how they make me feel

3. **If I have an argument with someone, I am affected most by:**
   a) how they look at you and their body language
   b) the sound of their voice
   c) their emotions

4. **When I operate new equipment I generally:**
   a) read the instructions first
   b) listen to an explanation from someone who has used it before
   c) go ahead and have a go, I can figure it out as I use it

5. **When I am anxious, I:**
   a) visualize the worst-case scenarios
   b) talk over in my head what worries me most
   c) can't sit still, fiddle and move around constantly

6. **When I am choosing a holiday I usually:**
   a) read lots of brochures
   b) listen to recommendations from friends
   c) imagine what it would be like to be there

7. **When I am learning a new skill, I am most comfortable:**
   a) watching what the teacher is doing
   b) talking through with the teacher exactly what I'm supposed to do
   c) giving it a try myself and work it out as I go

8. **When I listen to a band, I can't help:**
   a) watching the band members and other people in the audience
   b) listening to the lyrics and the beats
   c) moving in time with the music

*If you got **mostly A's** you likely have a preference for visual stimulation.*

*If you got **mostly B's** you likely have a preference for auditory stimulation.*

*If you got **mostly C's** you likely have a preference for kinesthetic stimulation.*

From the questionnaire you may have noticed how the way you interact with the world is influenced by the sense/s on which you are focusing on most during the experience. The questionnaire may have also made you think of a friend, partner or family member you think tends to have a certain preference. Let them try the questionnaire and see if your powers of perception are on the money.

Now let's focus on the style of words people use to communicate with you throughout the day. Like when developing any new skill it may be a bit tiring to maintain the level of focus needed, but practice long enough and it will form part of your intuitive, effective communication skill set. It's very simple and much like your emotion detection BOP. So let's clean out your ears and tune in to what people say to you throughout your day.

1. **Focus**
Provide the speaker with your undivided attention.

2. **Sense preference detection**
What kinds of words does the speaker uses? Visual, auditory, kinesthetic, olfactory, gustatory?

3. **Respond**
For now try not to think of how to respond appropriately, just respond as you normally would and get ready to listen to their reply.

HINTS & TIPS

- If you commonly have confidence or concentration issues that leave you with a frog in your throat, you may find that the thinking about what they are saying too much is preventing you from responding properly, which can be a mood and conversation killer. This is a common problem, to begin with. Don't fret. You can train your listening powers behind closed doors by watching people interact in reality TV or a chat show, and pressing pause for your own verbal response. Then after a little virtual training, move on to conversations in real-time.

BOP 2: PLAYING WITH COMMUNICATION

Have you ever been observing two friends as they fail to see eye to eye on a matter, when really they are saying practically the same thing. This is an all too common occurrence for matters both big and small, from how the baby should wear its diaper to how to develop your business or invest your money. Even when two people have very similar and complementary viewpoints they don't seem to hear one another as their style of communication is different at the time. To become a master communicator you need to be able to change your dominant style of communicating to match that of the person you are speaking with, with grace, skill and ease. How do we do that? BOPs. BOPs, BOPs and more BOPs!

You can use this next technique for a visualized conversation that is real or fictitious, occurring in the future or the past or ultimately during real world conversations. Whichever you feel most comfortable with at first. If you don't feel ready to jump into real world conversations you can practice this with a video of dialog by pressing pause and stepping in and responding appropriately.

1. **Focus**
Provide the speaker with your undivided attention.

2. **Word and phrase preference detection**
What kinds of words does the speaker use? Visual, auditory, kinesthetic, olfactory, gustatory? Take notice of commonly used words and phrases.

3.   Respond
Make your response fit those holes in the speakers head. Ask clarifying questions and restate what you perceive the speaker to be
saying. Make use of their use of words and phrases.

BOP 3: MAKING CONNECTIONS

Now let's put your new listening and speaking skills together with your
keen observational skills and get knocking heads and syncing up brainwaves
as you make stronger and deeper connections with everyone you encounter
in life.

1.   Focus
Provide the speaker with your undivided attention, let distracting
thoughts and self-reflective tendencies float away just as if you
were focusing on your breath.

2.   Matching body language
Adopt a similar posture as they are talking and look out for gestures. With visually inclined people this will help greatly. Paying
attention to facial expressions are particularly important with
kinesthetic individuals as it is a key route for communicating
emotions.

3.   Matching breath
If someone is breathing more rapidly than you normally would
and breathing with their upper chest, up the tempo, if it's slower,
deeper and more from the belly, crank it down a notch.

4.   Matching tonality and speed of speech
It's not what you say it's how you say it. Match the tone and speed
of speech. This is particularly helpful with those with a preference
for an auditory stimulus. As tonality of voice is a common way to

convey emotion, tonality is particularly relevant to the kinesthetically inclined.

5.   Word and phrase preference detection
What kinds of words does the speaker use? Visual, auditory, kinesthetic, olfactory, gustatory? Take notice of commonly used words and phrases. Prepare to respond to the emotion with appropriate tonality and body language as well your choice of words.

6.   Respond
Make your response fit those holes in the speakers head. Ask clarifying questions and restate what you perceive the speaker to be saying. Make use of their use of words, phrases, body language, tonality and speed of speech to help build rapport.

7.   Hush
Don't feel you must have an immediate reply. Often if you allow for some quiet after a pause in speech, they themselves will break the silence.

HINTS & TIPS

•   Take time to reflect about what is important to the people in your life. These are good lines of conversation to have with others. Try talking about what interests other people. Not necessarily what you find interesting, just because you find it so, it doesn't mean that anyone else will.

•   **Another vital component of successful communication is observing how someone likes to receive information. Do they like lots of little details or like things explained short and simple or perhaps they prefer hearing about the bigger picture.**

•   From paying such keen attention to others' words you will find you can more accurately guess the underlying aim or intention someone has when they say something. If what they say is negative, bear in mind that everything we say has a positive intention at the root of it all. Even if their behavior is considered bad the person may get a 'benefit' from it. For example the positive intention behind name calling may be a way for the name caller to feel less vulnerable.

•   If this is all too much too soon. Break it down. Just like when you focused solely on the listening or the speaking part of communication in BOPs 1 and 2. Similarly, why not train your visual perception and get that skill feeling more habitual, by paying attention to and matching body language only. With another attempt try only to match your breathing during the conversation. Or similarly focus only on matching the tone and speed of your voice. Then try to match the various forms of communication in unison, keep introducing another communication behavior for you to match until you feel you can easily incorporate them all.

NeuroLogical Brain Training Goals

COMMUNICATING BRAIN

Notes

Notes

CHAPTER IV:
FOCUSING ON SUCCESS

"I do not think there is any thrill that can go through the human heart like that felt by the inventor as he sees some creation of the brain unfolding to success...such emotions make a man forget food, sleep, friends, love, everything."

~Nikola Tesla

Part I

EXPANDING CREATIVITY

"There is no doubt that creativity is the most important human resource of all. Without creativity, there would be no progress, and we would be forever repeating the same patterns."

~ Edward de Bono

Understanding Creativity
What is Creativity?

The philosophical take and various understandings of creativity are the subject of many a good book. We will certainly touch on some of these points as we go. But for us to truly understand it, let's start with a sound, basic explanation. Put simply creativity is how we combine elements of thought and of action together in a way that is useful and fulfills the requirements needed to fit the creative idea's purpose. The further apart or loosely connected the thoughts are for generating the creative idea and the creative idea perfectly suiting its purpose, makes an idea all the more creative.

We are Creativity
It Shapes Our Lives

You may safely say that creativity is the architect of human civilization. All our progress and innovation depends on the use of imagination or original ideas to create something new, the product of creativity. Without creativity, we would be stuck in the dark ages depending purely on random luck to miraculously invent modern marvels like space travel, nano-technology or even something as creatively simplistic as your average household toaster—my bets are we would be waiting a looong time!

It Invents the Future

However, creativity is not just a magical, mysterious phenomenon, restricted to profound inventions and producing famous works of art. Creativity is an eminent component of our everyday lives. We can be creative in how we convey and discuss ideas with ourselves and one another, when tapping out a drum beat on the dashboard on your way to work, improvizational cooking in the kitchen, with how we get down on the dance floor, doodling, crafting your weekly schedule, paying your bills or writing a witty text message or Facebook post.

Anything and everything is subject to the creative process! Whether we are raising a child, planning a party or helping a friend work out their problems, creativity is part of how we as humans operate, be it in generating novel ideas or solutions to problems, or in expressing our individuality. Take a look around you for a moment. Every man made thing that you see—EVERYTHING—was once just a thought or idea in someone's creative imagination. EVERYTHING!

A Creative Conundrum

Creativity is such a vital component of our existence. Yet exactly how we problem solve and create with an innovative or novel outlook is poorly understood. As with all these fundamental questions in life such as, "What is love?", "What and where is consciousness?" and "Where does creativity come from?", the meanings of the key words (love, creativity and consciousness) are so all encompassing and subjective that simply defining what they are is a complex task.

Thanks to creativity fueling the development of new technologies and new ways of thinking we are finally at the foothills of understanding such far reaching and subjective concepts like love, consciousness and creativity, with neuroscience spearheading the journey. We are living in truly enlightening times.

Creativity Data on the Brain

Understanding our creativity and more importantly, related issues such as "How we can become more creative?", are tricky riddles to solve, especially when looking into your brain! We can't just shove anyone into a brain scanner and say, "Now be creative!" Similarly we can't expect the creativity required to paint the Mona Lisa will be exactly the same in the brain as developing a mathematical algorithm, as the tasks themselves are completely different. In the past few decades there has been a magnificent upload of neuroscientific data on creativity that (due to the many complexities inherent to the study of creativity) paint a complex yet intriguing picture.

Solving Creativity with Creativity

Researchers, like Arne Dietrich have remarked that, "It is high time that researchers became more creative about creativity". Now that we are beginning to creatively approach the study of creativity, a paradigm shift is underway, with a glimpse of the true face of creativity in the brain finally beginning to emerge. The use of innovative experiments includes tackling the scientific challenges of studying creativity outside of the lab in the real world.

Also by using the current data we can define the many flavors of creativity in more intricate detail and standardize criteria for studying them so that we can make revealing comparisons. Getting scientifically creative with out of the box thinking is forging a new understanding of our most valuable asset to success in life, our creativity! Using creativity, to understand creativity and unveil the best ways for us to enhance our creativity.

Components of Creativity

One way of looking at creativity's many forms and solving data related scientific dilemmas is to divide creative experiences into more comparable groups. The three main classes of creative thought and action are thinking processes used to problem solve and come up with novel ideas: artistic expression in music, dance and the arts; and insight, those eureka moments where a creative idea seems to burst forth out of nowhere.

While comparing these different kinds of creativity, both within and between the three classes, a general consensus is emerging. There is not as yet a special home or brainwave for creativity or its subtypes in the brain. Instead it's the goings on at the level of neural networks that ties together all forms of creativity and holds the key to harnessing the truly miraculous powers of creative thought.

Creativity in the Brain
Where is Creativity in the Brain?
Dispelling with Old Ideas

Studying creativity in the brain is a creative conundrum! There is a long history of studying creativity in the brain and as such, it has its own fair share of erroneous brain myths. You may have heard that the right hemisphere is the seat of creative thinking? It's actually a modern myth of learning that arose from the split-brain experiments of the 1960's, sounds catchy, and so this misnomer is still haphazardly thrown into the creativity debate.

As you may have gathered, complex brain processes such as creativity and its brain ability opposite, rational in the box thinking, are both whole brain phenomenon. When they occur many regions all over the brain are active, there is no one hemisphere or one singular bit of the brain solely responsible for creative thinking. We may in the future identify specific brain areas with specific functions in the creative processes, but this endeavor will require more of that creativity solving creativity for fine-grained analytical experimentation.

Welcoming New Ideas
Cognitive Contradictions

Creativity it seems, perhaps even more than with love, is not set in stone in the brain. The myriad of possible brain activation and deactivation patterns that allow for creative thinking is reflective of the varied and complex ability that is creativity. Creativity involves many cognitive processes including working memory, defocused yet sustained attention and mental flexibility while still maintaining cognitive control—there is clearly a fine balance of contradictory abilities that nurtures creative thought.

Creativity is a Balancing Act

Imagine you are an inventor and you have been asked to create a must have product that uses 1 million units of rocks, that's right, just rocks. If you are too zoned out it is difficult to be focused on the topic enough and if you are too focused on the topic it doesn't allow you the mental space to think outside of the box. If you are too flexible in thinking, the design will lose its purpose. Perhaps this lends itself as to why we bump into mental blocks to our creative potential; when we upset this intricate balance of networks too much. And FYI, in the 70s an inventor did make multimillions out of a pile of rocks, he invented the Pet Rock!

Neuroplasticity
Nature vs. Nurture

Creativity clearly influences neuroplasticity and the effects of neuroplasticity in the brain clearly affect how creative we are. Many studies have compared the creatively gifted with the creative norm to identify which regions of the brain are more neuron rich in creatives. At the same time, some of these beefed up regions of the brains in super creatives such as artists, musicians, inventors and comedians, will be a direct result of repeatedly turning to creative thought. Other daily practices that at the face of it seem unconnected to creativity may also affect a part of the brain useful for creativity. Some of us also have creativity boosting genes that influence the neuroplastic shaping of a highly creative brain. Creativity is clearly a complex case of nature versus nurture.

Neuroplastic Fattening

Employing a broad range of cognitive function means that creative thought is associated with increases and also decreases in grey matter (and white matter, see 'White Matters' below) all over the brain. Neuroplastic changes throughout the whole brain have an impact on creativity: from the midbrain sitting atop of the brain stem that relays auditory and visual information; to the multifunctional subcortical striatum involved in both planned and habitual thought and movement; as well as a specific area of the frontal lobe that is hyper connected to the thalamus and hippocampus in planning, organizing and regulating thought. A common theme is that regions of the brain that are information highways and are highly specialized for processing and relaying information around the brain impart greater creative abilities.

Neuroplastic Thinning

Conversely, there are bits of the brain that are also neurologically diluted in more creative people. One clear example is the less dense parts of the frontal lobe involved in signaling the expected reward or punishment associated with an idea or action. It would make sense to be able to judge your thoughts less and allow for more creative flow—think first and judge later.

Nonetheless, the list of different brain areas that are tuned up or tuned down that aid creativity are all over the brain and we are likely to discover many more similarly affected areas as research continues. Moreover this highlights the fact that regions all over the brain are employed, as well as inhibited, for creativity, depending on what we are being creative for.

Creative Brainwaves and Brain Regions
Frontal Alpha's Role Is Clearest

Creativity is similarly promiscuous in its use of brainwaves, as it is with the regions of the brain that are activated for our creative thinking and doing. Even the classifications of divergent thinking and problem solving, artistic expression and eureka moments show much variety in scientific data depending on the specific creative task at hand. One thing is clear that the use of alpha waves in the creative process, particularly their synchronization, is pretty important.

In artistic expression and divergent thinking alpha synchronization in the frontal lobe is commonly reported. By slowing down and relaxing the work of your frontal lobe this allows for freer interplay with different networks in the brain, allowing us to meander through our mental landscape and link more loosely connected ideas. This is opposite to intelligent convergent thinking where we want to take the fastest route to the most logically connected piece of information.

Alpha Desynchronization and Other Waves

You certainly need more intelligent like convergent thinking to push a creative idea or seed of an idea forward in your mind, to prod and poke it and see if it suits before continuing on with the creative process. This is likely why there are also reports of alpha power decreases and desynchronization, particularly for those eureka moments of creative insight. The picture is even less clear for other waves, but beta and gamma boosts seem to be reported more often in tasks that require more focus.

Similarly more beta desynchronization is reported for tasks that are more mind wandering heavy. Delta, whose hunting grounds tend to be in the more primal subcortical and subconscious neighborhoods, likely has roles in using your mind to paint creative pictures, presumably allowing you to dip into your memory bank to fuel such imaginings. Delta may have other roles when memory is involved. What we can safely conclude at the moment is that when it comes to creativity, different networks are operating with different brainwave frequencies, helping the defocusing and focusing required to nurture creativity.

Rap Battling May Hold the Key
A Relaxing Task

Researchers have gone the eighth mile and possibly found the key to understanding creativity in a brand new study of creativity in rappers. Freestyle rap, where a rapper improvises with unrehearsed lyrics is a masterful skill highly prized in the hip-hop scene and a shining example of creativity in action. In the experiment, they compared brain scans of rappers when they are being creative and improvising, with when they are repeating memorized lyrics. What they found was that one region of the frontal lobe that is part of the DMN (your default mode network employed for internalized thought and mind wandering) was activated, while another part of the frontal lobe that is part of the TPN (your task positive network employed for focusing on getting a job done) was deactivated when improvising.

Network Interplay

These simultaneous deactivations and activations are thought to relax your executive functions enough to allow you to defocus your attention for expansive yet directed creative thought. This has lead to the conclusion that the interplay between the DMN and the TPN is key to acquiring the contradictory forces that allow our mind to wander the realms of possibility (divergent thinking to discover and expand thought), while still maintain the focusing powers to direct the creative flow towards the desired outcome (convergent thinking to define and consolidate thought).

This network interplay would explain why alpha waves sometime flood the frontal lobe and other regions in one creativity experiment and not in another. Similarly this is why some studies see activations and others deactivations in the same regions of the frontal lobe (and other regions) depending on the type of creative task at hand. Does freestyle abstract painting of love require the same kind and consistency of cognitive focus as an off-the-cuff freestyle rap or improvised jazz piece on love? Unlikely!

Dopamine, Reward, Love and Salience

Other main parts of the brain activated during the creative process are within the salience network and dopamine system in the brain including the ACC, the insula and striatum that are also associated with love. Salience refers to trapping an object or idea in our mental spotlight and incorporating it into our thoughts and behaviors. The salience network is associated with dopamine in focus and attention switching, and in processing goal directed behavior. These regions are also lovey dovey brain regions and are thought to control the interplay between the TPN and DMN (as found in other studies on network interplay outside of the rapping scene). The more their creativity grows, the better control they would have over this switching process, with clear network links to passion and drive!

You wonder why the stereotype of a troubled youth that turns to rap or any other creative art form, becomes madly passionate about their new creative love in life, proclaiming that they have finally found something rewarding in life and learn to regain control of their focus and drive. By being more creative, the associated neuroplastic changes can help with other network functions in the brain. Expect a continued flood of creativity research which should allow us to further explore these concepts and learn how best to un-lock our powers of creativity.

Connectivity within the Creativity Network
White Matter Matters

If you start making creative thought a regular practice you can make the creative process a more natural and easy state to achieve. Why? Because the white matter of the creativity circuits get denser. This thickening of the axons and heavy coating of myelin helps speed up the connectivity between these brain regions. Interestingly the more creative you are the more the white matter of the corpus callosum thickens, giving you a faster set of tracks to navigate about your brain with.

This bestows the ability to have diverse hemispheric brain activation and more efficiently integrate information across the hemispheres, to coordinate the diversity in cognitive functions needed for expansive and creative thought and action. However, certain regions of the corpus callosum, such as the sple-nium that connects the parietal and occipital lobe, are known to be less dense in creative characters. The impaired connectivity in the case of the splenium, is thought to alter how we think in the visible space within our minds eye, allowing for creative mental explorations of visual imagination. When it comes to the matter of creativity, we will have to investigate why all matter matters to get a better picture.

Mad Man or Creative Genius?

Lower white matter density in some regions, as well as brain activation of dopamine affected brain regions that are associated with creative individ-uals, has striking similarities with patients with psychosis. In creatives and those suffering from psychosis, having loads of receptors for dopamine in your thalamus is thought to impede the filtering of information as it is trans-mitted onto the cortex for processing. With people with schizophrenia for example this leads to being overwhelmed with thoughts and disorganized thinking.

The capacity to think about many things at once however is also integral to creative thought. The difference with creativity is that it requires getting positively focused and re-routing these thoughts in reality. Yet if we attach meaning to any random wandering thought our ideas may be considered that of a madman! We all know of, or perhaps even know, people that have been highly creative yet troubled with mental health issues. Take Vincent Van Gogh for example. He may have created exquisite and masterful pieces of art, but lopping off your ear and gift wrapping it for your favorite prostitute is not exactly the healthiest manifestation of creativity!

SUMMARY

- The many uses of creativity and different kind of creative experiences (divergent thinking, creative expression and moments of insight), as well as the subjective nature of creativity assessment, are part of the many reasons that studying creativity in the brain is challenging.
- **Creativity is a whole brain process, with effective creative thinking being a fine balance between many different and sometimes contrasting cognitive functions.**
- When enhanced by neuroplasticity, structures that are information highways specialized for processing and relaying information around the brain, such as the thalamus, midbrain and striatum, impart greater creative abilities.
- **Deactivations and the resultant negative impact on neuroplasticity in some brain regions, include parts of the frontal lobe that assess reward and punishment, allowing for uninhibited thoughts and ideas.**
- Frontal lobe relaxation and excitation through enhancing or inhibiting alpha waves in the frontal lobe may support the expansion (divergent) and contraction (convergent) of thought required to develop creative ideas.
- **Improvisation (in rap and jazz at least) activates part of our DMN network and deactivates a part of the TPN network, both in the frontal lobe, which is thought to reflect relaxing your executive functions to allow for flow of creative thought.**
- Future studies will investigate the interplay between the DMN and TPN and our ability to integrate and switch between them as

well as the role played by the salience network and dopamine in controlling this interplay.

•   **White matter density increases in the corpus callosum (allowing for greater interhemispheric communication) and decreases (that alters the flow of information in certain regions) imparts powers of creativity.**

•   Differences in white and grey matter as well as changes to the neurochemical dopamine signaling in the brain are highly similar in both creative individuals and those that struggle to turn off a more creative-esk disorganized divergent way thinking in conditions such as schizophrenia and psychosis.

Up Next...

It's about time we stop using the word creativity and start getting our hands dirty. You will be pleased to find out in the following pages that all this learning about creativity in the brain may actually give you an extra creative edge.

EXPANDING CREATIVITY
BRAIN OPTIMIZATION PRACTICES

Creativity Training
You were BOPing and You Didn't Even Know It

The unlimited potential of creative thinking supports creativity's exalted value as a skill for improving all aspects of modern life. Being of such high value, there are well established training courses for creativity training. One clear message from scientific research on creativity training course participants is that their success crucially depends on developing a sound knowledge of creative thinking. Many studies have shown that if you were to go on such a course your creativity would definitely increase. But it is the latest study that is the real shocker. If you introduce the neuroscience of creativity into your understanding, you double your powers of creative thinking—at least when it comes to divergent thinking tasks. So simply by learning about the brain and creativity you have already been enhancing your creative potential, once you get BOPing that is.

Learning, Believing, Practicing, Acting

To make your creative potential a creative reality we need to do a little more than just learn. Firstly, limiting beliefs can be a fly in the ointment when trying to enhance creativity (see BOP 1). Secondly, you need to practice putting your neuroscience based knowledge on creativity into action (see BOP 2). Lastly, real world practice is what harnessing these creative powers is all about, so you need to get exploring with how you perform in the field (see BOP 3).

BOP 1: LIMITING BELIEFS

Let us put first things first. You may never enhance your creativity if you if you have a parasitic belief sucking away all your creative juices. So let us make things clear from the get go: you all have creative potential, can encourage greater creativity and you are creative with many things already even if they seem mundane. Have you ever heard someone saying "Well, you know, I was never any good at art or music in school, I'm just not a creative person". Or "I just don't know how to be creative, you either have it or you don't". In reality even the most basic choices we make in life involve divergent thinking as well as convergent thinking. Whether it's deciding what to wear, to buy, say or to literally do anything, at some point or other we think outside the box, even if it's just a little.

Take the time to think if you have this kind of limiting belief, especially if you think you can ONLY be creative at one thing, thats a limiting belief too!

Return to Chapter 1's BOP section on beliefs and habits and break down those negative beliefs and unleash your creativity.

BOP 2: PRACTICING SWITCHING NETWORKS

Let's practice putting your neuroscience based knowledge on creativity into action. You know that different kinds of tasks use creative, rational and logical brain processes to varying degrees and that creativity comes in many forms and flavors. And you also know that one of the keys to mastering creative thinking is in utilizing components of both DMN and TPN networks to stimulate expansive creative thought.

We use divergent thinking and the DMN to make loose associations between the object of your creative thought and all other things that float about in your mind. This is great for discovering and exploring new ideas. This line of thinking however, is pointless without convergent thinking and the TPN to focus on ideas that are useful and constructive for your purposes and to further define them. DMN activity is again needed if you want to improve an idea be it an expressive painting, invention or tonight's dinner. While convergent thinking will again be required to refine the improvement and fill in the details. So let's get practicing expanding and contracting our thinking focus in this simple, rigorously tested and infamous divergent thinking BOP.

Write down as many uses as you can for a brick in 5 minutes using the following technique. It is worth keeping a note of the number you get and to change the object each time you practice this BOP. Practicing this daily or every couple of days will help hone the networking switching required in virtually all forms of creativity. Remember that divergent thinking is an expansive process that we use to lead us towards novel ideas, and convergent thinking is a process of focusing a line of thought, leading it to usefulness.

1. **Convergent thinking**
Rattle out the obvious ones that first come to your head.

E.g. Build a house.

2. **Creative thinking**
Now expand your thinking. A nice trick here is to take a deep breath and relax. If a random thought doesn't pop in that is useful to you (insight) start thinking of something that on the face of it has nothing to do with a brick and that should get you started. A single word is more than enough to get the cogs turning (see below). Then as different thoughts come to you try and make a connection with a brick. If the next thought that comes into your head doesn't stimulate an idea, then move along. Remember it's a

timed BOP. Or, just think of literally anything that an object, person or any living creature does. Then see if you can think of a use for the brick in that setting. Just let your mind wander through the infinite possibilities.

E.g. Swimming>water>BOAT aha tie some rope to it and it could be the weight of an ankor. NEXT! France>Paris>PLASTER OF PARIS aha crush up the brick and make mortar out of it.

3. Convergent thinking
Have convergent thinking processes at the ready to pluck out those initial seeds of thought that show potential as shown in the example above. BOAT and PLASTER OF PARIS are the initial creative starting points.

4. Convergent cont.
Are there any more logically connected uses to the novel use you just came up with—convergent thinking? Define more possible uses that seem like a logical extension to your last idea

5. Repeat
Repeat steps 2-4 as many times as you can in the time available.

BOP 3: REAL LIFE CREATIVE THINKING

1.   Get creative

For now all you have to do is pick three random aspects of your day tomorrow and try and be more creative with them by exploiting switching thinking styles. Your cup of coffee in the morning? Your afternoon jog? Quite literally absolutely anything. And in the next section we will ask you to use your reinvigorated powers of creativity to truly get what you want in life and help you achieve your goals. Make it a point to practice creative out of the box thinking for both the mundane and the grandiose.

HINTS & TIPS

•   It is worth considering your physical environment as well as your mental environment. If you are stuck in a rut, a relaxing environment (cue bathroom) and your relaxation BOPs should help. However, there is far more to it than that. There have been many studies into what makes for a creativity stimulating environment. Simple things such as the observing the color blue when trying to be creative and observing red can make a difference to our creativity. It seems that blue boosts creativity, while red has a more profound effect on making us pay more attention to the details. Other studies have also indicated that the noise level around you influences your thinking processes. Too loud or too quiet music isn't the best for performing some creativity tests, while a moderate level of music is better. Experiment and get creative with your environment and see what works best for you. You find a certain color really stimulates your thinking, decorate you office with the color. Play with lighting, shapes, textures...have fun!

•   **Relaxation and mediation are pretty helpful in getting access to those alpha waves needed for uninhibited divergent thinking when you are stuck in a rut and aren't making enough ease of access to creativity promoting DMN action.**

•   Speak to people that know next to nothing about a problem you are trying to solve or anything you are trying to approach creatively. They may give you some atypical ideas to fuel your creative thought and lead you down a line of thinking you may never have touched on.

NeuroLogical Brain Training Goals

CREATIVITY

Notes

Notes

Part II

GOALS & DREAMS— THE NEW PATH

"You are never too old to set another goal or to dream a new dream."

~ C.S. Lewis

Where Are The Secrets Of Goal Success?
Success vs. Failure
The Stuff Dreams are Made Of

Can you remember what you wanted to be when you grew up? A doctor? An explorer? A policeman? A ballerina? We have been dreaming of bigger and better things since we were knee high to a grasshopper. For some of us, making dreams a reality is a piece of cake; while some have never been good at knowing what they want. Others dream away to their heart's content, getting nowhere fast. And, a very sad bunch of us have given up on achieving our goals altogether.

You've Had The Secret All Along...

So what is it that separates achievers from non-achievers? Having money? Connections? Good looks? Even a drop dead gorgeous billionaire who's best friends with the Queen of England may never achieve his true goals in life. While someone who is less than blessed in the looks department, has less than two cents to rub together, and has been living like a hermit half their life can do a 360° and become a dream-pursuing success story seemingly overnight. Well inadvertently, or through being well informed, some of us use how the brain deals with goals in their favor, while others make the repetitive mistakes that wire the brain for failure. You have had the secret to success all along, your brain! You just need to learn how to use it to your advantage. It's really that simple.

How Do We Best Set and Achieve Goals?
There are Many Answers In the Brain

Some practices keep your brain on target, helping you inch closer to success. Other practices keep your brain forever toiling to reach your targets, gradually killing off your confidence and motivation to seek what you truly desire. The way in which we deal with our goals in life can make or break us. Some types of goal setting are even known to lead us to and perpetuate depression and other mental nasties. One example is unrealistic conditional goal setting. I think we can safely say that at some point or other in life we have been guilty of negative conditional goal setting.

One Example: Get Real!

What is unrealistic conditional goal setting? "I can only be happy if I have a nice car, fancy mobile, clean house, good-looking spouse..." Put simply, to achieve a greater goal such happiness, we have directed our focus towards superficial means goals that may or may not result in happiness. Sadly to say this all too common way of thinking is also a classic hallmark of depression. What strategic, logical, tried and tested process was used to connect an honorable and highly important end goal like happiness with these kind of jumped up, nonsensical and superficial intermediary goals? Our sources say...there wasn't a logical strategy. And herein lies the problem. But by taking a peak into the brain we can learn the secrets of how best to set and achieve our life's ambitions.

Goals in the Brain
Our Dreams Are Already Achieved
Personally Attached

What is a goal to your brain? As you well know your inner world is pretty real to your brain and how you live in your inner world affects how you deal with the real outer world. Well the same goes for goals. Goals and dreams, no matter how large or small, are actually seen by parts of the ToM network as something that makes you you. Our dreams and hopes in life are very much real and a part of us in our minds. Have you ever come up with a potential idea for a goal in life that you shared with your friend who in some way or another lets you know that they think your idea is pretty bogus? How did you react? Like it was nothing? Or like your friend turned around, kicked you in the shins, pointed at you and shouted "fugly, fugly, fugly"!?

Keeping it Real

It's hard not to take the criticism of our dreams to heart. Or should that be, to the brain? This is partly why we feel motivated to fulfill this internal, dream molded vision of ourselves. The contradictory juxtaposition of our inner world reality (you're dream is real) and outer world reality (you're dream is unachieved), creates a tension within us that makes us crave to make our inner world dreams an outer world reality. The 'realness' of our goals is also why failing to achieve them can feel so tragic, like we have lost something that already existed, or a part of our potential. It can feel so heartbreaking that it can scare us into avoiding our life's dreams altogether.

Risk vs. Reward

We dream up an idea and become attached to it as a goal in life by assessing it's achievability, what the risks involved are and does the reward that we seek outweigh the potential risks. We do this for both the tiniest goal to the most profound. You dream up the idea to have breakfast and once you weigh out the advantages and disadvantages of popping out for an all you can eat fried breakfast against staying home, you become attached to an idea. It becomes a goal. You may in the end feel the motivation to eat a piece of fruit for breakfast, as it prevents the risk of an empty wallet, being late for work and gaining a few extra pounds. You can learn loads more about mastering risk taking and using it to your benefit in the next section.

Love and Our Goals Are Much the Same
All Over the Brain

Words like attachment, reward and motivation may be bringing back recent memories of Chapter 3's section on love. Well it should. How we hold both goals and people important to us in our minds are surprisingly similar and involve many similar areas and chemicals in the brain. As you may have suspected, there is not one single brain structure responsible for dreaming up our aims in life and setting out as intended. Instead, how we approach our hopes and desires involves the brainwave coordinated action of many regions of the brain.

Execution, Memory, Guts and Emotion

Clearly, decision making is involved in goal setting and parts of your frontal lobe are roped in. Researchers have found that activity in the frontal lobe related to your working memory (and alpha wave activity) is needed to update a goal we have in mind with any new information we find out about that goal. The 'gut feeling' producing part of the cortex, the insula, as with love, is also active when dealing with our goals. Another expected player in the goal setting game is our emotional circuitry and memory. You have been working on your frontal lobe activity, emotional circuitry and improving your memory when practicing our BOPs. You see? You have been preparing your brain for setting life altering goals all along.

Setting Goals in the Striatum
Achievement Bonus!

One of the brain areas that has been prodded and poked the most when it comes to our goals and desires is the striatum. As you well know the striatum is a multifunctional structure that is involved in the formation of habits and in dopamine signaling and feeling a sense of reward. The striatum has specific sets of neurons that are activated differently depending on whether the bonuses you receive for achieving a goal are in the near future or if you will have to wait to see the benefits.

Big Goal, Long Wait, Big Bonus!

The bigger the bonus the higher the activity is in your delayed benefits neurons, presumably making it more rewarding to go after your long-term goals. The important thing to note here is that the brain treats different kinds of goals and rewards differently. Moreover, if we have far-reaching goals and dreams (which we all should!), the bigger the bonus we make for achieving that goal, the bigger the activity will be in the striatum and so the greater the motivation and will-power you experience will be. Moreover, the striatum's multiple roles in goal setting, reward and habit formation hints at how success or failure can equally become forces of habit.

Getting Things Done Gets You High
Addicted to Success Too!

You have already discovered that dopamine is a desirable neurotransmitter that creates pleasant feelings and keeps us focused, or even obsessed with an idea, person or event. It has roles in our loving relationships, creativity as well as goal setting and taking risks (see the next section). Low and behold dopamine is integral to all those wonderful feelings you get with the sense of accomplishment that comes with achieving your goals and desires.

You Need Pleasure for Performance

A lack of dopamine is part of the nasty wash of feelings we get when we experience failure to achieve our goals and desires, which if left unchecked, manifests itself in anxiety, guilt, worthlessness and fear. Loss of your one true love and loss of that goal that your brain thinks is part of you are both associated with cutting off the dopamine drip. In both instances it feels as if you are losing an extension of yourself. You're cut off from pleasure and left with the pain. And so, as a person can relentlessly go after love, they can similarly refuse to fail when going after their goals and dreams, no matter how many times they are rejected or put down.

SUMMARY

- Having a brain based goal setting and achieving strategy provides the resources and flexibility required to successfully achieve your goals and dreams in the most direct manner possible.
- **Brain based goal setting requires that we distinguish clearly between our means and end goals (see more in the next BOP section).**
- The juxtaposition between the 'realness' of our goals in our minds and the reality that we haven't achieved them yet is what motivates us to go for them. On the flip-side this juxtaposition can make failure feel like a tragedy.
- **Risks and reward related brain circuitry is involved in the process of setting and trying to achieve our goals, with important roles for dopamine (see more in the next section).**
- Goal setting activity includes: frontal lobe activity in decision making and updating goals with new information, striatum activity in reward evaluation, insula activity in signaling gut feelings, brain structures associated with emotion and memory also influence goal related processing.

Up Next...

Goal setting is integral to directing yourself along the path to success. Granted some of those that aimlessly wander through life can also be successful, however, their numbers are far fewer. Why? Because it's far easier to wander through the sea of bad goal setting practices than to randomly stumble upon a perfect recipe for goal setting success. Similarly there are people that continually set goals yet still seem to walk through life backwards! Why? You can set goals all you want to no avail. Healthy goal setting BOPs are the logical alternative— goal setting practices that make goal achievement habitual and carve a positive use out of the word failure.

GOALS & DREAMS—THE NEW PATH
BRAIN OPTIMIZATION PRACTICES

Goal Setting With Your Brain
In a Nutshell

Taking all that goal related information into account, how should you work with your mind to maximize the benefits of goal setting? And how do you avoid the negative spiral devoid of dopamine that can come from failure? Which is well worth avoiding as it can lead to depressive thinking, senseless pleasure seeking and an aversion to seeking what you deserve in life. It's simple. Play by your brain's rules and set goals your brain likes!

BOP 1: USING MEANS TOWARDS YOUR END

By collecting many little wins (baby steps) along the way to achieving a monumental goal (no matter how big) we will sufficiently fuel ourselves with regular bursts of dopamine. These little bursts of joy will keep you motivated and focused on the task at hand. It was Martin Luther King, Jr. that once said, "Faith is taking the first step even when you don't see the whole staircase."

But the route to success is seeing all the steps on the staircase and acknowledging that each step towards their successful fulfillment is a mini-win to boost you along the way. We can dream big and have an ultimate end goal, but if you truly want to achieve it, break the journey to success down into mini-steps that your brain loves. The key to creating your own cycle of pleasurable productivity is to set a grand vision and work your way there with a few, achievable goals that increase your likelihood of experiencing a positive outcome.

Don't forget that you can also utilize the mind altering powers of rewards to influence your goal achievement success. The further you are from the ultimate end goal, the bigger and bigger the rewards need to be as you climb the ladder to success.

When you write a set of goals you should always have two lists: One for what you want to achieve and one for what this achievement brings you.

When your dreams and goals are far-reaching there tend to be many steps along the way and it is often the case that we get no real sense of reward for achieving them. And you know where that leads you, dopamine withdrawal. So as a failsafe mechanism make it standard practice that you reward yourself for achieving even the tiniest step in your master plan. So that even if achieving your mid-step goal isn't rewarding in itself, you are always sweetening the deal with yourself and getting the love buzz you deserve.

BOP 2: A GRAND VISION IS ACTUALLY THE END

OK so we need to break things down a little, but beware! We are suckers for getting stuck in a sea of middle steps and can easily lose sight of our grand vision all together. This is why it is key that we all keep in mind what we are working towards. The difference between means and ends goals should be clear in your mind. An end goal should really highlight exactly what it is you want and why. Means goals are dispensable; there is always more than one way to cook a chicken.

Let's take a typical scenario. Say someone's ultimate end goal is to become the CEO of the company that they work for. So WHAT they want more than anything in their career is to work?!? In reality, that's not truly what they want. What they want is something that they consider a benefit that they imagine being the CEO would bring. This is truly WHAT they want. Maybe those benefits are to be more comfortable with money, to have the means to support their family and pay for their children's college education or traveling around the world with their job. These could truly be end goals. Getting that particular promotion was mutton dressed as lamb and really a means goal all along. If we lose sight of what we truly want, we can waste years and years of energy and time pursuing the means and never getting to the end. Remember that in our brains we own our dreams and goals; they become part of who we feel we are. Make sure your goals are truly WHAT you want so that you don't become someone you never intended or wanted to be.

When you perform goal setting exercises return to your list and be sure that ALL your dreams are end goals. Then focus on the means goals knowing that they are just that, a means to an end.

BOP 3: FAILURE IS ACTUALLY WINNING

Our end goal should be epic and unwavering if it's what we truly want, but we should lighten up a little when it comes to the means goals (the steps in between). Means goals are just the HOWs. They are a list of sequential how to's that you can follow in order to reach that ultimate end goal. Means goals aren't actually what you WANT and as such shouldn't be taken so seriously. How does that saying go? For every problem there is always more than one solution.

Failure to achieve a means goal is really a WIN. Failure gives you the opportunity to determine what went wrong and may hint at what you need to do to get it right. When you fail to achieve one of your means goals and you come up with plan B (or C or D or E...), it is a cause for celebration. Again treat yourself to some kind of reward, be it a night out with friends or cooking a special meal, whatever floats your boat. Failures, that result in a new plan to take you a step closer to achieving your end goal are well worth celebrating, giving you a dopamine boost to keep on trucking.

Practicing seeing failure as a sign to get analytical, and even forcing a little smile and a few deep breaths can be enough to help prevent getting emotional about it.

Be analytical when it comes to failure, take an emotional step back and look around for the clues that will help you discover what best to do next. If you are too tense, try a relaxing BOP of your choice (focusing on your breath may be more than enough). You can even practice failure by playing online or offline games with friends and monitoring your emotions. This is such a vital key to success in life you will hear a bit more about failure in the next chapter too.

BOP 4: BRAINWAVES AND GOAL SETTING
Good Times and Bad Times

While next to nothing is known about goal setting networks and brainwaves there is one very important thing we all intuitively know about brainwaves and goal setting. Sometimes we just aren't in the best state of mind to set the best goals for ourselves. Have you ever been stressing out and had to make an off-the-cuff important decision that wasn't the wisest of choices? Or, while fussing over one problem that you are frantically trying to fix you inadvertently shoot yourself in the foot and mess something else up and make matters worse? The flip side of this is when we or someone we know has a problem and we calmly think about the solution, considering various possibilities and settling on the best course of action.

Goal Setting With Quality Thoughts

It all depends on our brainwave state. Being in beta mode is great for rapid brain processing: scoring a goal at soccer, passing an exam or multi-tasking but it's not the best state of mind for goal setting. The best mental environment for goal setting is one in which you have quality of thought, not quantity. An explorative state of mind, that processes thoughts slower and with less chance of error, allows us to explore multiple possibilities and take the time to nurture creative ideas. Alpha waves play a particularly strong role with this kind of thinking, which you already know from the previous section on creativity.

Creativity Au Naturel

It would be perfectly good practice to dip into the alpha waves by using meditation to slow things down a little. However, there is an even more natural way to use your brainwaves for successful goal setting. Have you ever been drifting off to the land of nod when ZING the solution to a problem or answer to that bothersome question you had is answered seemingly without conscious thought— a creative eureka moment. Almost as if the thought was teleported to your brain?

Or are you one of those people that think they do their best thinking in the shower or bath? Well it's because you DO do your best thinking there. It's all about brainwaves and the relaxation of your brain. When we wake up and when we go to bed we are transitioning through beta and alpha waves that dominate our waking lives, to the waves of theta and delta that dominate sleep and subconscious processes. This is the same as when we go into states of relaxation, like in the bathroom, or if we are to meditate or perform any other relaxing BOP.

Experiment using these special times when you are in need of goal setting and goal evaluating sessions: after you wake, before you sleep, places of relaxation and following meditation and exercise.

BOP 5: END GOAL SETTING

Finally we move on to actually setting some goals. Individually, all of the aforementioned goal related BOPs will make a great improvement as to how well you are able to attain your goals. However, when combined they form the ultimate recipe for success. Now we will focus on actually bringing your goals and dreams to life in your mind and then devise a goal achievement plan, using the other BOPs accordingly.

For now, so as not to get your means and end goals mixed up, we will focus solely on your far distant future end goals. Similar to a bucket list of things you want to do before you kick the bucket, these are your bucket goals. Imagine money, time, your current skill set or any other factor is insignificant and doesn't limit or direct your goal choice. Don't limit yourself one iota; imagine that time, money and resources are infinite. Imagine doing, thinking and experiencing what seem unimaginable to you right now.

So without further ado here is a short 9 min technique for goal setting. All you will need is a piece of paper, a pen and some way of timing yourself. **Skim read the steps through first, just once, and without thinking too much about your own answers** and then get the timer ready and focus only on the bold text. Timing yourself helps focus the naturally meandering creative flow of your thoughts and prevents stagnant over thinking. Write as much down within the time limits as possible, let your thoughts pour out on to the paper, you can come back to it and make sense of it later. So get ready to set life goals that will change the course of your life forever. Let your imagination run wild!

1. Focus on your breath (1 minute)
Draw your attention to your breath and let your mind go. To make the most of your brainwaves try the following steps during

times of brainwave relaxation throughout your day (e.g. in the toilet or just before bed) or following a meditation practice. Being relaxed and flexible is the key here.

2. Focus on yourself (2 minutes)
With all your answers let them flow, don't think too hard and give as much detail as you can. If you pause for more than a moment or two, recollect your thoughts and move on. You can come back to it later.

1) What personality do you have in the future, what kind of person are you?

E.g. Friendly, loving, compassionate, organized, centered, wise...

2) What experiences will you be having and where?

E.g. Travel the world (especially Africa)/meeting new and enlightening like-minded people / living in eco house on the beach with family / activities with friends and family outdoors as much as possible...

3) What skills will you have in the future?

E.g. Intellectual skills such as learning a language / communication skills like being able to give stimulating speeches and have engaging discussions / practical skills such as household DIY or cooking...

3. Focus on your health (2 minutes)
1) What does your body look and feel like in the future?

E.g. Pain free / gained weight / lost weight / strong / energetic / flexible...

2) What healthy habits that are good for my body and mind are a part of my normal day?

E.g. Loving my body / mastering LKM / mastering mindfulness / stopped smoking/ take pride in eating and preparing healthy food for family and friends...

3) What different forms of exercise do you enjoy or perhaps

even teach?

E.g. Master climber / sailor / martial artist / yoga / footballer / walking with dogs / playing with grandchildren...

4.   Focus on others (2 minutes)

What have you done for the other people in your life?

What have you done to enrich their happiness, lives and well-being?

Answer these questions for the following groups of people in your life. Remember, what would you want to do for them if money and time were of absolutely no consequence?

Family
E.g. Buy house for parents / pay off siblings school fee.

Friends
E.g. Organize regular camping trips with old school friends.

Town/City/Community
E.g. Start or be a part of a local charity / volunteer

Country
E.g. Start after school summer camp teaching kids about happiness and well-being.

World
E.g. Invent an app for reducing waste in the home

5.   Focus on success (2 minutes)

Bear in mind there is no obligation for you to be 'working'. Time and money are meaningless here, imagine you have just been given an unlimited bank fund and you have been told you never have to come back to your current job. It's not too unusual to hear of lottery winners that continue with regular jobs out of a love for what they do. While others may start their own business or charity and others may want to enrich their lives and the world in a non-career orientated manner. This is for many of us the most difficult part of the session as we have all been exposed to the stereotypical career path orientated life that can limit our minds dreaming capabilities. However, if you can break free of these outdated constraints this section of the BOP is perhaps the most enlightening. You may have already touched on a career goal from answering the previous questions.

What achievements have you made in your life?

E.g. being a loved and respected teacher / was always a devoted and dedicated friend / brought up happy healthy children into adulthood / spent my years having fun / founded a stray animal center / wrote an inspirational book or work of art.

BOP 6: MEANS GOAL SETTING

This is where we break down your well-formed end goals into yearly, monthly and then weekly goals for you to set. This technique also involves revisiting your goals daily. You may carry out the full visualization BOP every evening to explore how you may get one step closer to your end goal the following day. Similarly, when failure to meet a means goal signals to you that revisiting the HOW would be a good idea, this is the perfect BOP to come to an alternative solution. However, simply a quick review of your list of goals before bed will also be of use. Whether you are reviewing your NeuroLogical journal or you have them in a personal book or folder, simply taking a few minutes before the end of each day reviewing your goals in light of your plans for the next day will keep you on track.

1. Getting focused
Bring the end goal associated with the means goal to mind. Recall why this is important to you.

E.g. To regularly play in a band as a guitarist. Why? Because I would like to explore and enjoy creative musical flow by jamming with others.

2.   Write down the WHATs

No HOWS yet please!!! Think of a list of WHATs that any human being would need to do to achieve the end goal. Think of these WHATs as intermediary end goals. Think of what resources you don't currently have that you would need to achieve your end goal. Draw a line on a piece of paper to represent the time line you may follow in trying to achieve these intermediary WHATs on the way to your ultimate end goal. Write down the order in which you will need to acquire these resources in relation to the time line.

E.g. Have access to guitar, have access to lessons of some form, practice, join band, practice with band.

You may have thought 'Pay for Lessons' was a WHAT, but this is a HOW. Think to yourself if anyone in the world was to achieve this goal would they HAVE to do this, or is this really in matter of fact a way of doing something. Be wary sometimes as the distinction can be difficult to notice. In a way, these are mini-end goals, but don't get too attached. There may be a better an option or even multiple options that were not available to you or you didn't think of at the time.

3.   Checking in

With the first intermediary goal on your list in mind close your eyes and focus on your breath. Harnessing your creative thinking in the next step will be helpful. Especially if you are using this BOP to revisit how you should address a failed means goal. So if needed take checking in a step further and use the time of day, state of mind, other BOPs and your environment to your advantage.

4.   Down to the means

Now take the first step on your goal time line, and think of as many possible ways in which you can achieve the goal. Don't bother writing it down if it isn't actually relevant to you. For example stealing a guitar might not be the most relevant if you value being an honorable, trustworthy individual.

E.g. Borrow a friends spare guitar, buy a guitar

5. Visualization

Explore your inner world and the various means possibilities and how you would achieve them. You may discover a flaw in one plan and the key to success in the other. It is always good practice to visualize your goals in a dissociated manner instead of first person to keep you action-focused. Cycle through the various options to see which one works best for you. Really bring the scene to life with details, follow the story through and see where it takes you.

E.g. Buy a guitar turned out to not be the best choice right now as I may struggle with paying the bills at the end of this month. Steve and Natalie came to mind as people who might have spare guitars. However when exploring the possibilities I realized that Natalie is the better option as she may also have the time to teach me too.

6. Get specific

Write down the specific steps needed to achieve your means goal and the associated reward you get or will give yourself for achieving it and then go, go, go!

E.g. Call and ask Natalie and pick up guitar are the steps and do a little happy dance and organize the first lesson are the rewards.

7. Repeat

Repeat the process in steps 3-6 for every mini-end goal on route to the ultimate end goal. The closer to the end goal you get the more you will have to rely on visualization to explore the possibilities. Perhaps aim to repeat the whole process for one new end goal each week as you get better and better at this BOP and will be able to juggle more goals.

8. Visualize to actualize

For any step along the ladder, using visualization to enact achieving a goal the day before you go for it is great mental preparation.

NeuroLogical Brain Training Goals

GOALS & DREAMS

Notes

Notes

Part III

DO & DARE

"A ship is always safe at the shore - but that is NOT what it is built for."

~ Albert Einstein

Life Is a Risky Business
Evolution or Devolution Depends on Risk Taking

Mentioning the taking of risks usually brings thoughts of gambling and recklessness. Yet the ability to take calculated risks is actually an essential human characteristic. Risk taking has forever been crucial to human development. Imagine three cavemen, Bill, Bob and Bart. Bill is a calculated risk taker. Bob is over bold and lives recklessly. While Bart likes to stay in the comfort of his cave and shies away from risks all together. One morning as they wake with their respective families, the putrid stink of death and menace swaths their noses—the beast is outside.

With a primordial monster at their doorstep how do they ensure their families survival? Bob, not thinking before he leaps instantly rushes his family out of the cave in the hopes of reaching safer ground. "Look before you leap!"

Acting without thinking things through, he grabs his family by the hand and seals their fate: tasty appetizers to wet the beast's appetite. Bart, who never takes risks, stays in the confines of his cave, hoping the monster will go away. "Up an' at 'em! Don't rest on your laurels!" Unfortunately for him the beast doesn't get bored and go on its way and instead follows its nose straight into Bart's families cave to feast on a cave-wrapped family sized treat.

And then there is Bill. Bill sees that he needs to take a risk so he sets to thinking first about how to minimize the risk (being eaten) first, making success a safer bet. Able to keep his cool in a tricky situation, the decision is made quickly and he darts out of their homely cave to face the beast. Waving his arms about frantically, he boldly stares death in the face, as his family slinks off to safety. The beast draws in closer and Bill forgets all about waving his arms about as the Earth shudders violently with every encroaching step it makes, hulking its immense weight from foot to foot, bone, shatteringly, slow. Resisting the urge to succumb to fear and run away, the beast looms over him, just one swift movement away from bending down and swallowing Bill whole. With one final daring move Bill whips out a mouth-watering hunk of cured meat they had saved for the winter, and waggles it around to get the beasts attention, before lobbing it into a nearby bush. Just like a puppy the beast scampers off to munch his treat, leaving Bill to catch up with his family. While they lost their food store and the safety of their cave, they didn't lose their lives. All thanks to calculated risk taking. As the saying goes, fortune favors the brave.

Risk Taking in Today's World

In the here and now, the chances of you being stalked outside your home by a prehistoric beast are pretty slim. However, engaging in activities that are risky—that is, we are uncertain if the outcome will be good for us—is a part of day to day living. Confronting your belligerent boss, asking that special someone out on a date, applying for a new job, bringing up a touchy subject to a friend or spouse, even wearing an unusual outfit can be risky in today's world.

Some scientists believe that risk taking is essential to success in life. As with caveman Bill, calculated risk taking is what allows us to not only survive in tricky off-the-cuff situations, but to also walk the path less traveled and is how some of us dare to run for office, run with a revolutionary new business idea, lead a civil-rights demonstration or any other bold endeavor. However, just as Bill the caveman did, taking steps to minimize the potential risk can save us from the beast that we call failure.

Risk Taking in the Brain
Risky Networks

Two particular networks in the brain are of importance when we are calculating risk, your reward and motivation related circuitry and your cognitive control network. As you are aware, reward related networks include the striatum and amygdalae and their interaction with a part of the frontal lobe in modulating our emotions and motivation. The release of dopamine in the brain affects this network and is what gives us a mental pat on the back and the motivation to see something through.

The second network is your cognitive control network. This network actively maintains the patterns of activity that represent your internally generated plans and the means to guide ones behavior to achieve them, will power if you will. This network also involves parts of the frontal lobe and the frontal most part of the ACC and insula. Put simply, the reward network helps us with the motivational *why* we should do something and the cognitive control network aids it in assessing the *how* . What researchers have found is that how well these two networks interact with one another dictates how we approach decision making and the taking of risks.

Risky Brainwaves

You may have noticed that your reward circuitry is predominantly found subcortically while your cognitive control circuitry is cortical. Well this is where brainwaves come in to mediate network communication. As you know, slow waves like delta and theta are fond of the inner subcortical regions of the brain. Well, researchers think that it is the syncing up between the beat of the slow subcortical waves and the faster cortical waves that allow these two systems to communicate.

When your fast and slow brainwaves are coupling, the exchange of information between the two networks complement one another, allowing you to calculate the potential reward and punishment risks effectively in relation to how best to achieve your goals. The flip side is when your fast and slow brainwaves are singing to their own tune, the communication of potential reward and punishments associated with regulating how we achieve our goals is fuddled up. Researchers also think this partly explains why teens are big risk takers; communication within and between these two networks is wired differently in their still maturing brains.

Scared to Take Risks
Risk Isn't Dangerous but Regret Is

Success comes from taking calculated risks, resulting in either the achievement of your goals or learning from setbacks. Setbacks can however, if we take the failure too heavily, make us averse to taking risks all together. Have you ever tried something once, had a bad experience and then avoided it in the future? OK if the thing you did was actually bad for you, we are glad you avoided it.

On the other hand, what if it was something fun or useful that you are avoiding: an opportunity to sky dive, the world of dating, speaking up or letting go of your inhibitions? Well if you don't know the tricks of the brain it's not surprising that you start to avoid taking risks. Regret is a powerful emotion that leaves emotional signatures on the brain. Learning to manage regret is key, not only for giving yourself the mental faculties to take calculated risks and achieve success but it also bolsters our happiness and well-being in life and helps us avoid depression!

Regret and Disappointment in the Brain

Regret and disappointment are two sides of the same coin. However, disappointment is much kinder to us and should really be the emotion of choice when something goes to pot—unless you really have been naughty that is! Regret is a more intense emotion where we *focus* on how *our own* poor choice resulted in a bad outcome. Disappointment, on the better hand, is less intense and results from us *not focusing* on and blaming *our own* choices being at fault and instead, simply feel disappointed with the results or situation itself. This trivial looking difference is far from trivial. It profoundly affects how we approach risk taking, which is clearly reflected in the brain.

Compared with when we feel disappointed, and instead choose to feel regret, we have decreased activity in the striatum, which dampens our sense of reward. Meanwhile, increased activity in the amygdalae enhances our emotional response. What's more is that other regret related brain activations make us more likely to avoid taking risks in the future. Researchers think that regret enhances the processing of the punishment of failure, marks it as being emotionally important and then stores that intense regretful emotional memory via, respectively, the increased activity of the medial orbitofrontal region, the ACC and the hippocampus. This makes it much easier for us to readily anticipate failure and shy away from being bold and taking a risk. All the more reason to steer away from misplaced regret.

Dopamine Starvation and the Wild Side of Regret

Risk aversion and the associated reduction in dopamine from a lack of experiencing wins in life can actually turn you on your head 180°. A lack of dopamine in the brain starves the brain of pleasure and promotes negative pleasure seeking activities such as drug abuse and gambling. You are essentially making yourself a dope fiend by starving yourself of potential rewards.

Many recreational drugs induce very large and rapid dopamine surges to make up for all the dejected feelings that come with a lack of dopamine such as guilt, regret, shame and depression. But our brain in turn responds by reducing normal dopamine activity even further. Be careful with regret! The spiral of disrupting the dopamine system renders people incapable of feeling genuine pleasure with or without drugs. Don't look back in anger. An optimistic, no regrets attitude can alter the course of your life!

A Life of No Regrets

Let's not oil up your regret circuitry and see a failure as a signal to feel like crap. Say no to regret and see failure as a fact of life that can be used as a trigger for decisive action, signifying that something needs to change in order to achieve success. Learning to simply adapt your emotional response to failure is a key feature of healthy aging. With research into the brains of those who have aged unsuccessfully and are unhappy and regretful about life and are starving themselves of dopamine, feel more depressed and more likely to engage in unhealthy pleasure seeking behavior.

It is essential for our emotional well-being that we develop positive strategies for dealing with failure. And that we don't shut ourselves off from happiness through a fear of taking risks. If feelings of regret sneak up on you, don't fret, transform those feelings into disappointment by reminding yourself that the outcome was bad and so the methods used should be looked at again. Get back on the horse, rethink your strategy and get galloping towards your goals.

SUMMARY

- Having the mental capabilities to efficiently calculate risk is one of the evolutionary forces that have forged the brains and minds we have today.
- **Engaging in activities where we are uncertain of the outcome is a regular part of normal day life.**
- Deciding if something is worth the risk involves the interaction between reward related brain structures and the cognitive control network, whose activity represents how we plan to do something. This allows you to calculate the potential rewards and punishment risks effectively in relation to how best to achieve your goals.
- **The interaction between slow subcortical brainwaves in the largely subcortical reward circuitry and faster brainwaves in the cortical cognitive control network, allows these two systems to communicate.**
- Learning to manage regret is key, not only for giving yourself the mental faculties to take calculated risks and achieve success, it also bolsters our happiness and well-being in life and helps us avoid depression!
- **Compared with when we feel disappointed, with regret we have decreased activity in the striatum which dampens our sense of reward, as well as increased activity in the amygdalae, which enhances our emotional response.**
- When we experience regret, activity in the medial orbitofrontal region, the ACC and the hippocampus, researchers think that these structures, in their respective order, enhance the processing of the punishment of failure, marking the memory as being emotionally

important and then store that intense and regretful emotional memory.

• **Avoiding risk and other means of dopamine starvation can lead us to surprisingly negative and risky pleasure seeking behaviors such as gambling and drug abuse.**

• Learning to simply adapt your emotional response to failure is a key feature of healthy aging.

Up Next...

In our final set of BOPs we take a look at how best to calculate risks and how we dare to be bold. With your sound goal setting techniques you can ensure a healthy approach to achievement. We combine this with the creative skills required to envision new possibilities and innovative ways to go for your wildest dreams, while minimizing the potential risk should you fail first time round. So let's get taking risks—calculated ones that is—and be successful in achieving our wildest imaginable dreams.

DO & DARE
BRAIN OPTIMIZATION PRACTICES

We Tricked You!
BOPs Within BOPs

We will be totally honest with you here and tell you that we have been deceiving you just a tiny little bit (it was for your own good, we promise!). If you have been practicing our previously mentioned BOPs and thus self-directing neuroplastic change and re-wiring your brain, you have been unwittingly preparing your brain for this moment all along.

The various states of mind that your brain orchestrates for you to get about your day have been fine tuned and optimized so you can present your better self in life. However, they do far, far more than all that. Our earlier BOPs are really a build up to these BOPs right here. These BOPs are the true life altering BOPs that can propel you onto life paths that before you picked up this book, may have been vague and uncared for pipe dream. Now in our minds and daily practices let's make those dreams a reality!

A Brain Trained For Risk

There are so many aspects of the truly astonishing changes you have been making to your brain (well done!) that make you better able to make good decisions and better calculate risk. Henceforth, you now have the power to be one of those 'lucky' people who seem to put themselves out on a limb and come back time and time again with a resounding success story.

You have been balancing your emotional circuitry, making you less likely to make rash, hot headed or emotionally laden risky decisions. Also, many network tweaks from various techniques have been boosting your sense of fair play and team spirit with a greater ease in making selfless, altruistic decisions. You are now more able to focus your attention and perceive far more from your inner and external worlds, as well as being better able to filter through this information with new found efficiency, allowing for the extraction from your experiences of the useful and relevant information as opposed to the disruptive and irrelevant information. This enhanced perception gives you the ability to have more at your disposal and perceive potentially unforeseen bonuses and pitfalls when making any decision, risky or not. Your enhanced creativity should also allow you to come up with novel solutions to your problems and goals in life, so that you have a larger repertoire of possible paths to pick from.

The list goes on and on and we would bet includes other brain based beneficial effects that haven't even been tested for yet. So get ready, get set, use all your new brain powers and have the courage to go for the 'ungettable' and dare to live your wildest dreams!

BOP 1: DONT LET RISK TAKING DIE

Creativity and Risk Taking Have a Closely Intertwined Relationship

As you are in the know, it should feel clear to you that creativity is the product of the brain making long distance connections. Yet if you are scared to take risks your creative forces may be stifled seeing as you are less likely to consider 'crazy' alternatives that may actually be the beyond perfect solution for you. And similarly, when we are presented with a potentially risky situation, creative off-the-cuff decision making may be the very thing that saves your ass! So here is a fun and simple BOP to reignite even the most risk-averse individual with the joys of taking creative risks.

1.   **Notice your fears and take note**
This BOP builds on the creativity BOP where you played about with

your daily routines. Now let's take things a step further and be creative with the things that you are scared of. In this sense, your fear and fear of displeasure, along with the upsetting emotions that can result are actually very, very useful emotions and you shouldn't be afraid of them. Like any other emotion, if you can take a step back and see it for the signal that it is, it's invaluable, whether the emotion is perceived as a good or bad one. Fear and the fear of feeling unpleasant are 'call to action' emotions. It's a call for you to write your fears down so that you can explore that fear and overcome it in your BOP sessions. It may be useful to think of a few of your fears and write them down now. Let's start with the silliest little ones. Here are two examples (that may be silly fears to some but major ones to others):

> 1. Being in 30 minute long queues in the bank (or anywhere else) in your lunch break gets your blood boiling so much that you tend to avoid queues completely even when there is no other alternative.
> 2. Looking like a fool in public is a common fear many people have.

2. Use creative thinking to have fun with taking risks

Now harness your creative thinking powers and think of out of the box ways in which you could flip the experience you fear into something more interesting, maybe even something you will enjoy! We all love to see Youtube videos of people doing daring, creative and inspiring things with their day, why can't that person be you?

> 1. Buy a jumbo pack of muffins and doll them out to fellow bored individuals in the queue. Then proceed to make use of your lunch break by making balloon animals that you learned to make online to keep their minds occupied! Now neither you nor any other person on their break need fear that queue today!
> 2. Suggest a charity fundraiser at work or join, or even start your own charity event out of work. You and your workmates could pick a theme and dress up like fools as you collect charity money. This way it is actually your job and duty to look like a fool in public!

3.   One risk a day challenge

For a full week try a 'one risk a day challenge'. Before going to bed try and think of one aspect of your day the next day that could be transformed creatively into something a little more daring. Commit to doing that act and you may be amazed at how quickly you master fearful feelings, allowing you to be less afraid to take risks, opening up your mind and life to new possibilities.

HINTS & TIPS

•   Please record share and document these wonderous acts of daring and creative risk taking so that you can inspire others too! However, use the next BOP when you should really think a little harder about the consequences of such a risk or when you really need that extra brain boost to overcome any fear of failure.

•   **For one week at least (or even for life?) make time for creative risk taking. Simply before going to bed take a few minutes to write in your NeuroLogical journal. Write three normal parts of your day where you will mix it up a little and dare to do things your own way in spite of your fears.**

BOP 2: VISUALIZE TO EXPERIMENT AND ACTUALIZE
Visualizing Risk

You have been harnessing your visualization powers ever since that introductory visualization BOP back when we were dealing with stress. By now you should be pretty good at painting vivid and sensation rich scenes in your mind. You will likely have heard that visualization can make or break achieving your goals. Why does it work so well? The language of your dreams and goals is pure visualization. You have to mentalize and imagine achieving a goal to even want it in the first place. Brain science heavily supports the use of visualization in achieving your goals. Perhaps more importantly, visualization provides a space for you to experiment with the best way to achieve your goal by comparing the alternative solutions in your mind.

And on that note when it comes to making decisions, visualization is never more important than when making potentially risky decisions. And low and behold, navigating your way through a sea of potentially risky decision making pitfalls is the art, that when mastered, will make the direction to your hopes and dreams feels as intuitive and simple as taking a walk in the park.

Imagining with the DMN

Being the braniac you now are, could you hazard a guess as to what networks are involved when you are simulating reality in your mind? That's right, you guessed it, the DMN! As you know, this network is active when we are not focused on the external world. Also, there is a striking similarity between remembering the past when using this network and imagining something fictitious, be it pigs flying or you imagining how to deal with a future, risky goal-oriented situation.

Imagining is Different To Remembering

While strikingly similar, the differences found in the activation of a subset of brain bits set the two main types of visualization apart from one another, that is imagining something new and revisiting memories. Research indicates that the process of imagining encodes this new imagined information and stores it as a pseudo-memory in the brain by integrating bits and pieces from your memory bank. Remembering on the other hand, doesn't encode new information and it's more like hitting a playback button. This may be part of the reason why many famous thinkers, speakers, actors and sporting celebrities alike use visualizing achieving a goal to mentally time travel into the future and implant a pseudo-memory of their up and coming success. This makes success feel so real to them in their mind, that it actually increases their chances of success in the real world.

Goal Directed Imagining Is Different Too

What's more is that there is a clear difference between your non-goal related imaginings like tea parties with unicorns and Santa Claus (although these may be real goals for a select few *special* individuals) and your future personal goal imaginings, be it your plan to move home, change jobs or even BOPing plans. Such goal-directed autobiographical planning engages the DMN, with specific frontal lobe activations for self-reference.

More importantly, your DMN's intricate coupling and neural connectivity with executive regions helps your imaginings become goal-directed cognition. We suspect that in the future we are likely to find that those of us that use visualization to achieve our goals will not only be more successful as past experiments have shown, but will have greater connectivity between the DMN and executive functions to support the success. This is amazingly something that is found in the brains of meditators! Presumably this gives them more controlled use of mind wandering and imagining. Haha! Your journey through Mind Your Head and meditation may not as yet have been for focusing on your most daring, putting yourself out there, more to gain-more to risk goals, but you have actually been training your brain for this moment all along.

Imagining is Real

Imagining is so real to us humans that when a group of skiers mentally rehearsed their downhill run, their brain contacted their muscles as if they were actually out on the slopes navigating the real run itself! Whether you are imagining performing an activity or actually performing it, neural pathways are similarly activated. This just goes to show how important watching what you think is. Imagining disastrous results may have disastrous consequences. .

The real world consequences of imaginings can similarly be seen in stroke patients simply imagining moving their limbs that, due to brain damage, cannot be moved correctly. This actually helps to repair damaged neurons and get that limb moving again. The power of your mind is truly magnificent, you have had the powers to dust yourself off from failure and achieve the unimaginable all along. Now it's your time to use the power of visualization to dare to imagine yourself achieving your wildest dreams.

How to Get the Most Out Of Visualization

Some researchers suggest the importance of having a first person view when visualizing something we wish to really impact our behaviour in the real world. In this manner one would more accurately represent the neural activations of someone actually performing the action. Although to our knowledge this hasn't been tested we would suspect that if we imagined in third person view, more ToM specific activations would occur.

Another really useful hint when visualizing is to break the visualisation down into stages. This is to give your posterior parietal cortex a little helping hand. This part of the cortex helps us model plans for movement before we act and is responsible for generating a navigational plan of action. Breaking visualizations down into action stages may ensure that the posterior parietal cortex is not overloaded with information and can more easily plan your route to achievement.

Now let's think of one of your more significant goals that you feel would benefit from some brain boosting, one that you could actually do in the real world in the near future. Not your grand distant end goals but some more readily achievable means goal that you plan to do sometime soon. This could be starting a new job on the right foot or leaving a good impression on a date, literally anything. Firstly, think for a few moments of one way you can imagine yourself achieving that goal, break it down into steps and then get started.

1. **Checking in**
Focus on your breath and use any relaxation technique you choose to get you into a relaxed brain mode for visualization.

2. **Visualize the scene in the third person**
As if seeing yourself in a movie scene, play the scene out step by step. Pay attention to how you feel, think and do in the situation and how the environment responds, be it a social one or not. Try

not to rush through the scene and maintain deep steady breathing to keep your mind in a relaxed state. Was the outcome as you had hoped? Could the same behavior result in a different outcome? If so, rewind and replay in your mind any other ways the scene could play out.

3.   Try alternatives in third person

You may have thought of various alternatives when devising means goals in the last section but now is the time to really play around with the specifics. What could you say, do or think differently in the scenario to make for a better outcome. Be daring, imagine yourself doing things in ways you perhaps wouldn't normally. If you are normally shy, imagine yourself feeling strong and confident. Play with your mind's lead character and explore the various roles in the scene that you could play in your imagination.

4.   Which version had the preferred outcome?

Reflect for a moment on the various alternative scenarios you have just played out in your mind. Which outcome best served your goals, needs and desires?

5.   Imagine the best scenario in first person

Now is where we really want you to break down the scenario into three or more segments. For example if getting a point across successfully at a meeting with a client was the goal, the steps could be: meeting the client, approaching the subject, delivering the point, closing the subject, closing the meeting. In first person mode, visualize each individual step. Again try to let your breath guide a slow and steady visualization that allows you to pay attention to the details.

6.   Move your imagination into the real world

So it's the big day where you can finally put your imagination where your mouth is. You may have spent a moment, day, month or even year visualizing achieving a particular goal. Now it is time to switch to actuation mode. The moment before you perform the activity, task or event that will achieve your goal, focus clearly again on that picture in your mind, take a deep breath, centre yourself and GO!

HINTS & TIPS

- Imagining yourself winning is not the key. Imagining yourself doing in order to win is the key. Studies in visualization in dieting and in sports support this idea.
- Third person view is a great time to play with imagining behaving in a way that may at first seem risky to you or for when you may be dealing with potentially risky situations. It's important in this instance to focus on alternative endings that may result from the same action. Is there a fly in the ointment? Is there a potentially unforeseen risk factor that will affect your choice of action? Your creative powers will serve you well here.

BOP 3: BRING YOUR ACTIONS TO LIFE
Print Out Your Mental Visualizations

From the previous section on goals you should have a whole load of notes on what you really want in life (end goals) and the ways you propose to achieve them (means goals). While you may be some way off yet on the road to achieving them, vision boards have been known to help many achieve their goals. Simply put, a vision board is any sort of board on which you display images that represent whatever you want to be, do or have in your life. They can be physical and made from newspaper and magazine clippings, pictures and printouts or be digital and made on your computer.

Go for the Action

However, you can fantasize and dream all day long and never get a step closer unless you take action. So instead of creating vision boards we are going to have the actions needed and means goals in mind as we create ACTION BOARDS!

With action boards, the image or typography that represents the end result is great for a little focus and motivation, but should be relatively small and not dominate the page. Images and words that represent the steps and actions you need to take to achieve the goal on the other hand are more important here. Make them big, bold and beautiful and really call out to you. One or two letter sized pages should suffice for each end goal. If you can do this for all of your main end goals you can literally hold your dreams in your hands and review them whenever you feel you need to.

Protection From Failure

When you feel there is a lot to risk involved in a step on the path to achieving your goals, reviewing your action board can help you to visualize alternatives in light of how they may affect achieving your goals. Similarly, some people find such tools are really quite handy when they feel life has begun to take over again and they have lost sight of what they should be getting on with. That is ultimately the most profound and simplest key to success when daring to take risks in the bid to achieve your dreams: always being able to regain your sight no matter how many times you may lose it.

Get your scissors, glue and glitter out and hold your dreams in your hands, never lose sight and always know that it is action that will truly free your life!

NeuroLogical Brain Training Goals

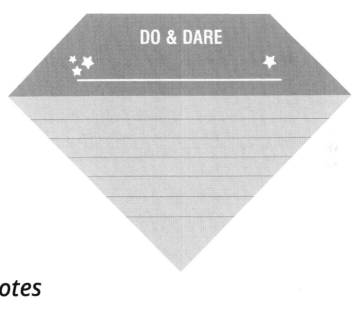

DO & DARE

Notes

Notes

Power Resources

MINDING YOUR HEAD NEVER ENDS: MORE USEFUL RESOURCES

Welcome to the Mind Your Head Community!

Now that you have learned the BOPs and the latest practices in Mind Your Head, we are excited to share many continually evolving resources for brain training knowledge, experts and insights. All our Mind Your Head related resources are designed to make enhancing your skills and life fun, while meeting other wonderful people who are learning and practicing too. So we welcome you to a community like no other, where you'll meet other fellow brain trainers and fascinating experts who want to get the most out of life.

From Sue Stebbins, Dr. Carla Clark and the global Mind Your Head team and community.

Brain Training Audios

Releasing Overwhelm

http://successwaves.com/products/catalog/Releasing_Overwhelm.html

Quantum Weight Release

http://successwaves.com/products/catalog/Quantum_Weight_Release.html

Authentic Power

http://successwaves.com/products/catalog/Authentic_Power.html

Letting Go of Pain

http://successwaves.com/products/catalog/Letting_Go_of_Pain.html

Mind Your Head Contact Information

MindYour HeadBook.com/references

MindYourHeadBook.com/freegift

1.866.758.3433

info@mindyourheadbook.com

Ultimate New Life System Website

UltimateNewLifeSystem.com

Social Media Channels

Register for news, brain science updates, events and special offers:

www.Facebook.com/MindYourHeadtheBook

www.Twitter.com/TheMindYourHead

Workshops, Courses and Group Training

There are many different ways to learn more about training a happy, healthy, social and wealthy brain and getting expert training and guidance – coming 2014

Mind Your Head BOP Groups

Want to lead a brain optimization group and train your brain on being happy, healthy and wealthy? Online Training – coming 2014.

Small, friendly and remarkable. Contact info@mindyourheadbook.com if you'd like us to start a group for you and some friends.

Brain Training Workshops and Courses

Courses on brain training for happiness, healthy body and weight, relationships, wealth creation and more to be announced in 2014.

More Possibilities

If you'd like to introduce Mind Your Head to others, or know someone who could benefit from Mind Your Head's insights and what you learned from the book, we love providing interviews, keynotes, and custom programs—please feel free to reach out to us about how we can bring the best new brain science to you, or your organization, or your personal sphere.

Ultimate New Life System

Ultimate New Life System is a digital brain training web portal being launched in 2014 with radical new social capabilities for collectively re-wiring our brains and optimizing our lives. Ultimate New Life System will be home to the brain training audios, community portal and web journal already mentioned in this book, for accelerating, recording, improving and sharing your BOP journey. Stay Tuned.

Glossary

ACC: Anterior Cingulate Cortex: Involved in blood pressure and heart rate regulation and is more active when we exercise. It is also involved in error detection, monitoring conflict and decision making outside of exercise. The ACC helps the brain in handling conflict better, with more efficient error detection and in turn better decision making.

Action-Perception Loop: A real-time loop of information formed between our brains and our environment that allows us to interact with and learn from our environments.

Alpha Brain Waves: Relaxed wakefulness, bridge the conscious to the subconscious, general knowledge ('knowing'), easy listening and calm reasoning, inhibitory roles.

A-O System: Action-Outcome System: A system in the brain whereby, a new behavior, prior to enactment, will involve some relatively complex thoughts in thinking about the outcome of your intended actions.

Beta Brain Waves: Associated with alert and focused on task consciousness, unlike the relaxed conscious awareness of alpha. It is your alert and ready to respond 'action stations' wave associated with motor systems in the brain.

BOPs: Brain Optimization Practices: Simple steps of thought and action, that with simple repetition alter network functioning in your brain, allowing you to more easily and rapidly move your life toward optimal well being.

Brainwave Entrainment: Any technique aimed at promoting synchronization on neuron activity with the assistance of a periodic stimulus (like a drum beat or strobe light) that has a frequency equivalent to the intended brainwave state.

CBT: Cognitive Behavioral Therapy: Centers on how we think and feel (cognitive), which in turn influences the way we act (behavioral).

Cerebellum: A region at the back of the brain with major roles in motor control and newly found roles in memory, learning, language, behavior and emotion—including the feelings of pleasure and affection.

Cerebral Asymmetry: When equivalent structures, one from each hemisphere, are unequally activated.

CFT: Compassion Focused Therapy: Used clinically to treat mental health problems. It allows you to make contact with, build on and develop your inner compassionate self.

CM: Compassionate meditation: Aims to cultivate compassion or deep, genuine sympathy for those stricken by misfortune, together with an earnest wish to ease this suffering.

Corpus Callosum: The largest white matter structure in the human brain that is crucial in maintaining the independent processing of the hemispheres and in communicating information and coordinating activity between the two sides.

Cortex: A structure formed by the outer layers of the brain that is divided into four lobes, each with specific functions.

Delta Brain Waves: Brain waves that dominate the realms of slow wave, deep, restful sleep. Involved in memory encoding during sleep, in motivation and has a dark side.

DMN: Default Mode Network: A network within the brain that is in control when you are not busy or on task, being most commonly used when you are engaged in internal thoughts

ECG: Electrocardiograph: An instrument used to measure the electrical activity of the heart.

EEG: Electroencephalograph: An instrument used to measure the electrical activity of the brain.

End Goal: Should really highlight exactly WHAT it is you want.

Executive Functions: An umbrella term for the regulation and control of cognitive functions including working memory, decision making, task flexibility and problem solving.

Frontal Lobe: Part of the brain that deals with the executive functions.

Fusiform Gyrus: A brain region that is active only in loving mothers when viewing their children.

Gamma Brain Waves: Involved with fast brain processing for peak performance, short-range network integration, has implicated roles as a unifying wave in binding theory and is a neuroplasticity booster.

Grey Matter: Mainly consists of the cell bodies, dendrites and unmyelinated axons of neurons.

HFOs: High Frequency Oscillations: Also known as the epsilon band, HFOs in the brain's electrical activity.

Hippocampus: Part of the brain that encodes, stores and retrieves information for learning and memory.

Hypothalamus: The part of your brain that tells your glands what hormones to produce to keep your body stable without you having to think about it.

Hz: Hertz: Is a measure of the number of times per second a periodic phenomenon occurs, called the frequency.

Infra-slow Brainwaves: Little is known about them. They could be the glue that links networks together.

Insula: A region of the brain's cortex, that when activated is associated with generating our 'gut feelings', as well as sensations of 'emotional touch' that enhance the pleasure of loving skin-to-skin contact.

LKM: Loving Kindness Meditation: Has a unique focus on cultivating positive emotions and heartfelt unconditional kindness for the self and others.

Means Goal: Means goals are just the HOWs. They are a list of sequential how to's that you need in order to reach the ultimate end goal.

Meditation: Generally, meditation is thought of as a sitting practice, although does not have to be, that trains your brain and mind and alters your state of consciousness.

MEG: Magnetoencephalography: A technique for mapping brain activity by recording magnetic fields produced by naturally occurring electrical currents in the brain.

Mindfulness: The ability to stay aware and play close attention to the present moment, where you tune into everything both outside and within you with calm acceptance.

NAA: N-acetylaspartic Acid: A substance made by neurons that influences how neurons perform and is the most abundant chemical compound in the brain. It has many beneficial functions in the brain and its production is increased by exercise and meditation.

Neuron: Neurons are the building blocks of the brain, communicating information electrochemically from one neuron to another, where a dendrite of one neuron meets the axon of another, an inter-neuron region called the synapse.

Neuroplasticity: Essentially neuroplasticity is an umbrella term that covers all changes in the brain occurring at the cellular level that alter the connectivity of networks in the brain in response to everything that we experience.

NLP: Neuro-Linguistic Programming: To use language and communication to reprogram the brain and enhance intra-personal and inter-personal relations.

Occipital Lobe: The region in the brain's cortex that processes visual input that is sent to the brain from our eyes.

Oxytocin: The 'trust hormone', associated with reducing panic and pain, important for the 'getting to know you' phase of love.

PAG: Periaqueductal Gray: PAG has been shown to have roles in humans in modulating pain and in defensive and maternal behavior.

Parietal Lobe: The region in the brain's cortex involved in integrating information from our senses.

QEEG Quantitative Electroencephalography: the numerical analysis of EEG brainwave data in the understanding of associated functional and behavioral correlates.

QEEG brain map: Quantitative Electroencephalograph brain map: Heat map of brainwave functioning.

S-R System: Stimulus-Response System: When a certain behavior becomes a habit, this system in the brain takes over, where little thought is required and the thought or event triggers an automatic response.

SMET Yoga: Self Management of Excessive Tension Yoga: A form of yogic exercise that provides astonishing brain balancing results from non-strenuous exercise in a very short amount of time.

Striatum: A multifunctional structure nestled deep in the forebrain. The more a behavior is repeated, the more neuroplasticity is activated in the S-R modules of the striatum as opposed to neurons of the striatum that are part of the A-O system. This enhanced neuroplasticity causes a snowballing shift from the A-O to the S-R system, which truly ingrains a behavior into our brains and bodies.

Telomerase: An enzyme that protects the ends of your DNA from degrading with time.

Temporal Lobe: The region in the brain's cortex important for integrating visual information from the occipital lobe with auditory processing, allowing us to interpret what a sound is and to understand the language we hear.

Thalamus: Located at the top of the brain stem, the thalamus acts as a switchboard for the hotel that is your brain.

Theta Brain Waves: Documented roles in REM sleep, memory fine tuning during sleep, memory, navigation and emotional regulation.

ToM: Theory of Mind: The ability to infer, understand and attribute thoughts, feelings and states of being to yourself as well as others.

TPN: Task-Positive Network: Takes over in place of the DMN when you are focused on a task.

Vagal Tone: The vagus nerve regulates the resting state of the majority of the body's internal organ systems and operates on a largely subconscious level. As with your biceps, the tone or tension in the nerve—vagal tone—is a good indicator of general health.

Vasopressin: Love hormone associated with the forming of attachment to your romantic interest.

References

The number of peer reviewed journal articles that went in to this book is astounding. Without the work of these dedicated scientists and thinkers the writing of this book would have been impossible.

www.MindYourHeadbook.com/references

Made in the USA
San Bernardino, CA
21 April 2016